D0752447

Tony Kushner in Conversation

TRIANGULATIONS
Lesbian/Gay/Queer ▲ Theater/Drama/Performance

Series editors:
Jill Dolan, CUNY Graduate Center, and
David Román, University of Southern California

Tony Kushner
in Conversation

EDITED BY ROBERT VORLICKY

Ann Arbor

THE UNIVERSITY OF MICHIGAN PRESS

Copyright © by the University of Michigan 1998
All rights reserved
Published in the United States of America by
The University of Michigan Press
Manufactured in the United States of America
⊗ Printed on acid-free paper

2001   2000   1999   1998   4   3   ·2   1

No part of this publication may be reproduced,
stored in a retrieval system, or transmitted in any form
or by any means, electronic, mechanical, or otherwise,
without the written permission of the publisher.

A CIP catalog record for this book is available from the British Library.

Library of Congress Cataloging-in-Publication Data

Kushner, Tony.
    Tony Kushner in conversation / edited by Robert Vorlicky
      p.   cm.
    Includes index.
    ISBN 0-472-09661-3 (alk. paper). — ISBN 0-472-06661-7 (pbk. :
alk. paper)
    1. Kushner, Tony—Interviews.   2. Dramatists, American—20th
century—Interviews.   3. Politics and literature—United States—
History—20th century.   4. Art and state—United States—
History—20th century.   5. Social problems in literature.   6. AIDS
(Disease) in literature.   7. Gay men in literature.   I. Vorlicky,
Robert, 1950–   .   II. Title.
PS3561.U778Z476   1997
812'.54—dc21
    [B]   97-31754
                                                          CIP

Acknowledgments

I'd like to express my heartfelt gratitude to those whose assistance was invaluable in preparing this book and made this project possible: LeAnn Fields, Tess Timoney, Laurie Clark Klavins, Melissa Holcombe, Sarah Stevenson, Kurt Lancaster, Una Chaudhuri, Michael Mayer, Mark Oram, Pat Kozma, Nicola Scadding, Ben Krevolin, David Román, Lacy Torge, and Ellen Bialo. Many thanks to the interviewers without whom this book would not be, to theater personnel, and to photographers who met pressing deadlines with utmost professionalism—to you all, my appreciation.

Several important interviews could not be included in this collection; some are readily available in other publications, while others, regrettably, may be less well known: Wendy Arons, "Preaching to the Converted?" (*Communications from the International Brecht Society,* fall 1994); Jarrod Hayes, Lauren Kozol, and Wayne Marat VanSertima, " 'Stonewall: A Gift to the World': An Interview with Tony Kushner and Joan Nestle" (*Found Object,* fall 1994); David Savran, "Tony Kushner Considers the Longstanding Problems of Virtue and Happiness" (*American Theatre,* October 1994); Mitchel Raphael, "Oh God! I'm Only a Playwright" (ICON, October 1996). All excerpts from *Angels in America, Part One: Millennium Approaches* and *Angels in America, Part Two: Perestroika* (New York: Theatre Communications Group, 1993 and 1994) are reprinted courtesy of Theatre Communications Group.

Words cannot express the depth of my admiration for Tony Kushner, writer and friend, nor the honor I have felt to work with him on this collection. Thank you, Tony, for this once-in-a-lifetime experience. We all look forward to "more plays, more plays" from your blest pen.

To our friends and families, both known and unknown, with love.

Contents

Works by Tony Kushner

*Angels in America, A Gay Fantasia on National Themes,
Part One: Millennium Approaches*

*Angels in America, A Gay Fantasia on National Themes,
Part Two: Perestroika*

A Bright Room Called Day

Henry Box Brown or The Mirror of Slavery (in progress)

Hydriotaphia or The Death of Doctor Browne

The Illusion (freely adapted from P. Corneille)

In Great Eliza's Golden Time (children's play)

The Protozoa Review (children's play)

*Slavs! (Thinking about the Longstanding Problems of Virtue
and Happiness)*

*Thinking about the Longstanding Problems of Virtue and
Happiness: Essays, A Play, Two Poems, and A Prayer*

Yes Yes No No (children's play)

Adaptations

A Dybbuk: Between Two Worlds, based on *The Dybbuk*
by Sy Ansky

The Good Person of Sezuan by Bertolt Brecht

Stella by Johann Wolfgang von Goethe

Introduction: "Two not One"

Robert Vorlicky

Tony Kushner: One of the things that we were talking about talking about . . . this sort of mutual conversation thing, it's very strange!

Anna Deavere Smith: Well, let's test the form. Let's test the form of supposed real-life conversations in front of eight hundred people.

—"Why Get Out of Bed?"

Tony Kushner, the playwright who burst upon the international scene in the early 1990s, is an anomaly in contemporary American art and life. Kushner's identification with marginalized communities, most noticeably gays and lesbians, Jews, socialists, agnostics, political activists, and artists, marks him as an outsider and as a primary target for invisibility in the "don't ask, don't tell" climate of America's dominant culture. Nonetheless, he has been bear-hugged by the media, by critics and academics, and by the arts world since the London and New York premieres of *Angels in America: A Gay Fantasia on National Themes, Parts One and Two.* To their credit, Kushner and the various cultures in which he is an active participant have survived one another and they have lived to tell their histories as a prelude to their evolving future together. *Tony Kushner in Conversation* connects the dots of Kushner's immediate past by means of the interview format, while presenting the evolution of an artist who has become one of America's most revered playwrights in the last decade of the twentieth century, the nation's voice for the turn of the millennium.

During the relatively short period since he emerged on the

literary scene, Kushner has proved himself to be neither a Warholian fifteen-minute success story, in which a meteoric rise matches a crashing decline, nor a vacuous talking head whose opinions are unfounded, unintelligible, and exaggerated. Kushner has emerged as a major cultural figure at a time when America gleefully disposes of its idols and celebrities as quickly as the next newscast, film, and web page can trumpet their demise. He attracts large crossover audiences when he appears live (whether as interviewee, panelist, or speaker) and assumes the burden of representing the widely diversified groups who claim parts of him as their own.

The key to Kushner's appeal is his attention to issues of immediate concern to many Americans. For example, people who highly regard the place of the arts in American cultural life have waited a long time for a young artist to emerge whose sensibility includes political awareness and who can strongly articulate an argument for government support of the arts. Kushner speaks and writes boldly, courageously. He's extremely effective, whether serious or ironic, in voicing his opinions. He is cordial and sensitive to those whose opinions are different from his, and in an old-fashioned, "town hall" manner, Kushner takes his show out to the people, both nationally and internationally. While not insensitive to others' criticism of his opinions and art, Kushner never holds back. Perhaps we care about what he has to say because his survivor instincts are a rare model for those who are otherwise suspicious of the hope he expresses in the future. For many, he articulates their fantasies. For others who are eagerly pressing for material change, Kushner suggests concrete steps that can be taken toward social and personal change, as well as offering encouragement amid difficult realities that appear fixed. Essentially, he has taken center stage on issues about which he is passionate and has justly won rave reviews from his public for his tireless and daring performances.

Tony Kushner in Conversation presents selected interviews from the 1990s. The personal interview—though not among Kushner's favorite literary genres—nonetheless provides interviewees with the opportunity to construct an image through the media on their own terms, which is determined by how they answer questions and how they act, or perform, before the public.

The interview form has a politics of its own. Since the focus usually remains on interviewees in this format, they can generally determine or control *how* they want to appear and to be evaluated—whether it be by their words alone, their voice quality, bodily expressions and gestures, physical appearance, or the appeal (or not) of their personality or *character* as represented "on stage." The interview format is a spontaneous performance of multiple selves (each attendant to the various communities of identification for the interviewee) that is fostered by the flow of impromptu questions, answers, pauses, and interruptions providing an edge of the unexpected to a live occasion.

In many ways the interview format perfectly matches Kushner's political and aesthetic appreciation for preserving a dialectic. Time and again, throughout the collection, Kushner refers to the value of community, to the vital necessity for discussion and argument between and among peoples—to his belief that the human species is "two not one." The interview format encourages and preserves Kushner in dialogue with others; it complements his sense of the dialectics within life and theater—whether off- or onstage. As such, the interviews stand beside his plays and essays as a significant body of literature in their own right, distinguishing themselves from the latter by their spontaneity, candidness, and variety, as well as by their immediate awareness of and responsiveness to the audience.

The interviews, then, are records of Kushner's unscripted performance of Tony Kushner, as he moved from his thirty-fifth to fortieth birthdays, a period accented— in the professional sphere—by numerous awards for *Angels in America:* a Pulitzer Prize for Drama (1993), Tony Awards for Best Play (1993 and 1994), Drama Desk Awards (1993 and 1994), Evening Standard Award (Great Britain, 1992), Olivier Award nominations for Best Play (Great Britain, 1993 and 1994), New York Drama Critics Circle Award (1993), Los Angeles Drama Critics Circle Award (1993), Lambda Literary Award for Drama (1994). In addition, *Slavs!* was awarded a 1995 OBIE Award for Best Play.

This five-year span also contained the highly acclaimed, award-winning national tour of *Angels in America,* directed by Michael Mayer, along with countless international productions of the epic and the beginning stages of production of the film version. During this period Kushner also did his first adaptation (of Brecht's *The Good Person of Sezuan*) and experienced the premieres of *Slavs!, A Dybbuk* (adaptation), and *The Illusion* (adaptation). He took his first trip to Israel; participated in the watershed ACT UP action-protest at New York's St. Patrick's Cathedral in December 1990; was named 1993 "Man of the Year" by the *Advocate;* spoke at many college campuses, public readings, and demonstrations (including the notable ARTNOW demo-celebration of the arts in Washington, D.C., April 1997, as debates raged in Congress over continued federal funding for the arts in America); and published

3

numerous essays, poems, commentaries, and a book, *Thinking About the Longstanding Problems of Virtue and Happiness* (1995).

This collection of interviews begins and ends with pieces that are not interviews. Tom Szentgyorgyi's essay-profile of Tony Kushner opens the book. First published in January 1991 to coincide with the New York premiere of *A Bright Room Called Day*, it is significant as the first major article published on Kushner. The article, interspersed with Kushner's comments, introduces the reader to the playwright's Louisiana background, his college life in New York City, and his early days with the theater collective Heat and Light Company, where he served as director, actor, and writer. The collection ends with an afterword by the playwright himself. It is the first chapter of his novel-in-progress, "The Intelligent Homosexual's Guide to Socialism and Capitalism, With a Key to the Scriptures," and appears here for the first time in print. I am delighted to have it in the collection, as it beautifully demonstrates how fluidly Kushner moves among the genres of interview, playwriting, and fiction.

Half of the interviews in this book—in terms of sheer volume, the bulk of the collection—are previously unpublished material. I have arranged the interviews in chronological order according to the dates that the conversations actually occurred, to best capture the evolution of Kushner's thinking and feeling on a range of topics. When appropriate, I have included in the headnotes the size of the audience, the admission charges, and the distribution of proceeds from the events (when known) to charities or arts organizations. These latter, useful facts place Kushner within the business of exchange, that occurs between notable artists and the public. His appearances, among their many features, are also an active part of the circuitry of the marketplace and commodification.

My arrangement of materials reveals not only the month-by-month immediacy of this personal-professional evolution but also the extent to which Kushner is called upon as a respected and honored spokesperson at a broad range of cultural events (graduations, commemorations, celebrations, memorial services, rallies for a variety of causes, meetings for public policy, conferences, readings, et cetera). He occupies a kind of "poet laureate" position for many of the disenfranchised—for those who experience their lives as voiceless or marginalized—a position that Kushner fills (involuntarily but nonetheless graciously and knowingly) within the American media, if not the American psyche. As a "Reagan kid"—a post-hippie, pre–Generation Xer—he is one of the first of his generation to occupy a space that

4

other progressive artists may not have the means or access to attain. With Kushner a widely based, anxious American populace found an articulate, reflective, and future-oriented spokesperson for a generation that is, itself, a divided community. And while many in the American audience might not agree with Kushner's politics and views, he is nonetheless embraced by many Americans as one who is allowed, or invited, *in* to speak *out* on a diverse range of issues in a variety of forums.

The attraction *and* controversy that Kushner's outspoken public persona continues to command are fully captured in this collection of interviews—several of which were conducted before packed auditoriums or millions of television viewers. They reveal his eloquence, his humor, and his vast knowledge of many subjects. Kushner's voice crosses boundaries of intersecting, marginalized cultures as his subject position fluidly moves among a range of identities, all of which *are* Tony Kushner: son, brother, uncle, lover, queer, agnostic, Southerner, democrat, socialist, Jew, feminist, political activist, Manhattanite, and theater professional—playwright, director, essayist, and artistic collaborator. The complexity of his personae manifests a kind of counter-celebrity status, one that resists his falling into the demands of a predictable, singularly defined public personality.

Many in these diverse communities have located in Kushner a kindred spirit, a passionate soulmate. Nonetheless, any single identification of Kushner fails to capture the breadth and depth of who he is and the value of his public presence. He is among the very few living Americans under the age of fifty who have been able to carve out a public space in contemporary American life for the many who otherwise feel unaddressed and unheard—a space in which he candidly speaks out for the marginalized communities from which he derives a sense of being and strength of purpose. Kushner names his otherness boldly, actively, and proudly. He affirms our potential as a people to recommit ourselves to the ideals of living dynamically and democratically on a global scale. Not only is this no small task, it is one that has silenced many who went before, who grew weary of the opposition's combative, punishing strategies. Kushner believes in and offers in his work a "hope" for humans to locate the space within, the soul without, to live and work beside one another cooperatively and peacefully, always mindful of both our differences and sameness. He is also aware of the ambiguities of life that constantly challenge this vision and the crises of experience that make one wary of utopianism while wholly embodying its hope. He addresses what is ahead of us. And he does so as an extraordinary, public intellectual.

In editing the previously unpublished interviews (all of which were conducted live), I have made every effort to keep Kushner's remarks as close to the original comments as possible. In general, I have taken the liberty to correct some language usage, eliminate some repetition, and cut material within a given interview in order to include more conversations in the collection. I have deliberately retained those features, such as audience laughter and applause and speakers' pauses and attempts to find the right word, that preserve the liveliness of each public performance. With one exception, all editing of interviewers' comments was done by me.

Kushner's interviews span a five-year period of astonishing artistic achievement and public acclaim, during which he conversed with many of America's most noted social commentators and artists, as well as with lesser-known figures whose interests represent specific religious, political, sexual, and theatrical communities. As gathered in this collection, Kushner's interviews are framed by past and future productions of his work in London at Great Britain's Royal National Theatre. At the beginning of this period is film critic Adam Mars Jones's interview with the playwright in 1992 at the RNT's Cottesloe Theatre after the acclaimed British premiere of *Angels in America, Part One: Millennium Approaches*. Four years later, Kushner's dialogues with playwrights Anna Deavere Smith and Naomi Wallace anticipate the playwright's future return to London to premiere at the RNT his eagerly awaited *Henry Box Brown or The Mirror of Slavery*, under the direction of George C. Wolfe in his European debut.

Kushner once said to television host Charlie Rose that "the task of my life is, in part, to try to understand it" (*Charlie Rose Show*, December 1, 1993). For me, this phrase illuminates several of the striking moments throughout the collection. Progressing toward his goal is Kushner's June 1993 conversation with Patrick Pacheco, in which the writer is remarkably candid and explicit in discussing his own sexuality and sexual history, as well as adult gay life in general. This interview is noteworthy as a testament to Tony Kushner's commitment to AIDS activism and as an indication that future interviews will reveal the process of change, of Kushner's continued development and maturation as a gay man and an artist.

Kushner's voice becomes increasingly confident and direct on a range of issues, as suggested in his 1994 conversation with novelist Michael Cunningham. Here, Kushner's willingness to adamantly disagree over a response to his work—some claim that *Angels* does not adhere to a "gay political correctness"—frees the playwright to address his ideology and aesthetics, as the personal/social converge with the political. Yet Kushner comes across as more relaxed and playful in conversations with other writers, including Cunningham, Craig Lucas, Susan Sontag, Anna Deavere Smith, and Naomi Wallace. They provide a kind of "breathing space" for Kushner where the dialectic, the "two not one," casually exists in mutual recognition of art and community.

Kushner's June 1994 appearance on *Charlie Rose*, in recognition and honor of the twenty-fifth anniversary of the Gay Liberation Movement, is an extraordinary, watershed document in this collection. Up to this point, Kushner has been alone in dialogue with single interviewers. The roundtable discussion on *Charlie Rose* placed Kushner among three other gay contemporaries—including Andrew Sullivan, at the time the editor of the conservative magazine the *New Republic,* with whom Kushner would continue to engage in print over such issues as homosexuality, identity politics, and the various political and social avenues for change in America. The *Charlie Rose* segment is a highly volatile, inflammatory conversation, one in which Kushner does not back down, although he does face formidable, equally aggressive opposition to his views: Sullivan, for instance, accused Kushner and lesbian writer-activist Donna Minkowitz of being "stuck in McCarthy and the 1960s." There is much "crosstalk" identified in the transcript of the televised "debate," an apt metaphor, also, for Kushner's earlier stated goal to "try to understand" himself better. It is fascinating to hear him as a participant in a bifurcated conversation on gay politics with other prominent gays and lesbians. Kushner's voice is only *one* voice amid others who passionately speak out and address the diversity within the gay and lesbian communities, especially in terms of identity, politics, ideology, and notions of change. He and Sullivan are both combative here, as the two go head-to-head.

Another striking marker of Kushner's stamina, flexibility, and fullness of presence at any given occasion is vividly captured during the twenty-two-day period in April 1995 when he gives three major live interviews in three distinct formats. Each, in and of itself, is an extensive document in terms of the transcript's length and the range of material covered. Collectively, they capture the various venues in which Kushner, at any given moment, finds himself on stage to address the public within the interview format. Seven days after a one-on-one discussion with fellow author Susan Sontag, Kushner is interviewed by four theater scholars and practitioners in front of a packed house at Northwestern University (an occasion that provides a glimpse of the impact Kushner's remarks can have on a panel of interviewers and an audience); soon after, he is interviewed by Rabbi Norman Cohen, Dean of Hebrew Union College–Jewish Institute of Religion, before the student body and public on the eve of Holocaust commemoration. One is impressed not only by Kushner's endurance during these demanding, lengthy, public performances, but also by the vast fund of knowledge he always draws from in provocative, illuminating ways. His contributions galvanize on audience's attention, for he is one of America's few public intellectuals.

In these three interviews, as well as throughout the collection, Kushner repeatedly acknowledges the influences on him, such as William Shakespeare, Karl Marx, Bertolt Brecht, Walter Benjamin, and Tennessee Williams. From this strong foundation, Kushner readily speaks his mind on the connections among politics, art, and activism. Constantly adjusting the frame of any given conversation to include or to allude to his views on democratic socialism, capitalism, agnosticism, and their relation to social issues—such as AIDS research, homophobia, welfare reform, sexism and gender inequities, the abuse of women and children, the environment, class struggles and the economics of everyday life, and global politics—Kushner summarizes his thoughts on the value of adjustable framing when speaking to Dean Norman Cohen: he adheres to a political model of action whereby one should be able to "drop everything" at a given moment in order to "act," since "[one's] art is not enough." While acknowledging the significance of individualism, Kushner argues that the individual is alone, and that it is only through the dialectic with community—"two not one"—that life has meaning as community moves toward necessary changes.

Never far behind (or sometimes even preceding) his social declarations is the playwright's passionate willingness to discuss the emotional capacities for people to alter substantially the dialectic, whether one focuses on our capacity for and struggle with hope, forgiveness, and sentiment or our ability or desire to identify that which is unspeakable or unforgivable in life. This reflection, in turn, generally leads Kushner to consider his own moral position, which he expresses consistently throughout the collection. Whether in dialogue with Robert Altman, Gordon Davidson, Susan Sontag, or Carl Weber, Kushner forthrightly asserts the centrality of *words* as the core of his being, his morality, and his aesthetics. He has reinvigorated our belief in the theater of language, and in the power of the written word in performance. Kushner is unwavering, interview by interview, in expressing his deep commitment to one's responsibility toward others, without which the belief in the materialization of joyful, supportive community is much harder to imagine, let alone to create. As an artist he accepts an ethical responsibility toward his craft and his audience, one that challenges his fellow artists and himself to consider their own positions and contributions as creators within the world. He remains committed to growth, to the possibilities of transformation as an individual, citizen, artist, and a member of various communities.

> I think that this is the most fertile period of American playwriting ever. . . . [W]e certainly have many, many more really good playwrights right now than we've ever had in our country's history. . . . I think that's true. It really is a weird little sort of tarnished golden age.
> (Tony Kushner, "The Theater and the Barricades")

For me, reading and seeing Tony Kushner's work does indeed evoke a contemporary renaissance, a "tarnished golden age" that has been generated by other American playwrights of the 1980s and 1990s.

I vividly recall numerous moments over the past six years when Tony Kushner's words leapt off the pages of his plays and grabbed my heart and mind, awakening in them a passion of acute recognition, if not a kind of momentary healing power. My first reading experience of Kushner's work was during a summer residency at Williams College in 1991, when a close friend sent a typescript copy of *Millennium Approaches* for me to read quickly and return just as quickly.

I sat in the quiet of the Berkshires (a treat in and of itself for a New Yorker) and turned pages seemingly faster than I ever had before. I pulled out the cast of characters so I could keep track of everyone. The script sailed by . . . my imagination was wildly free to see the staging, to hear the glorious words, to experience the various worlds that Kushner opened up. It was like no other play I had read previously. What made it captivating for me, however, were the odd echoes, the shadows of other presences hovering within and without the text; among them were Tennessee Williams, Gertrude Stein, George Jessel, Abraham Lincoln, Bertolt Brecht, Herman Melville, Lewis Carroll, the homeless kid in the building next to mine who sits nightly on the stoop, the faces of the dead, and my own faceless body. The text was compelling, compassionate, and humorous. Unrelenting. Thought-provoking. Then Belize spoke:

> *Belize:* I've thought about it for a very long time, and I still don't understand what love is. Justice is simple. Democracy is simple. Those things are unambivalent. But love is very hard.
>
> . . .

Soon, this . . . ruination will be blanketed white. You can smell
it—can you smell it?

Louis: Smell what?

Belize: Softness, compliance, forgiveness, grace.
(*Angels in America, Part One: Millennium Approaches,* 100)

I tried very hard that day to smell the ruination "blanketed white," but
I couldn't. I knew my own continual struggle to understand and to
feel deeply "forgiveness." Renaissance and transcendentalist thinking
washed over me, their differentiation between the powers allotted to
the human heart and the divine soul. Kushner had linked centuries-
old questions to contemporary ones. The play's poetry, its humility, its
political edge, and most of all the grace it hints at in life completely
filled me with joy and, yes, fear. I am astonished that I still carry with
me the emotions evoked by Kushner's words when I first read them
beneath lush mountainsides. I cherish them no less amid the relatively
treeless, urban island I now call home. Thus, the collection of interviews, to my complete gratification, enriches and enhances my earlier
memory, as it galvanizes the demanding challenges before us today
and in the future. And it does so not at the expense of one's loss of
hope.

As the collection quickly reveals, Kushner's talents as a playwright
soar far beyond the page. His work, after all, is meant first and foremost for live performance. His plays, as with all plays, are to be
performed—to be seen and heard before audiences. Kushner's sense
of captivating theatricality, his firsthand knowledge of the formidable
tasks that face a director and cast with any material, and his eagerness
to wholly embrace the power of storytelling before live audiences are
unique. Writing for the stage, Kushner is free to unravel, for himself,
the complicated relationship between ritual practice and theater practice, a topic that he engages with some frequency throughout his
interviews: the "spirituality" offered through theater and performance, the political nature of spirituality as represented in drama and
performance, and the politics of theater. Acknowledging that evil can
exist in the world, Kushner, an agnostic, courageously pushes for
answers or awareness as to *how* one is to live with this truth. His plays,
to a great extent, ask the audience to explore along with him the same
question(s) or, more dramatically and perhaps more honestly, to come
up with their own set of questions in an effort to unlock the mysteries
of the known and the unknown.

Look Back—and Forward— in Anger

Tom Szentgyorgyi

The following profile essay is significant because it is the first published piece to focus solely on Tony Kushner. The occasion for the article was the New York premiere of *A Bright Room Called Day* (Public Theater, January 1991). Tom Szentgyorgyi's discussion with Kushner took place in December 1990 at the Public Theater.

"Leaders like Reagan and Bush are essentially as morally debased as the people who followed Hitler. Bush may not be as psychotic—I think Reagan probably is—but whether or not they sound as crazy or have the same mustache, these are people who fundamentally place all sorts of ideological agendas and personal success above human rights. I think one of the things pushing Bush toward his holocaust in the Gulf is a slip in his popularity.

"It may be the case that because of the media, and the pressures of public life, most of the people that we elect to public office are not morally fit to be in a position of leadership. That's terrifying. And I think we have to be willing to look at that, in spite of a strong desire not to want to."

A Bright Room Called Day is a play born of bleak days.

In 1984 its author, Tony Kushner, recently deposited in the wider world from the New York University graduate program in directing, entered what he now calls "a very, very black time." A close relative died; a good friend and collaborator was in a serious car accident; his theater group, 3P (for the three P's of theater: poetry, politics, and

From *Theater Week* 6, no. 1 (January 14–21, 1991): 15–19.

A scene from the Epilogue of *A Bright Room Called Day,* directed by Michael Greif at the Joseph Papp Public Theater, 1991. Left to right, Zillah (Reno), Agnes Eggling (Frances Conroy), and Die Alte (Marian Seldes). (*Photo by Martha Swope © Time Inc.*)

popcorn), came apart; his mentor at NYU, Carl Weber, left to teach on the West Coast; and Ronald Reagan was reelected president. Somehow that last fact, and the dark political future it promised, seemed caught up in all the personal trials Kushner was facing. "The desolate political sphere mirrored in an exact and ugly way an equally desolate personal sphere," Kushner wrote in a recent essay.

Kushner developed a voracious appetite for literature dealing with German refugees in the 1930s (a response, he now believes, to the departure of the German-born Weber). And so he began work on a play "about Germans, refugee and otherwise, caught on the cusp of the historical catastrophe about to engulf them." He found his title at the Lincoln Center Library, where he misheard Agnes DeMille on videotape describing a new dance. "From across the room I thought she said it would be titled 'A Bright Room Called Day.' Which sounded lovely. Then, when I actually walked over to the videotape monitor, I discovered the dance was in fact called 'A Bridegroom Called Death.' But the other title stuck with me."

Written "very quickly," the play had its first production in 1985, in a six-performance run at Theater 22 directed by Kushner himself. Oskar Eustis, then artistic director of San Francisco's Eureka Theater, saw the play and brought it to his theater in 1987; the following year it was produced in London. Now it has returned to New York, to the Public Theater, where it opened January 7 under the direction of Michael Greif.

Set in Germany during the last months of the Weimar Republic, *A Bright Room Called Day* portrays the dissolution of a small circle of friends under the pressures created by the Nazis' rise to power. Kushner, an admirer and student of Brecht, was inspired by *Fear and Misery of the Third Reich* to juxtapose trivial and momentous events. "I love the idea of these little scenes showing daily life while the world was going to hell," Kushner says.

Daily life in the play takes place in the apartment of Agnes Eggling (named after DeMille, in thanks for her titular inspiration). A minor film actress, she is "the center of a group of extraordinary people who is herself not especially extraordinary," according to Kushner. As the Nazis ascend, she and her friends are forced to choose the course of their lives, forced to respond to the demands of an exacting and terrifying moment in history. For most, the choice is, finally, exile; for a few it is continued resistance. But for Agnes there is no choice; she experiences a slow collapse into passivity and solitude inside her Berlin apartment. "In a way the play is the story of the failure of these four people who are Agnes's friends," says Kushner. "Within the context of an entire social movement failing, that is. The collapse of Agnes's little coterie is in no way removable from the collapse of the German Communist Party, or the entire progressive movement for that matter."

The story of Agnes and her friends might evoke little more than what one of Kushner's characters angrily calls "elegant despair" were it not for another character in the play: an irritant, a contemporary provocateur, a guerrilla theatrical presence. Her name is Zillah, and in the New York production she is played by the lesbian Lenny Bruce of our day, Reno.

"There are moments in history when the fabric of everyday life unravels, and there is this unstable dynamism that allows for incredible social change in short periods of time. People and the world they're living in can be utterly transformed, either for the good or the bad, or some mixture of the two. I think that Russia in 1917 was one of those times, Chile under Allende was one of those times. It's a moment when the ground and the sky sort of split apart, and there's a space, a revolutionary space. During these periods all sorts of people—even people who are passive under the pressure of everyday life in capitalist society—are touched by the spirit of revolution and behave in extraordinary ways. These spaces only exist for very limited periods of time and then somebody's going to get control. And what happens frequently is that the Left doesn't get control. Because the forces are very powerful against a successful Left revolution. That's what the play is about, that's what a 'bright room called day' is. That space. If the Left had not lost heart at a series of critical moments, I think Hitler might not have been able to take power, or consolidate his power. And the fact that they lost heart and lost the struggle is a catastrophe for the entire planet."

Zillah interrupts *A Bright Room Called Day* with harangues to the audience on contemporary politics—called interruptions in the script—that are delivered with a blend of glee, malevolence, and semihysterical energy. "I added Zillah because I didn't want the play simply to exist as a metaphor," Kushner says. She is the play's immediate and irrefutable connection between Germany in the 1930s and America in 1990; and she's been known to unsettle some audience members. "Everyone came out of the play wanting to argue with her," says Eustis.

14

"We're so allergic to politics in the theater," says Kushner, "and I wanted to treat that. I wondered, while I was writing it, what if, in the middle of this well-made, little four-wall drama someone stood up and said well, what's the most obnoxious thing anyone could say in 1985? 'You've just reelected Adolph Hitler.' "

Zillah has changed over the years. In 1985 her anger was at Reagan himself; it was a response to the bleak political spirit his reelection and the absence of effective protest created. Today, in the kinder, gentler world, it is Reagan's legacy that Zillah must cope with, and in particular the challenge of mounting opposition to the Right when the Left's death knell is being sounded all over the world. "I feel one of the legacies of the Reagan era is to drive a very powerful wedge between the American people and their political reality," says Kushner. "There's a kind of amnesia that the country has always been guilty of but that has now become a national political style. I think the Reagan administration was a major beachhead for that style."

Zillah now addresses the audience from Berlin, where she has gone "to see the Wall come down." She has taken an apartment—Agnes's old apartment—and the play is in part the story of the two women making contact. "Zillah is concerned with not remembering history, not being able to learn from history," says Kushner, "so she goes to Berlin to reconnect with history in as visceral a way as possible at the very time the Right is claiming that history is over. She's trying to make contact with a ghost, with some embodiment of the past, and she does." In the end Zillah leaves Berlin to return to the United States. "It's a kind of reverse exile, a decision to reengage."

Some critics have made the assumption, usually on the way to an unfavorable conclusion, that Zillah is The Author's Voice. This irritates Kushner no end. "There are a lot of political positions trotted out in *Bright Room* that are informed by the histories of the people that hold them. Zillah is one of those people. It's not me getting up on stage."

Tony Kushner, New York born, was toted down to Lake Charles, Louisiana ("No one asked me if I wanted to go"), at the age of one by his musician parents. When he left Lake Charles it was for Columbia University and a medieval studies major. After college he spent three summers teaching back in Louisiana and directing his young southern charges in plays by Shakespeare and a Brecht Lehrstucke, *The Baden Play for Learning: On Consent*. "That was pretty weird. All these little kids mouthing this cryptic Stalinist stuff. The parents loved it. It was a real lesson in how ineffectual theater can be, because the audience was made up of completely reactionary yahoos who I'm sure all voted for David Duke." His interest in Brecht led him to NYU. Kushner then did stints as a director at the Repertory Theater of St. Louis, at the New York Theater Workshop, and at the Theater Communications Group, where he was—briefly—director of literary services, before what he calls "this playwriting thing" began to offer a living wage.

These days Kushner can't write fast enough to please people. In addition to *Bright Room,* his adaptation of Corneille's *The Illusion* has appeared in New York, Hartford, and L.A. It so impressed the locals in the last town that Universal Pictures snapped up the film rights; Kushner is now working on the screenplay. He has also been working with Ariel Dorfman on an adaptation of the Chilean writer's play *Widows.* And then there is *Angels in America,* the opus that has occupied much of his time for the past three years. Subtitled *A Gay Fantasia on National Themes,* it is a massive work, intended to be performed over two nights, that explores AIDS, the age of Reagan, and the same question that bedevils the Berlin cadre of *Bright Room:* What do you do when you face a calamity of historical proportions? "It's about people being trapped in systems that they didn't participate in creating," Kushner says. "The point being we're now in a new world in so many ways, we have to reinvent ourselves. It's the reverse of *Bright Room;* the characters need to create their own myths to empower themselves. I think that's the whole point of liberation politics: to try to create new systems." Parts 1 and 2 of *Angels in America* will premiere at the Eureka Theater in San Francisco from May 18 to June 30.

"I have a kind of dangerously romantic reading of American history. I do think there is an advantage to not being burdened by history the way Europe is. This country has been, in a way, an improvisation of hastily assembled groups that certainly have never been together before and certainly have a lot of trouble being together, but who recognize that our destiny is not going to be a racial destiny. Anyone who thinks that completely self-interested politics is going to get you anywhere in America is making a terrible mistake. Which is why I object to Louis Farrakhan. Which is why I object to gays and lesbians in ACT UP who say 'I hate straights.' Or to Jews who think that the only thing that matters is Israel and defense against anti-Semitism. People who don't recognize common cause are going to fail politically in this country. Movements that capture the imagination of people are movements that deny racism and exclusion. The country is too mongrel to do otherwise. This country is made up of the garbage, the human garbage that capitalism created: the prisoners and criminals and religiously persecuted and the oppressed and the slaves that were generated by the ravages of early capital. That creates a radical possibility in this country that's unique."

Tony Kushner at the Royal National Theatre of Great Britain

Adam Mars Jones

Part One of *Angels in America, Millennium Approaches* premiered at the Royal National Theatre on January 23, 1992. The following evening, after the play received overwhelming acclaim in the London press, Kushner was interviewed by Adam Mars Jones, an author and film critic for the *Independent* since 1986, at the Cottesloe Theatre.

ADAM MARS JONES: Your play *Angels in America* has two controversial words in the subtitle: *A Gay Fantasia on National Themes.* One is "gay," the other is "national." Which would you rather talk about first?

TONY KUSHNER: What was important to me was the conjunction of the two words. I felt that a lot of what you could identify as gay theater in America (and I don't know if it's as true in England) in the late sixties and seventies was focused very extensively on domestic issues and relational issues. That was appropriate to its historical moment and to what was of concern to the community at that time, because the notion of gay liberation was relatively new. I think there's a shift in attention happening now, and *Angels* is an example of that. There are other lesbian and gay writers in the States who are beginning to address issues that connect personal dynamics and questions of relationships with the political issues that are of such tremendous significance to the lives of gay men and women. In American drama, politics tends to be very, very deeply embedded in psychological, familial, relational

From *Platform Papers 2: On "Angels in America,"* published in August 1992 by the Royal National Theatre. The interview took place on January 24, 1992, at the Royal National Theatre. Over one hundred spectators paid the equivalent of $5 to attend the event.

issues and I think that American playwrights in general are beginning to feel more and more comfortable with making overt the politics that our relationships are always riven with.

AMJ: The play premiered on the West Coast and has had two productions there, and has yet to make an appearance on the East Coast. Is that intentional?

TK: That is completely by design. It's coming to New York next year. New York is a scary place because of the critical establishment there, but it's very important to me to bring the play there.

AMJ: It's still important?

TK: Well, it's about New York, it's where I live and in a certain sense I feel that it's more my community than the San Francisco gay and lesbian community is, though it was commissioned and written for San Francisco. I don't know if people in the audience have been to San Francisco?

AMJ: How important is that?

TK: It's only important in that, of the places that I've been, it's the most "gay positive" (a stupid expression, but it's true). It's a city where the gay and lesbian community wields an enormous amount of political power, where homophobia is simply no longer acceptable in the general political discourse. That's absolutely not the case in New York, where homophobia can win you elections. A few months ago Pete Wilson, the governor of California, refused to sign a law legitimizing gay and lesbian domestic partnership. There was yet another riot in San Francisco and the state building was completely trashed. My former lover called me from the middle of the riot. He had just moved there from New York and was standing there in astonishment. It is Oz in a way, it's not real. It's this wonderful city on the western end of a vast nation of homophobes. You can't imagine a more congenial place to put this work forward. The audiences and the critics simply accepted the sexual politics of the play as a given, and that's been a real blessing.

AMJ: In a program note you say that because you were getting federal money, you felt the play had to have a national dimension. I thought in a way you were disowning your own perfectly legitimate ambitions. I notice in your biography you've had money from the Princess Grace Foundation, but you didn't write a role for a soignée blonde. You wanted to write a play that is as broad as possible, and that in itself is new and doesn't need to be apologized for, coming from a gay playwright. Do you think there are particular problems because of the sort of country that America is? One of the strongest speeches in the play is also the one that comes under fiercest attack: the one that says socialist views are different in America because America is different, that race is different in America because all the races are somehow contesting more equally than they do elsewhere. As there is no primal race, there are not native Americans in positions of power. So even race is different in America. Is that the problem, that America is different? Even an issue like AIDS, which seems universal in that every country has it—there were two cases reported on Easter Island last week—AIDS is everywhere but it is different everywhere. Is that a problem when you're exporting a view of your whole country?

TK: The play felt so much addressed to Americans and about America that I never really imagined it was going to go anywhere else. A German publisher called to ask if I had a new show a couple of years ago and took a look at it. He said, well it's a nice play but we wouldn't understand it here. So I was surprised that the National wanted to do it. I now believe it works here. I don't know if this is an answer to the question.

Another change that is happening, completely as a consequence of the AIDS epidemic, is that it's becoming clearer and clearer to the gay and lesbian community in the States, and probably elsewhere, that there are life and death consequences to homophobia. We always knew that. There was always gay bashing and bloodshed and emotional violence, but it's not until you realize that people are simply willing to let hundreds of thousands of people die and not extend simple human compassion because of their sexual preferences, that you realize how deep the hatred goes. It's become clear, as a result of this, that what seemed to be a marginal issue was actually very deeply rooted in American consciousness. Whatever the root causes of homophobia are, they are very deep and must in some way be integral to the structure of the heterosexual majority consciousness. Gay theory and gay art in the States are beginning to roll around to this point of view. We've come to reconsider the ways in which the oppression of minority groups is actually part of the central project of the majority. There's a new book by a woman named Eve Kosofsky Sedgwick called *Epistemology of the Closet,* in which she says that the closet is really the central space in Western consciousness from the beginning of this century, that the dialectics of heterosexuality and homosexuality are incredibly central when you take an overview of Western literature and thought in the last century. It's a very persuasive argument.

AMJ: Would it be fair to say that *Angels in America* is as much about gay obligations as gay rights? For instance you do imaginatively re-create Roy Cohn, a self-hating gay person, who would be the very first person thrown out of the balloon in a balloon debate amongst gays. In a discussion on who of our persuasion we least want to acknowledge has anything in common with the rest of us, he would be first to go. Also there's a certain amount of drag (which is fairly incidental) and quite a lot of camp in the play, which is the flavor of gay culture which was most stigmatized. Was this consciously done?

TK: There are two questions in that. The issue of dealing with Roy, I think I've mentioned in the program. (The thing about national funding in the program note*—I wrote that very quickly, and it was supposed to be a joke, but I left the punch line kind of open so it sounds like I'm completely serious.) When we got that federal grant, it was in the middle of the Reagan years (or at the end of them, but he was still in office). The application for it was very honest. I said I was going to write a play about gay men and Mormons and Roy Cohn, sent it in to the federal government under Reagan, and thought, this will come back immediately with no money attached. Then they gave us this huge check and it was the first federal money I'd ever gotten. In the United States there's a very strong feeling of power being invested in the federacy and in Washington. It was Washington money with an eagle stamped on the check. So I felt, when I was writing it, that it was taxpayers' money, and I do think that had some impact on the play's scope.

I think the play has become—and I didn't intend this when I started writing it—a play about the extent of a community's embrace. I think what you're saying is interesting, that one side of that question is whether or not it's possible to feel any kind of kinship or solidarity with someone like Roy Cohn, who was one of the most hateful men that ever lived, a tremendously evil man. I'm a little worried that in the process of figuring that out I've overdone it and he's maybe too sympathetic a character.

AMJ: I don't want him to leave the stage, but he's not sympathetic.

TK: It's interesting to examine questions of forgiveness and communal embrace when you're dealing with somebody as unacceptable as Roy was. On the other side of the equation, the question of drag and camp: I think that the community has grown up a lot, especially in the last few years. When the epidemic first hit, the first reaction, especially

---

*The program note ends with: "Since the writing was funded by a Federal grant, I felt the play ought to have a National dimension, and as it was a considerable sum, I wanted to give the taxpayers their money's worth."

among many gay men, was a complete repudiation of sex: saying we've made a terrible mistake, we should never have been screwing around as much as we were and now we're paying the price. They adopted the response of the Right, and said maybe they were right, we should have been aping a monogamy model, and all of that backroom stuff was terrible. The Stonewall riots happened in New York in 1969, the night that Judy Garland died, when all these drag queens refused to be arrested and taken out of a bar—the beginning of the gay liberation movement in the States and I guess elsewhere. The moment we said we're not apologizing for the sex, and we're not going to stop having it, we are involved in a very legitimate experiment, we're not going to be embarrassed or ashamed, or deprived of something we're working on, that our historical mission is to investigate—that was the first moment of real political sophistication in gay liberation since Stonewall.

AMJ: When was that moment? We may have missed it. I can see what you mean about the political realization, but what public event crystallized it? The foundation of ACT UP?

TK: ACT UP is certainly a big part of that. I'm thirty-five, there are gay men now who are fifteen years younger than me (of course I still think of myself as being ten) who grew up post-Stonewall all over the United States, in a world where the struggle for the establishment of gay subjectivity instead of subjection was really under way. They're much less apologetic.

AMJ: I should explain that ACT UP is the Aids Coalition to Unleash Power. There is an equivalent in this country, I think a little less aggressive because, for instance, on medical issues, the existence of a National Health Service does make a difference. If you're not paying directly for medication, you're less likely to picket Burroughs Wellcome for the price you have to pay for it. But is it the case that the second play is going to have strong ACT UP themes, or is it too early to tell?

TK: There's the beginning of it. The first moment of the second evening is the angel saying "Boogie boogie" and then going away. The first act takes place on the same night but you don't see what happens with the angel, and the second act starts three weeks later, then skips back to that night, and takes the entire act to show what the angel has done. In the course of the second evening, Belize (the nurse, and Prior's best friend) becomes, through a series of coincidences, Roy Cohn's live-in nurse. He takes the job with Roy Cohn because Roy has gotten his hands on an entire private stash of AZT, which at this point was being tested in Bethesda [Maryland], as his doctor mentions in Part One. It's a drug, one of the only drugs (there are three now) that prevent viral replication, but it's terribly toxic and hard on the body. There's a huge controversy in the AIDS community about whether or not it's better to just stay away from it. Roy clearly was killed by it. He was overmedicated and died from it. It's just being tested at the time of the play, and Belize decides that he's going to steal it, so accepts the job with Roy. That's the beginning. In 1985–86 there was no activist movement like ACT UP, but people with AIDS had formed all sorts of informal networks, basically to get their hands on medication. It was the beginning of what I think is a real phenomenon of the AIDS epidemic, which was a community of people suffering from a disease mobilizing themselves and claiming power and demanding rights, confronting not only government but the medical establishment. Driving their doctors crazy, demanding good health care. It's becoming a model. In the States now there's a drastic increase in breast cancer among young women. Clearly part of the problem is that, because it's a woman's disease, not enough research has been done. Also about abortion. There are political groups now beginning to form around medical issues.

AMJ: There is a sense in which the logic of solidarity leads to a different sort of insularity. Outing for instance—you can see the logic that says "If we are all in it together, and it is life and death, then you, my gay brother who is in the closet, have no right to remain there, and I will destroy you rather than let you remain there." At what point do you feel that logic has gone far enough, or do you follow it all the way? If so, it's strange to be able to forgive, imaginatively, someone like Roy Cohn, but not be able to forgive people who are doing much less obvious damage in the present, other than committing the terrible crime of not acknowledging themselves. How far do you go with outing?

TK: I don't know what the answer to it is. I personally don't like it. I certainly would have supported anyone with information about Roy Cohn outing him at any point. Unfortunately he was outed by an American journalist named Jack Anderson who got his hands on Roy's medical records when he was in treatment in Bethesda, and announced to the world that Roy Cohn was dying of AIDS. Everyone knew that Roy was gay but there had never been any proof, he had always denied it, and in fact if you said it in print he would sue you. He was the most litigious man that ever lived, he sued everyone all the time. So, he was outed by having AIDS and the response that the press made at the time was really revolting in all sorts of ways. I find it very unacceptable to take actors or writers who choose to be in the closet, and feed them to what is largely an antigay press so that people can make horrible comments about them. I do think they should all be out. I think it's morally incumbent on gay people to tell the world they're gay, because we need to have a presence in the world. Being in the closet is personally disempowering and not something that anybody really ought to do. In the States there are a lot of actors who are in the closet, in the theater and in movies, and I don't think they need to be. They'd be surprised at how acceptable they would be if they came out.

AMJ: Except you can't take it back if it doesn't work out! There is this logic that says once you come up with the phrase "Queer Nation" then "Queer Treason" becomes part of the description of some people.

TK: Queer Nation leads to Queer Nationalism and who wants Nationalism? I have a problem with that, although the group Queer Nation is rather remarkable.

AMJ: Where would you draw the line? With politicians?

TK: The assistant secretary of defense in America is a gay man, whose name is Pete Williams. He's the spokesman for the Pentagon, he's always on television, and he's known by everyone in Washington as being gay. When he was outed in the *Advocate,* which is the national gay and lesbian news magazine, most of the straight press wouldn't pick it up because they felt it was unfair. But the armed forces in the United States are tremendously discriminatory against gay men and women, and this man is assistant secretary of defense. I think he deserved it and they deserve it. It provoked a lot of useful discussion. I don't feel quite as sympathetic with politicians if they're involved actively with discrimination. There is a gay movie star, who I won't name, who has made a film that is hideously, hideously antigay. I have great respect for this particular person but the movie is a nightmare, and shame on this person.

AMJ: Of the three themes of this play, Mormonism always seems to come third for some reason. We'll give it a little bit of a run for its money. Have you spent time in Salt Lake City? Did you choose Mormonism because it's the American religion that is most folksy and strange, or were there other reasons?

TK: I have spent time in Salt Lake, but that's not particularly where the theme came from. Mormonism is a theology that I think could only really have come from America. The *Book of Mormon*—since I don't believe it is actually from God—is fairly clearly a work of nineteenth-century American literature. It's not the most readable book, but clearly of a tradition that also produced *Moby-Dick* and *Huckleberry Finn*. The theology is an American reworking of a western tradition that is uniquely American: the notion of an uninhabited world in which it's possible to reinvent. It's part of the political project of westward expansion and genocide against native American populations, because it gives a moral ranking to color of skin: the darker you are, the farther away you are from goodness. I think the Mormons in Britain have a very different reputation. They seem to be more "cultey." In America, when you visit them in Salt Lake, they have a kind of indigenous dignity that they may not have when they travel abroad. They're very interesting people, the ones that I've met and known personally, I've always liked them a lot. They're very decent, hardworking, serious, intelligent people. But they're very reactionary.

AMJ: But the two go together. You can't be surprised that being hardworking and reactionary should go together. When you're a pioneer they must, if you're to survive.

TK: And it's very much a pioneer religion. That conjunction is intriguing to me. Reactionaries like Roy are a lot of fun but they're as lousy as you feel the consequences of their ideology are. Mormons always seem much nicer people than what they wind up visiting on themselves and the rest of Utah. That contradiction is very interesting.

AMJ: I remember talking to a Mormon who said he was retired and did Temple work. It turned out that Temple work meant being baptized in other people's stead. That meant he was being washed on the nipples and genitals hundreds of times a day so that other people's souls could be sealed for all eternity. That sounds more fun than most religious vocations.

TK: In a way it reminds me of Judaism in that they have an interesting ambivalence toward sensuality and the flesh. They are actually a very "touch-ey" bunch of people and yet they have a lot of strictures about physical contact and sex that are as puritanical as one can imagine. It's older and far more confusing in Judaism. There are a number of similarities.

AUDIENCE MEMBER: About casting—in New York will it be star casting or will it be an ensemble piece right from the start?

TK: It was originally written for eight main actors. Roy, Joe, Louis, Prior, Harper, Belize, Hannah, and the Angel. Those characters play all the parts, crowds of them in Part Two. The Rabbi, Roy's doctor, Hannah, and Ethel were written to be played by an actress that I know in New York. Martin, the man who pressures Joe to take the job in Washington in the restaurant scene, was written to be played by Joe's wife Harper, which adds a certain twilight-zone dimension to that scene. Declan [Donnellan, director] and I talked when we were casting

25

and the National were very generous and said if you want a ninth actor you can have one, and I'd always wondered what the dynamics would be, especially in the scene with Roy and his doctor. The woman that I wrote the part for is very good at playing men—but we felt it would be very interesting to try it this way, so that's how we did it. But the doubling for me is very important. I think it makes it into a community. To see Roy come in as the second Prior ghost is important somehow. It adds up. All the characters double at some point. They all appear as angels in Part Two.

AMJ: Why is the angel such a western-tradition angel? Would Mormon angels be different?

TK: The thing that appeared to Joseph Smith, to tell him where the book was hidden, was not ever actually described as an angel in his writing. He calls it a personage in robes of surpassing whiteness. It's not described as having wings. This is Prior's angel, not Joseph Smith's. Prior's angel would definitely have wings.

Five of the eight parts were written for specific actors in San Francisco, they've been playing it since I first started working with it, and they'll stick with it until they go stark raving mad and have to be taken home and replaced. They'll do it in Los Angeles in the fall and then they'll travel with it, practically all of next year in the States, and arrive in New York next spring.

AUDIENCE MEMBER: Could I ask you about the Jewish side of the play? Do you think Jewishness is a main theme or an incidental issue? Also I'm interested in the fact that both of the main Jewish characters are quite unsavory and unpleasant. Obviously Roy Cohn is, but I wondered why you chose to make Louis such a miserable individual as well.

TK: Oh God, *I* don't think he's miserable! He's certainly miserable in the sense that he's incredibly unhappy. I have to say that question has come up before. Judaism isn't what the play is about, but I'm Jewish and it took me by surprise that it wound up being all over the play. Louis is an interesting character to me. I think one of the wonderful things about Marcus [D'Amico]'s performance is that, much more than any other time I've seen the character played, I think that he's tremendously "empathizable." I think Louis carries the biggest burden of the play. One of the things it's about is that it's incredibly hard to take care of someone who is catastrophically ill. I think this is going to become an issue that is inescapable, because people are getting sicker all the time. We live in a very bad time for the human body and this is a problem that all of us are going to have to face at a much younger age than our parents did. Louis wrestles with that particular angel and sometimes people are very upset by the choices he makes, but he's struggling tremendously with it. I'm very critical of Jews because I am one and, for instance, Jewish homophobia makes me angrier than Goyische homophobia. I think, good God, after what we've gone through for the last six hundred years and before . . . surely suffering should teach you compassion. So I've been kind of hard about it. But there are also two other Jews in the play, there's Ethel—you see a lot more of her in Part Two—and the Rabbi.

AUDIENCE MEMBER: There are two main women in the play, Harper and her mother, Hannah. I know there is a Part Two, but the three scenes that Hannah has seem inconsequential to what's happening to the main characters. I'm curious what happens to her and to Harper.

TK: I can't really deal with the two women as being equal. Harper is very central to Part One. And what Hannah does, in the phone call with Joe, is not in any sense inconsequential because her response produces the next scene, which produces the next act, which produces what happens at the end of the play between Louis and Joe. She is, in a certain way, a Part Two character, as are Belize, and the Angel. They are characters who have a bushel more in Part Two. I hate playwrights who talk about their plays as if they were music because they're not, but you think of it sometimes that way. I don't know how to explain why those two women (Hannah and Ella Chapter) come in at the end of the second act, except that emotionally and textually it's an introduction of another kind of music, another theme. Did it bother you?

AUDIENCE MEMBER: It's just that we're seeing Part One without Part Two.

TK: Well, you had to do it with *Star Wars* . . .

AUDIENCE MEMBER: Could I ask about positive images? What I found fascinating and exciting about the play is that it seemed to have moved beyond simply doing a glossy propaganda exercise in a very good cause. You didn't seem to be too worried about possible homophobes in the audience maybe drawing the wrong conclusions. There seemed a much more relaxed attitude toward presenting images of gay people. What do you think are the benefits and restrictions of a positive images policy?

TK: It's a very complicated issue. I think one really has to trust that the good cause will speak even through bad characters. It's just no fun to watch polemics. If you're telling a story it has to be full of all the twists and nooks and crannies that people's stories are full of. If you're really committed, and you want badly to see the world change, because you believe it's very screwed up right now and people are in great danger, and you're engaged in the struggle in your own life, you can trust more that it will come across in your writing. This sounds pompous, I don't mean it to sound like I'm an example of this because I think sometimes I'm not. But I do think that if your politics are good enough it will come through. You don't have to go about saying it, the characters will say it.

AUDIENCE MEMBER: I must say that at certain points of the play I could not see you anywhere behind the characters.

TK: The great thing about being a playwright is that you never have to take responsibility for anything. It's my second play. With the first play that I wrote, I was much more conscious of a design and plan. It was about Reagan's reelection, although it was set in the Weimar Republic. It was a very angry response to Reagan. When I started writing *Angels,* I deliberately set myself the most weird assortment of things and had no idea how to tie them together. I trusted that connections would become clear. You read about Chekhov that he desperately wanted plays to turn out differently and they just wouldn't. The Democracy in America scene happened like this: I had written acts 1 and 2, the Eureka people [Eureka Theater, San Francisco, who commissioned the play] were screaming at me every day, "Where is the play, it's six months late and we have to go into production. What are you doing?" I was contracted to write a two-and-a-half-hour play with songs—that was the original contract for *Angels.* I had no way of resolving it. I started to sketch in an outline. It was clearly two evenings long and went on forever. So I actually sat down and asked Louis (who is the character I identify with most, not for autobiographical reasons, but just as a person) to tell me what the play was about so I could end it. This sounds silly but I just started writing and that scene came out in twenty-five minutes. It just poured out and that was tremendously exciting. I really felt like there was this other person. It sounds a little schitzy, but that's what it felt like. Sometimes there are things that characters just won't do and if I ask them to do it, the scene is lousy.

Nobody knows the answer to any political problems any more. We've lost our way so profoundly, we're in such a complete miasma, theoretically and politically. Systems have really collapsed around us. Whether you were a socialist or not the presence of socialism, even if you were vehemently anti-socialist, gave a dialectical depth to the world—the fact that there was this other place. It really wasn't socialism in the sense that people talked about in the nineteenth century, but the world had two sides in a certain way, there was a space held out and that's gone now. There's a terrible sense of flatness, or it feels that way in America. The play can't help but reflect that sense, that people are looking all over the place for answers and making great messes in the process.

The Eye of the Storm

Craig Lucas

On January 20, 1993, during Bill Clinton's inauguration as the forty-second president of the United States, Tony Kushner and Craig Lucas, two of America's most prominent playwrights, met privately in a small office at the Theatre Communications Group, the New York–based national organization for nonprofit theater. Lucas, author of such plays as *Prelude to a Kiss, Reckless, Blue Window,* and *God's Heart,* and screenwriter of *Longtime Companion,* conversed with Kushner as auditions were being held in the same building to cast the New York premiere of *Angels in America, Millennium Approaches.* Part One of the two-part, seven-hour epic would open at the Walter Kerr Theatre on May 4, 1993.

CRAIG LUCAS: It must all be overwhelming.

TONY KUSHNER: Yeah, it is. It's been a very, very strange time. I feel very lost and confused and sort of unclear about what I should be doing with the play, where I should be going with it and where I should be going after the play is done, and it's not going to be done for quite a while because we're not even going to open *Perestroika* until October of next year, and then it'll be opening in London at the same time.

CL: Will you get a chance to work on a production of *Perestroika* before it comes to New York?

TK: I'm going to workshop it with some NYU graduate students. That's probably all I'll do with it. I'm beginning to run out of steam, because I've been working on the play pretty much since 1988; I wrote

From *BOMB* 43 (spring 1993): 30–35.

one play in the middle of working on *Angels,* but that was an adaptation [Corneille's *The Illusion*]. So I feel like it's time to move on. I don't want this to be the only thing that I ever write. And I have a lot of plays that I've backlogged in the meanwhile, so I wanted a director that I could just give the play to for New York and not really have to sit and watch very closely. I hope that I am banned from rehearsals. It's like being in therapy with somebody for a long time. I've done as much work with these people as I can possibly do. It's time to go and find another gig.

CL: It can turn into a cottage industry, and you don't want to be that mother hen following it around.

TK: And the question of whether you want to make it into a film, or whether writing a screenplay is a good idea. You can spend years and years and years, and it's probably a terrible mistake. One thing the play's taught me is that I can let it go.

CL: What you have in your favor is the force of your clarity, a lucidity. So much modern art is about ambiguity and what one is going to read into it. You've created a moral universe which allows audiences to watch your characters run 180 degrees in the *wrong* direction. It's enjoyable to watch Roy Cohn, and at the same time even the most right-wing fundamentalist homophobe would not suspect that you were endorsing this man's values.

TK: Yeah, I hope not. I mean, I still feel—especially in *Perestroika* —there were people in the audience in L.A. who cried when Roy Cohn died. And the audience was kind of shifting in their seats and thinking, "Well, *should* we be crying?" Which is, I guess, the point. I'd like to explore being ambiguous a little bit more in the future. I feel sometimes that that's kind of a flaw in the work.

CL: It's not that there are no contradictions. I simply mean there's this sense of mastery. For a seven-hour play, it's very economical. There's not a lot of fat.

TK: Yeah. *Millennium* was about forty pages longer in its first draft and *Perestroika* was literally twice the length, so they've both been boiled down. I don't think that there is actually a great deal of fat. I've listened to *Millennium* now for a long time, and I'm a very fat writer in several senses of the word. *[Laughter.]* I've been working with a lot of very good editors and directors, and because we knew that the ultimate thing was going to be as prodigiously long as it is, we couldn't really afford to be sentimental about anything, everything that could possibly go would go. One of the things that worries me about the play is that everybody in it, except for Roy, is sort of a decent person trying

31

their best. And that's part of the appeal of the play, but it's the part of me that I worry about being excessively liberal, that I genuinely believe people are primarily motivated by the good. And I wonder if that makes everything a little bit vanilla. There's a certain kind of writing that starts with a more cynical set of assumptions about people, that produces a harsher picture of reality. And the world is a harsh place, so I'm trying to figure out what it is in myself that resists seeing the world that way. Excessive optimism or sentimentality or something . . . I don't know.

CL: Well, I'm here to dissuade you from this delusion. I think you picture a complex universe.

TK: I'm not sure that I'm explaining myself correctly. You want to believe that people are usually behaving according to standards that they've set for themselves that are assigned qualifications like good and bad. And the thing that works about Roy is that I proceeded from the assumption that his world made sense to him and that he wasn't operating with conscious knowledge of being a bad man. And I think that people do proceed, for the most part, from that assumption. But—

CL: Hitler.

TK: Hitler. Well, yeah, *exactly*. Where does evil come from? Is Bush really proceeding from just a very bad ideological system that he's being true to, that he's consequently doing very bad things because of his fidelity to that? Or is there something else at work? Because when you look at somebody like Bush, you see a monstrously cynical man, or one reading of Bush might be that. He'd be an interesting character for a play because the question is whether or not people that do really terrible things are always self-justifying in the way that I have Roy self-justify, or whether or not there's more clarity about the malevolence that they're creating.

CL: Like Richard the Third.

TK: Yeah. Which is a very daring . . . or Iago. There are characters in Shakespeare which at some point say to the audience: "There is no human justification for what I am, and I represent a kind of evil that's more radical and more profound than human evil." That's the question that Hannah Arendt asks or gets asked when she puts forth the notion of the banality of evil in *Eichmann in Jerusalem*. For somebody like Eichmann, for a petty demon, that seems a sufficient explanation, but for somebody that really does immense historical damage, not a Roy Cohn, but an Adolf Hitler, how do you describe that evil, what do you call it, and how do you account for it in a system that doesn't have a very clear spiritual dimension? If there isn't a devil, then what is that evil? I mean, I feel that maybe the plays are a little too forgiving. But I don't know.

CL: Do you think there is a devil?

TK: I just had a big argument with a friend of mine who was telling me that he fears the devil and believes in the existence of the satanic. And I guess I don't. But then maybe I just don't want to believe it. That's what I mean by saying that I worry about being too liberal. So much of what we've lived through in the last twelve years has shown us that these people really are murderers. They're very, very, very evil people.

CL: Yes, I agree. But you know you can be a murderous villain simply by virtue of leading an unexamined life.

TK: Yeah . . . you can be that. But do you want to say then that all evil is to be ascribed to ignorance and a lack of examination and a lack of analysis? There's something very comforting about believing that, because it suggests a continuity between yourself, the people that you know and love and have conversations with and reason with, and those people who are doing this terrible thing. It suggests that Bush or Reagan or a Hitler or the neo-Nazi skinheads who are now beating up disabled people in Germany, that these people are really just part of the human community, and that there's some way . . . if their *system* is bad, as long as they're basically faithful adherents to a system in the way that you are faithful to a moral vision that you have, then you should be able to convince them of the inappropriateness of their system and reason them out of their evil behavior. But that may in fact be wrong. There may be something at work, and I don't know what that something is, but there may be a kind of active malevolence that's beyond . . . that has to be resisted, *I think,* finally with force. So you have writers like Larry Kramer, for instance, whose anger clearly goes in the direction—I don't know whether Larry has actually ever advocated violence or not (but I guess he sort of has) but certainly people who have no real problem saying, "These people are our enemies, and there is no community between us." That may be the difference between being a radical and being a liberal. You're not sentimental about letting go of that continuum.

CL: Abuse, whether it comes in the form of poverty or ignorance or sexual molestation, can actually twist a mind and a psyche to such a degree that you have Jeffrey Dahmers on a mass scale.

TK: Yeah.

CL: Witness the fascists in Germany. Those are, I believe, sociologically induced psychoses.

TK: Yeah.

CL: They're not going to be changed in individuals who are over a certain age.

TK: Right.

CL: But perhaps the way the next generation is raised can be changed. By force, I agree. It's a curious contradiction, though. In your play, *A Bright Room Called Day*, you call the Gulf War a misadventure, or your character Zillah does, and she states that the U.S. is trying to start World War III. But then another character, Paz, is held up to criticism for *not* shooting Hitler when he has the opportunity. I sometimes drop my liberalism when I think about Hussein or Milosevic who through the force of their will and hatred would certainly annihilate you and me. How far are they from Hitler? I'm not sure that *I'm* so far from Mr. Bush, though he may have had different goals in mind, surely he did, when he used force against a murderous dictator. What are your feelings about Serbia and Bosnia? Do we have any responsibility there?

TK: Those situations are terribly difficult. It's very hard for me to ever say that I think unilateral military action on the part of the United States can be a great thing at this point. The idea of the United States armed forces going in and suppressing and controlling a population of any sort is so fraught with history. And I don't trust our government, I don't trust our motives, so I don't think that I would ever really be . . . I mean, it's like in Somalia. It's hard to believe that the United States ever would act out of—or that any government really ever acts out of altruism. One would really like to see somebody go in and just kick the shit out of the Serbs in Bosnia; the situation is horrible, and it's terrible to watch a Holocaust unfolding, and to feel that we're sitting around and doing nothing, but it's also hard to feel that once you let that thing out . . . I mean, you're a fool to think that you're going to be able to control it. Congress doesn't control it. We don't know what we've been using; in Iraq they were using what I consider nuclear weapons—bullets covered with radioactive waste. There's those Tomahawk missiles which don't work and which basically are happier hitting things in cities than flying off into the ether. We've completely lost the possibility of limited warfare.

CL: By the same token, if there had been a way for us to militarily intervene in Germany in 1933, we might have prevented . . .

TK: Right, and there would have been a catastrophe if Roosevelt had not been president and we had not broken out of isolationism and stood up against Hitler. And so I'm not a pacifist in any way, I just

34

think that in terms of this particular situation it's very complicated. Ethnic cleansing and the progressive Balkanization of that entire part of the world has to stop somehow. Saddam is a danger, but I don't believe economic sanctions were given a chance. One thing that the cold war seems to have eliminated is an ideological wall that prevented a certain kind of discussion. There's the possibility now of the countries of the world acting in concert to manipulate trouble spots out of military conflict. That could have worked in Iraq. Of course that's also very problematic, because you wind up with kids not getting medicine and people dying of starvation in countries that are sanctioned, but the end of the cold war doesn't mean the end of American imperialism. And what one doesn't want to see is a failure to compete economically transformed into our becoming a bully with our weapons.

CL: This is the whistle Noam Chomsky keeps blowing. The more our economy fails to produce anything anybody needs or can afford, the more we put all of our eggs in the military basket and become this international arsenal, selling weapons to Iran *and* Iraq so that neither side can win, and all we see are dollar signs, and nobody's even looking past next month.

TK: Dollar signs and this national sense of failed virility, so that the minute we start dropping bombs on anybody, everybody feels very good for five minutes. And there is a fantasy sense that we're still the number one country on earth because we can go in there and kick this person, and we forget we're talking about this completely decimated country that was annihilated two years ago and has never rebuilt and has no military machine at this point, and what we're doing is going in and ineptly trying to bomb a couple of—I mean, they announce that we've gone in and it was very quick and here are a couple of videotapes, and then the next day it turns out they didn't hit any of their targets and they dropped bombs on hotels and on private buildings and orphanages, and everybody's shuffling and saying, "Well, we're *trying* to hit our targets." In addition to the fact that we're not much of an economic superpower, in point of fact, although we have the ability to destroy millions of lives, the army doesn't seem to be very good any more. It seems to be run by people who don't know how to run the technology that we've created. We spent so much money building machines, and none of these people really know how to work them. Which is one of the reasons that Desert Storm evaporated as an exploitable issue within days after the first shot was fired; it became clear that we were killing our own people, that we were doing things no civilized nation would ever want to admit to doing, like burying people alive in trenches. And, in addition to being an unsuccessful war, because we didn't really get rid of Saddam, it was an ineptly handled one against a vastly inferior enemy.

CL: While you were in auditions today we swore in a new president.

TK: Yeah, did you watch him? I heard the speech was like hot air.

CL: Maya Angelou was so moving . . . How do you feel about Clinton?

TK: I don't know. I'm really thrilled that he won, that those bastards are out, and that it's becoming a simple fact now that the whole twelve years of Reaganism was a horrendous mistake; it says a great deal about the American people, and about the way that this weird amalgam of different populations and this very troubled history still produce a country that's committed to participatory democracy of some sort. And to *not* finding easy, ugly solutions. Because the British couldn't get rid of Thatcher, they still have Major around. I thought the Republican National Convention was a watershed event. They saw that Reaganomics was failing, and they pulled out their witchiest stuff, and you could just feel it not working. Feel people sort of curdling.

CL: In *A Bright Room Called Day,* Zillah says of our much-touted "great communicator," "what Reagan communicated was that you can be even more divorced from History and Reality and Language than he was from Jane Wyman and STILL BE THE MOST POWERFUL MAN ON EARTH!" So many of my friends and I are critical of the status quo, and yet there isn't an explicit or articulated vision of how things . . .

TK: How to improve it.

CL: I often wish that there was a party I could belong to. Or a school. And I'm embarrassed and afraid sometimes to say that I am attracted to Marx, that I think there is something wrong with the division of wealth in our society, and I feel very vulnerable when I say this. I fear I may lose the ability to make a living as a writer and be vilified as a socialist—which certainly happened to many writers during McCarthy. Do you worry about these things?

TK: Oh yeah. I know exactly what you meant when you said you wished there was a party to belong to. The idea of socialism is still completely valid, and the collapse of the Soviet system doesn't in any way mean that capitalism has succeeded. Capitalism is always going to be successful economically in the sense that about 10 percent of the population will have a lot of money and 1 percent will have immense amounts of money and everybody else will live lives that are either full of fear or full of poverty, and there'll be huge numbers of people out of work. Socialism is simply the idea that people are better off if we work collectively and that the economic system we live in is made by people and therefore can be controlled intelligently rather than let loose. There's no way that can't be true. As long as there are decent people in the world, there's going to be a demand for socialism. The demand for health care right now, which is a demand that 80 percent of the people in this country share, is a demand for a certain kind of socialism. People wanted to get rid of Bush because they wanted the restitution of the social net that FDR put into place. We don't want to live in an outlaw, in a bandit country anymore.

CL: At the same time they want to see the end of welfare.

TK: Yeah, well, welfare is the demon and people don't even think about what it means. What it is basically is the fear and terror of being poor. Fear of the notion of being dependent in a country where dependency is a shameful thing. Everyone recognizes their potential for being homeless, for being on welfare, so we hate people that are because they frighten us. David Duke made great political hay out of welfare expenditures in Louisiana which, when it was examined, amounted to 5 percent of the state budget. So it's a complete, idiotic fantasy. What really makes you nuts is that people want health care and they don't want to pay taxes. But then again they don't get anything for their taxes. In Europe you pay a huge amount, but you actually get services that you would want. Here all you get are Tomahawk missiles. Here all you're doing is bailing out savings and loan associations. You don't get anything back. So you need to hold onto your money, because you're not going to get anything from the government. It's very embarrassing and difficult to say that you're a socialist at this point in history, but lots of people, I think, really still are.

CL: Another thing in your work that makes me feel less alone in the world is that it doesn't share the knee-jerk, dismissive attitude toward Freud. Have you been analyzed?

TK: Oh, yes, endlessly . . . I sound like Woody Allen, I really have been analyzed virtually all of my adult life . . . And I've just gone back in. I absolutely believe that the people of the Frankfurt school were on the right track in trying to come up with some political theory that incorporated Freud and Marx, because it seems to me that there's much consonance between the two worldviews. There's a direction you can take Freud in that's anticollective, just as there's a direction you can take Marx in that's antipsychoanalytic, but neither of them need to be seen that way. The deepest Freudians, including Freud himself, have acknowledged the existence of the collective, and have not seen people as being hermetically sealed entities, just as the best Marxists were very sophisticated and believed in psychoanalysis; Trotsky sent his own daughter into psychoanalysis. One has to acknowledge the profoundly antisocial dimension in people and recognize that it isn't truer—you don't want to privilege it above the social dimension, but recognize that these two things are thesis and antithesis, that they're in constant struggle with one another, and that a real collective doesn't annihilate the idea of people being differentiated from one another and having specific detail.

. . .

CL: The magician at the end of *The Illusion* suggests something which Christian theologists have been trying to articulate for two thousand years, that time and the physical universe are illusions which are created in the separation, and our belief in this world is the dream.

TK: Yeah.

CL: And he says it very beautifully in terms of love being perhaps the only reality.

TK: I also believe that it has a lot to do with being in theater . . . the whole thing of the real and the unreal, the uncertainty about which is which. I decided I really wanted to be a playwright and be in theater when my Shakespeare professor at Columbia read for us the Theseus/ Hippolyta debate at the top of act 5 of *Midsummer*. This sounds incredibly corny, but it's true . . . it's the closest thing that I've ever come to magic. And also to a sense of collectivity and a sense of energy that's not bound by physical bodies. Because sex, of course, requires a certain degree of . . . I mean, it's *better* when there's contact . . . but in the way that an audience and actors create something, and they really do create something. It isn't just an old theater cliché, the event that takes place on any given night is something that a bunch of people who are not speaking to one another and don't know each other make almost before the first line gets spoken . . . there's a kind of thing that will happen. Some of it you can tease out and say: "Well, this person coughed on that line and so he didn't get his laugh and so the whole play fell apart," but it's never reducible to that. There's something in the air . . . I feel in a certain sense that the theater is the closest that I come to a religion.

CL: The afternoon that my lover and I saw *Millennium Approaches* at the National, we were so invigorated. As you know he has AIDS, and I worried that the play was going to send him into a tailspin. We were so

The Angel (Ellen McLaughlin) appears at Prior's (Stephen Spinella's) bedside in *Angels in America, Part One: Millennium Approaches.* The Broadway production, directed by George C. Wolfe, opened in April 1993 at the Walter Kerr Theater. (*Photo copyright Joan Marcus.*)

elated, and so sorry when it was over, we were on such a theater high, we went and saw *Heartbreak House* that night. Which was how I came to be reminded that your subtitle, *A Gay Fantasia on National Themes,* comes from Shaw—something which nobody seems to have noted. How do you feel about Shaw?

TK: Oh, I love Shaw. Yeah, you're the first person. John Bellucci, the actor who played Roy Cohn in San Francisco . . . And *I* didn't know what it had come from . . . kept saying, "Something else is called that." It strikes terror in your veins because you're going to find out that someone else . . .

CL: Oscar Hammerstein.

TK: Or somebody your own age. And then he said it was *Heartbreak House.* I wanted a title that had a musical sound to it. Every playwright probably wants their plays to have a kind of musical structure, its themes and interweaving.

CL: Did you work from an outline? The design is so ingenious.

TK: I started to, but it just fell apart completely, and I had never really been successful at doing an outline. Because I really didn't know what I wanted it to say; I had no idea what the second part was supposed to be about. When I first started writing it, it didn't have a second part; it was three acts, they each had like fifty-six scenes in them, and I could tell that I was heading into trouble, but by the time I got past the end of the second act, and there were things that happened in the second act that I hadn't planned for . . .

CL: Such as?

TK: Well, Joe's mother coming out at the end of the act and selling her house in Salt Lake. And I didn't know why she was selling her house or what she was doing . . .

CL: I love that the first part ends, she arrived in New York, it's a promise and it's completely unanswered and unaddressed. Obviously it throws you into the second play, but it also has the feeling of life lived. Change. And so much of the play is about change and how painful it is (I love what Harper says in *Perestroika* about God slitting you open with his thumb and pulling all your guts out and rearranging them and stuffing them back in, and that's how change happens) . . . It must have cost you an enormous amount of pain to shape these plays.

TK: Well, yeah. *Millennium* has been shaped a good deal, but the first draft of it and this draft are within shooting distance of one another. *Perestroika* has just changed and changed and changed and changed, and it's still changing, and that's appropriate, because that's what the play's about. It's a little miracle of compression at this point. *Millennium* introduces eight major characters, only five of which are dealt with substantively, and nothing happens in *Millennium*. And in *Perestroika* everything happens. Probably there could have been a third play. It was originally five acts long and a 293-page manuscript that I've had to just crush down. It's a little uncomfortable that it's happened in such a public way, because now the critics in San Francisco who saw the really long version wrote that I had ruined it, that I'd cut too much out, and I think that when people who saw it in L.A.—it's going to lose some more before it gets to New York—will say, "But what about that?" And everybody will say how their favorite things were lost. And that's been hard, but it's nothing compared to the thrill of getting it done. I can't think of any other play where there were two parts, and the first half went out and did its thing, and then the second part has to sort of live up . . . it's a really weird situation.

CL: Are you at all struck by the irony of those who saw nothing in *A Bright Room Called Day* now jumping up and down and screaming about *Angels*? I mean, the same person wrote these two plays.

TK: I know that while *Bright Room* would never be a big success, if you took Zillah out of it, and just did the German scenes, people would say, "Well, it's a nice play." Or they'd say it's not a good play, but it would be this tepid little nonevent. But having this character get up and say Ronald Reagan and Adolf Hitler are virtually the same thing, and that fascism starts at home and whatever it is that Zillah's saying, just made people ballistic. Even though Zillah comprises about 6 pages out of a 130-page manuscript . . . I didn't read any of the reviews in New York, because when it got trashed in London I stopped reading reviews forever.

CL: You don't read them now.

TK: No. I can't. I was reading Michael Billington's review in the *Guardian* of *Bright Room* in London, and it was so angry and he was so incredibly contemptuous of everything in the play, that I felt like if I read this all the way through and read any more of these, I'll never write again. And this isn't fair because I just started, and I don't think that these people are getting what's good about the play. It's sort of amazing to me that, from what I've understood of the critical response to *Bright Room*, virtually no separation was made between me and Zillah, and no one noticed that she is in fact a character, she *speaks to people*, and that she's full of contradictions and that she herself says to the audience that this is deliberately overstated, you need to overstate. Not five months later after everybody got hysterical, John Frohnmayer was standing in front of the National Press Club saying, "What's happening at the NEA will lead to fascism in America." By the time the Republican National Convention was getting reviewed and the farther reaches of Iran Contra, you had Murray Kempton and all the poobahs of the press saying this is fascism. All of a sudden it became sayable.

CL: Not to Al D'Amato.

TK: Well, he doesn't know how to pronounce the word. Dale Collins did this great column where she went to all the senate candidates in the fall and asked them to name the two books that they had read in the last year and liked the best and she cornered D'Amato without any of his aides around and he came up with one that clearly didn't exist, and then he said, "Oh yes, another book, *The Rise and Fall of the Second Reich*." Collins said, "Well, what's a Reich or two between friends." *[Laughter.]*

CL: To get back to change, I was thinking how it was within the last ten years that John Simon felt free to call a play "faggot nonsense" in *New York Magazine*. Things can seem to go along one way for so long and then be transformed . . . I don't think AIDS is the only force that has shoved homophobia and homosexuality out into the open, but it is nonetheless dazzling to me that now I can pick up the paper and read articles about gay people whereas ten years, fifteen years ago I could not. I'm frightened for what's to come because I feel we're a very visible target now—

TK: Yeah.

CL: We're not so very different from European Jewry in the '30s. We're accepted in certain sophisticated urban quarters, in our ghettos, and nice people don't openly say mean things about us, but lots of people would like to see us dead. Do you have thoughts about why homophobia holds on and what is under the surface now and . . .

TK: What one must understand is that when one examines any great social phobia, one will be examining really the heart of the society that hates. Sexual politics is the eye of the storm, and racism is the eye of the storm even though blacks are 11 percent of the population. That the oppressed minorities in this country's history, or anywhere in the world, are the thing by which the majority defines itself, and that it has no identity except as not being the thing that it's despising. The Catholic Church is an enormously complicated institution; it represents one of the biggest stumbling blocks that the progress of gay rights faces. Because how do you get around fundamentalism, how do you get around doctrine?

CL: With a certain amount of learning. John Boswell writes that early Christians honored gay marriage and that the earliest existing Christian marriage ceremony is between people of the same sex.

TK: Right.

CL: The Vatican may wish to tear the page out of the books.

TK: Well, they do destroy stuff, but they don't really need to. They're not like the Mormons who actually do have to put things in their secret vaults. The fact of the matter is that the holy texts of Christianity contain passages that clearly anathematize homosexuality as a practice. And if you believe in a fundamental reading of those texts or if you believe that the Vatican, that the cardinals and pope interpret doctrine, which they do, which is part of the doctrine of Catholicism, then you can't do anything about it. You either have to go for a reformation which is, I think, coming in this country, or you just sign on for the whole nine yards. Boswell's great, but a lot of what he's talking about is Christianity as it was practiced before Paul, before the gospels were really codified, and yes, there was a tremendous—Elaine Pagel's book also shows there was a tremendously weird bunch of religions going around back then that were all sort of vaguely Christian or Jewish or something.

CL: But so many Catholics are willing to put aside notions on contraception. They're just not willing to put other—

TK: Women are going to be the great beachheads for the church, because I don't think that women are really interested in backroom abortion anymore, or in having fifty babies in a row. They're really tired of watching successions of uninspired male priests tell them what the church is about. They clearly are the life force of the church. Just like the third world, there's going to be people of color in the church (who are far and away the most populous element) who are going to get tired of an endless succession of Europeans. And the first time there's a Latin American pope or an African pope, we can hope for certain kinds of incursions into church reactionary thinking that we're not seeing. I do feel, like you, things are changing remarkably. I mean, the plays you've written, *Angels*, there's a space for us now, and a way that straight critics and straight audiences can listen, and just didn't exist ten years ago. And it is going to make life better and also more difficult because there are going to be backlashes like what's happened in Colorado, all over the place.

CL: Well, I feel very strongly that you have opened that space out. Thank you.

43

Tony, Tonys, and Television

Charlie Rose

Kushner's first live television interview was on the *Charlie Rose Show,* hosted by the New York–based sociopolitical and cultural commentator. The interview was taped the day Kushner had been notified that *Angels in America, Millennium Approaches* had broken the record for the most Tony nominations awarded a drama in American theater history.

CHARLIE ROSE: We begin this evening with Tony Kushner. His play, *Angels in America,* is the talk of New York. It won this year's Pulitzer Prize for drama and has been receiving raves from critics and audiences alike. Today it broke a record by receiving nine Tony nominations, more nominations than any other drama ever! And all this is even more surprising because the play runs three and one-half hours, focusing on AIDS and homosexuality, and is only the first section of a seven-hour work. I'm pleased to have Tony Kushner join me now for his first ever appearance on live television, right?

TONY KUSHNER: That's right.

CR: This is a silly question, but how does it feel to have all these Tony nominations, and what does it mean to you?

TK: Well, it hasn't really sunk in yet. I just found out about it earlier today. It's very exciting. I think it'll make more people want to go and see the play, so I'm excited about that. And it's sort of unbeliev-

From the *Charlie Rose Show,* WNET-TV (Channel 13), New York. This previously unpublished interview was taped on May 10, 1993, and aired later that evening before an estimated audience of three million viewers of the Public Broadcasting Service in the United States and Canada. Courtesy of Charlie Rose Show/Rose Communications, PBS.

able. I would never have thought that this would happen. Last year, when Ian McKellen made that announcement on the Tonys about *Angels* winning Tonys, I thought that that was simply because he didn't understand that plays that weren't on Broadway wouldn't be eligible, and I never thought that *Angels* would make it to Broadway, so the whole thing feels kind of unreal.

CR: You never really thought it would make it to Broadway—

TK: No.

CR: —it was not the kind of drama that generated audiences, which Broadway needs.

TK: It's long, as you say. It's about gay people. It's about AIDS. It's very political. There are a lot of words in it, and it just didn't seem like the kind of thing that producers would find a viable risk for investment, so I thought that it would probably live out its life in regional theaters and at an off-Broadway theater, which would have been fine, but . . .

CR: And now it's the hot ticket in town.

TK: Well, I guess it is. *[Laughs.]*

. . .

CR: Nine nominations. When you look at what this means, it means box office. It means attention. The fact that it's on Broadway and that people are coming says what?

TK: I like to think that it's in part because it's a good play and it's done well. It's a wonderful production. George is a great director, and the cast is brilliant.

CR: Brilliantly staged, and George Wolfe did a hell of a job.

TK: Yes. He's an extraordinary artist. And it's done well in other places. It did well in London last year.

CR: Where Frank Rich first went over to see it, and he came back and just raved about it even before it came here.

TK: I think that the reason that it's gotten as much attention as it's gotten, and it's a sort of an extraordinary amount of press attention, is probably more due to the fact that it is happening coincident[ly] with a transformation in American culture and politics. This spring has seen a full public flowering of the change that's occurring in the political and cultural status of gays and lesbians in the United States. Any play that addresses gay and lesbian issues, particularly a play that addresses them the way the gay and lesbian issues relate to a national political agenda, which is one of the things that *Angels* is trying to do, is going to hook into a great political energy. That's one of the things that's happened to make the play get the attention that it's gotten.

CR: You have a hero here, and a villain—Roy Cohn being the villain—and the hero is a young man who's dying of AIDS and who . . . characterize him.

TK: There are two people with AIDS in the play. One is Prior Walter, who is the person that you're calling the hero, and I think in a certain sense, he is the play's hero. He is a young man who lives in the East Village. He's done drag, but he's not necessarily a drag queen. But he's sort of a—he works as a caterer-waiter, and he's a kind of a fabulous gay man. Stephen Spinella [the actor who plays Prior] said in an interview that he's the gay man that Stephen wishes he was, and I think that's probably true of me, too. He's somebody with a great deal of strength, a great sense of humor, a great deal of resourcefulness, which I think he discovers during the course of his struggle with the syndrome. And the other person with AIDS is Roy Cohn, who is certainly the play's villain and certainly was in real life a great villain, and who is a person who is a closeted homosexual, and a person who was actually . . .

CR: To his death.

TK: To his death, who was sort of outed, in a sense, by AIDS, and a person who worked assiduously all his life for homophobes and in homophobic causes. So he's a very complicated figure, and I was interested in writing him because I thought that he presented an interesting challenge. At the time that he died of AIDS, I was moved in a way that I never expected to be moved by Roy Cohn. I felt a certain sense of sorrow and grief for him, even though he was a person that I detested most of my life.

I was kind of upset at the way that he was discussed in the press at the time that he died because I thought there was a great deal of homophobia and homophobic gloating over the fact that he had died of AIDS. In a certain sense, his dying of this disease made him a part of the gay and lesbian community even if we don't really want him to be a part of our community. Dealing with those contradictions and with the complexities that his life and his death raised were what made him so much fun to write.

CR: Three and a half hours—did you have any trepidation about the length?

TK: Yeah. It seemed completely insane at the time.

CR: Not to speak of your producer.

TK: It's three and a half hours for the first half, and then you have another three and a half hours to go. Oskar Eustis, who commissioned it and who directed the play in Los Angeles, and I were kind of horror-struck because we thought that the play should be ideally about two and a half hours long completely, but as I was writing it, it just kept getting longer and longer and seemed to need more and more space and time. Eventually, we all sort of bought into the idea that it would be fun to see if something like this could work. And the fact that it does seem to work is something that we're all proud of because it's a trick. There's an assumption made that people's attention spans are very brief, and I don't think that that's actually true. I think that people need to be interested in order to engage, but if you can keep them interested, I think people like length, they like complexity, they like depth, and they'll respond to it. They like being told that they are capable of sitting for three and a half hours and feel good about themselves when they've done it.

CR: It's a little bit like respecting the intelligence of your audience, or respecting the capacity to want to open yourself to the experience.

TK: People like being challenged. People like difficulty. I don't think that it's true that people always want the easy thing and the simple thing. They want food that's hard to chew, but nutritious. If you give them that, they'll be excited.

CR: And you want them to walk out after three and a half or seven hours, coming away with what understanding about homosexuality?

TK: Because the play is an epic and because it has a very, very broad canvas, it doesn't really give you a single point to take home. I think that after people have spent three and a half or seven hours listening to gay people—various kinds of gay people—and thinking about ways in which gay issues are not marginal, but central to the American political and cultural agenda, I hope that people will come away with a sense of comfort, a sense of curiosity, a sense of excitement, a sense of having been exposed to something that maybe they thought they knew, but didn't know as well as they thought they knew, or hadn't known at all.

. . .

CR: Has there been a difference in the reception of the audience in London and Los Angeles and New York?

TK: Yeah, the audiences are very different. You can feel it's also played very successfully in San Francisco, directed by David

Esbjornson. Every audience has a completely distinct character. I've been waiting for four years for this play to come to New York because it is a play that's set in New York. I'm from New York. I live in New York. It's very much a play—as much as it is in a certain sense about being gay—it's a play about being Jewish, and I really felt that this would be the city that would embrace it most fully. So I'm excited to have it here.

CR: But how is it different, though?

TK: The audiences?

CR: Yeah. How is an audience in Los Angeles different than an audience in New York, and how is an audience in New York different . . .

TK: Oh, God, I'll get in trouble if I touch that.

CR: Oh, go ahead! I mean, you're on a roll tonight.

TK: Well, the London audiences were terrific. They were very, very smart. They're very quiet. They listen very intensely. The production there was very different than the production here. It was very passionate and very fast, and in a certain sense, not as funny, because, I think, partially, of the cultural differences. The audiences in L.A. loved the jokes and, I felt, responded to it with great excitement. It became a sort of a political event in L.A. It was sort of the first big gay play in L.A., and I think that there was a lot of partisan politics in the audience, and that was great. It was also during the election. So the day after Bush was booted out and Clinton came in, there was an orgasmic feeling in the audience. People were cheering at every joke about Reagan and Bush.

In New York, it's just . . . I think this is the smartest audience in the world. It's the best theater audience in the world. New York is the only city in the United States that has an old theater culture, so it does feel like London in that sense. It's a theater town.

CR: Someone who knows a lot about the theater said to me today, "It stuns me that it's on Broadway. It's mainstream America." This is the biggest marketplace for theater in America.

TK: Yeah.

CR: And here is the play that's about AIDS, about gays, about a culture and a lifestyle that . . . people now say that this is going to be the gay decade, and a lot of things are going on. But still, this person was saying, "It's an event that this is being accepted and awarded and honored so much on Broadway."

TK: It's pretty wild. I mean, I do think that the current political climate has a lot to do with it. I also think that it's important that it's on

Broadway. It's also important to remember that this is not a play, I think, that could have been created for Broadway. This play exists because of the regional not-for-profit theater movement in this country. Most serious, important theater in this country is created at regional theaters, including some in New York City, like Lincoln Center and the Public.

CR: A lot of people are unhappy about the Tonys because it does not recognize a lot of off-Broadway productions, and they will say that the most creative productions on Broadway today, with the exception of a couple of things, come off-Broadway—plays by Jon Robbie Baitz and other very gifted playwrights are not nominated for Tonys because they're off-Broadway. And they're upset about that and think that it robs the Tonys and it robs America's appreciation and honoring of theater.

TK: It's sort of like the Oscars only now beginning to recognize independent filmmakers.

CR: Sure. Suppose that *The Crying Game* was not nominated. It would be the same thing as, say, having plays that really . . .

TK: Yeah, if the Tonys really want to get exciting, they should include not only off-Broadway plays but off-off-Broadway plays and plays that are happening in regional theaters. . . . Chicago should be included. There is great theater in Chicago.

. . .

CR: Tell me a little bit about why an angel. What does the metaphor for angel mean? And what is your take on spirituality in America?

TK: I'm very ambivalent and undecided and confused about it. I'm a genuine agnostic. I don't know, but I think that as we approach the millennium, it becomes clearer and clearer that there are features of human experience that the Left has traditionally not touched upon, including a sense of the miraculous and a sense of the magical. And as the Left develops in the face of whatever kind of world we're looking at now, it's becoming clearer and clearer that the spiritual has to be factored in. The spiritual has to be examined in a new way. We don't know how to do that yet, but we're working toward that.

CR: Part of your statement is the political Left in America hasn't addressed spirituality.

TK: Traditionally, Marxism is a scientific doctrine, and there's much value in Marxism that still needs to be explored. One of the things that we have to explore is the way in which magic and the spirit

49

work in the world as well, and we have to be scientific about that, if we can be, but I think we have to investigate it.

CR: If I don't ask you this, somebody will get after me. I mean, is this a film?

TK: Well, I am talking to Robert Altman about the possibility. He's interested and I'm interested and we're sort of . . .

CR: And he's a director that would interest you to make it?

TK: He's the only director in the United States that I would consider making this with because I think he's a great director, and the play was, in fact, very heavily influenced by his work, especially *Nashville* in the length and the interconnectedness and the complexity. His work is just spectacular and smart and political, and I'd love to work with him. He's interested in this, so we're thinking about it.

CR: Do you, in your own mind, think of actors for the principal roles?

TK: Oh, I want all of my actors in the principal roles. *[Laughter.]*

CR: Ron Liebman plays Roy Cohn.

TK: And Ron is, I think, a national treasure. He's a really great, fantastical actor who is theatrical in a way that almost no other stage actor of his generation is, and I think that it's a brave and electrifying performance.

CR: I'd love to continue this. I hope you'll come back and do it again. It's a pleasure to have you, and your first live television appearance wasn't so bad, was it?

TK: Oh, it was a little scary, but . . .

CR: Thank you, Tony.

TK: Thanks.

CR: Again, the musicals *Kiss of the Spider Woman* and *Tommy* each received eleven Tony Award nominations. *Angels in America, Millennium Approaches,* received nine, the most of any play since the Tonys began in 1947. Tony Kushner, the author of *Angels* nominated, as were five of the eight actors in the play's ensemble. We'll be right back.

AIDS, Angels, Activism, and Sex in the Nineties

Patrick R. Pacheco

Patrick R. Pacheco, a freelance journalist, interviewed Tony Kushner at his home during the summer of 1993, just after the playwright had moved from Brooklyn to Manhattan. Pacheco's piece would be published in *Body Positive*, a monthly publication of Body Positive, Inc. of New York, a nonprofit organization that offers, as summarized by a staff member, "unique services in the community: lifestyle education, medical information, and support groups for people infected and affected by HIV."

PATRICK PACHECO: What is it you'd like to say to PWAs [People With AIDS]? Do you have a message for them?

TONY KUSHNER: I don't write plays with messages, so I don't know how to answer that question without sounding like an idiot. The last thing anybody with AIDS needs is to be lectured to.

When I started work on *Millennium* in 1988, a lot of what I was reading and seeing about AIDS was using the illness as a dramatic device, *Camille*-type model, a way of getting a guaranteed tearjerker finish. It was important to me to create a character with AIDS who was not passive, who did not die at the end, but whose illness was treated realistically. So it wasn't just one lesion on the shoulder and then a little coughing fit and then he dies in time for the surviving lover to make a moving little speech that gets everybody in the theater to cry and then leave feeling uplifted.

From *Body Positive* 4 (September 1993): 17–28. Copyright © by *The Body Positive*. Reprinted by permission.

If you're going to deal with a biological problem, you have to deal with the biology. So there's a good deal of time spent in *Millennium* with Prior [who has AIDS] enumerating his symptoms and speaking very specifically of what he is going through; that was modeled on what several of my friends had gone through. I follow the same line of reasoning with Roy Cohn in *Perestroika*, trying to be true to the course of the illness in terms of what was available in 1985.

The play isn't intended to tell seropositive people or PWAs that they should be doing this or that. I've seen people do the most heroic things in dealing with this illness; and it's changed a lot of what I understand about courage and bravery and the places it comes from. And I hope the plays reflect that.

PP: When you started *Angels* had you taken an HIV test?

TK: I hadn't. I started getting tested just before one of the first attempts at writing *Perestroika*. *Millennium* was already done. I think that then—it sounds like ancient history now—whether or not you should get tested was still controversial. AZT hadn't yet been approved; there weren't any good treatment options for opportunistic infections either. So why bother getting tested? All you were doing was providing information for the government to use to put you in a concentration camp.

PP: What were your results?

TK: I'm negative. I had a long discussion with Stephen [Spinella, the actor who plays Prior] when he was interviewed by the *New York Times* about the politics of saying or not saying when he was asked [Spinella was negative]. It's a complicated issue, but I think it's probably useful for people who are seropositive who go to see the play to know that it is written by someone who isn't.

PP: You mentioned in an earlier interview that you were a bit promiscuous in your early sexual experimentation. I think you said you'd gone to bathhouses. Did this cause apprehension when you were tested?

TK: Did I go to bathhouses? I went a couple of times. I'm incredibly shy and I've never been turned on by sex—or even nudity—out in the open. I'm embarrassed by it. The word "promiscuous" I have problems with. But I certainly have been sexually active for a good part of my life, and I've had many partners.

PP: Why are you uncomfortable with the word "promiscuous"?

TK: I don't know. Probably because it has that quality of judgment, that *Scarlet Letter* sense. But I really look back on the days when one could meet a lot of different people—you can still do it—and I think there was something wonderful about it. And I enjoyed it. Apart from the fun I had, I met an outrageous variety of people. Sex is a great leveler. You meet people in an intimate and complicated way that you wouldn't be able to do on the street. I had to write a piece about "Sex in the Time of the Plague" recently for *Esquire* and my first take was, "Everybody should go out and have as much sex as they can get." And then I read about the San Francisco study showing a sharp increase in HIV rates among young gay men. And so I reconsidered my position. How much do you want to know about this?

PP: I'm curious about your sexual history and how it shaped your work, particularly the process of going through testing.

TK: I've been tested several times, and every time I do it I think, "Oh, God, this is it. I did something unsafe somewhere along the line." The first time, I was still with my lover of five years and we'd been completely monogamous. Then I broke up with him and started going around again and my doctor said, "You know, you've got the gold standard now . . . "—I'd tested negative and I had a high T-cell count, but it seemed he was talking about currency devaluation—"you really want to think about preserving this." While I'd love to preserve it, I'd also like not to spend the rest of my life not doing anything. And I'm an immensely oral person. I had a long conversation with a group of friends, all serious people, about kissing. Because we didn't know—I guess we still don't completely know—whether it's safer sex. But we thought, "How could you live without it?"

PP: You mean deep tongue kissing?

TK: Yeah. Kissing. I've made out with guys that I've known were HIV+. And had sex with them. And I'm still negative. At least, I think I am. But I do think sex is incredibly important, part of what we are. And I don't think we should let a health issue dictate . . . Oh, it's so complicated. I do think people should preserve their health and take care of themselves whether they're seropositive or seronegative. But on the other hand, people shouldn't have to be . . .

PP: Hobbled?

TK: Well, we *are* hobbled. There are things people should not do. Many of us miss the taste of cum. But we've got to remain sane about it.

PP: You're saying that deep kissing someone who is HIV+ is okay?

TK: Well, what I'm saying is, I think it's okay enough to do it. I'll let you know if I'm wrong.

PP: Were you scared or frightened while waiting for your results?

TK: Oh, yeah. Although I've not done anything I consider unsafe in all these years. But there's always the fear and rumors going around about people seroconverting who have never done anything unsafe at all.

PP: Do you feel any guilt about your HIV+ friends?

TK: Sure, I feel guilt. I try to be sensitive about it. I don't go calling up positive friends and crow about my status. And I think there is a tendency among some gay men to turn it into a badge of physical and spiritual superiority in the way that they turn a gym body into that, because white gay men tend to be very status-oriented about a lot of that stuff. And that's particularly repugnant.

PP: How do you handle it, then?

TK: You keep it very clear that you've been spared by accident. I'm thirty-seven years old and this is a very hard world to survive in. But people do survive. I mean, it's really like Holocaust survivors have to think of it. There is a fantasy that a lot of survivors have that they survived because of some clever thing that they did, some way that they outwitted death. But in point of fact, they were just lucky. And luck is this blind thing that flies around and hits some people and doesn't hit others.

PP: Since you brought this up, I wanted to ask you about the Holocaust parallel with AIDS. I know it's a complex issue, but it's worth talking about.

TK: I firmly believe in using the Holocaust model, promiscuously. I think we should be very liberal with likening people to Nazis. I wrote a play about this [A Bright Room Called Day]. I think that the worst thing you can do to any historical event is to turn it into some kind of magic moment that happened for a metaphysical reason that doesn't have anything to do with the materialist conditions of history. The Holocaust has become the paradigm for human evil, and then we turn and say there was nothing like it before in history and nothing will be like it in the future. For the people who went through it, it's understandable to say that. But it's also a terrible mistake. Milosevic is a Nazi and Ronald Reagan is a Nazi. This is not to say that Reagan walks around in a black uniform. But he cynically manipulated an issue and allowed the situation to become more dangerous. I think the indifference the West has shown to AIDS in developing countries is genocidal and I wonder how many gay men, who have been so wonderful in responding to men in our own community, will continue to worry about it when, as I hope will happen, medical advances make it into a maintenance illness or get rid of it. There will still be an economics of infection and prevention in other parts of the world. And will we still care?

PP: Is it possible to say how being negative affected the writing of the play? Would the play be different if you'd tested HIV+?

TK: I'm sure it would have had a profound effect on me and consequently on my work. I just finished interviewing a lot of HIV+ people for *Vanity Fair*, and every single one of them said that before they'd gotten the results they didn't know how they were going to handle it and that the way they did only evolved after some time had passed. I'm sure that would be true of me, too.

PP: Within this context, it's intriguing to look at Prior and how he copes with his situation. Was it clear from the beginning of the writing that Prior would not die?

TK: I knew that Roy was going to die. The play was designed to culminate in a certain way with Roy's death, but the main person with AIDS was Prior. And the point is that people *do* survive. It's seriously underrepresented. You don't want to be pie-in-the-sky about it, but there can be years and years of very productive life. And I thought there was an incredible unwillingness to show that. That it was a widespread form of delectation among those who are not immune-compromised to show over and over again people dying these terrible deaths because it makes you cry. Unfortunately, it's considered one of the hallmarks of success in theater or film if you can make the audience break down at the end. And I think that's disgusting.

It's terribly important that *Perestroika* ends with an epilogue, five years into the future, and that Prior is still alive. He's having a hard time. He's not necessarily going to be alive a lot longer. And yet he *could* be. It doesn't end with that. And some people are pissed off at that.

PP: Why?

TK: Although the literature of AIDS has gotten more sophisticated, there's still the expectation that AIDS equals death at the end. Which is why I love the responses that audiences have at the end of *Millennium*. Because it's possible that Prior is dead at the end, but it's clearly not a scene that allows you to sit there and weep over somebody quietly expiring in a hospital bed. It's this wild event. And I think people really know he hasn't died. But I have had people come up to me afterward and say, "He didn't die at the end. Is that realistic?" They felt cheated of their deathbed scene.

PP: Have PWAs accused you of denial?

TK: No. But part of the struggle Prior goes through in *Perestroika* is specifically over this issue. I know I said I wasn't going to lecture anybody, but I will say this: In my experience with this as with other illnesses, it does make a difference how you live your life. Do you take care of yourself? Do you actively, aggressively seek out good medical attention? Do you question your doctor? And it's terribly hard to do those things. You have to resist both the notion that you can absolutely control this through will—which isn't true and only makes some people feel like they've failed when they've gotten sick—and the idea that it's a death sentence that will be carried out in a couple of months. In *Perestroika* I wanted to represent somebody having an immensely difficult time getting himself to do those things. One of the things I like about Prior is that he's someone who doesn't see himself as a strong person. He sees himself as a fragile queen who isn't going to be able to bear up under all the horror and abandonment. And he finds himself to be a tremendously strong person with great courage, which has been very true to my own experience in a lot of people.

PP: What's also intriguing to me about Prior is the idea that he's expected to be some kind of prophet. But he refuses that role, doesn't he? What does this mean?

TK: It's very complicated, and it's part of what my struggle over the rewrites of *Perestroika* have been about—exactly how clear I want to make this. I find that when I spell out the various possibilities of the meaning of it, it makes the play lose what is shaggy and strange, which is what I like. What Prior is refusing is a very specific message and a very specific part of himself that he needs to refuse in order to make his decision: not just *to survive* but that *he wants* to survive. I think these are very different things. I think that if it was anybody's decision to live, most people would decide that they would want to. But when you don't have the choice, then to make the decision that you *would like* to live is sometimes very difficult. Because sometimes death—for the planet, in a certain sense—has become an attractive option. What I'm trying to explore in Prior is one of the great mysteries. It's hard to explain without sounding sentimental, but this is why human beings survive things that seem so unendurable. It's not survivalism. It's not "fuck everybody else, I'm going to stay alive." It's the question of the will to live: Is it just biology? Is it just fear? Is it an addiction (which is what Prior calls it at one point)? Even when there is clearly no joy left in life, why is it that we won't surrender? And that's what *Perestroika* is all about, what Prior's struggle with the angels is all about. What they're offering him is what all religion offers—the solace of what comes after.

PP: And that's opposed to change, isn't it? The angels are reactionary; they demand paralysis.

TK: Yes. They want paralysis, illness, an end to change and progress. The Angel of History wants to go back and restore what has been destroyed. But the winds of time are inevitably blowing her forward.

PP: That's what I think gives the play such hope: the embrace of change, even in someone unexpected, like the character of the Mormon mother. What about the changes in your own personal life? How did you manage those? Say, in your search for sex, love, and affection?

TK: I have a tremendously strong mating and domesticating impulse. From the age of twenty-one, when I had my first sexual encounter, I began meeting guys and having sex, but I was thinking, "Oh, God, it's so empty." I'd had sex with three people and I was already experiencing this John Rechy–thing about it all being so meaningless. What I wanted was to have a boyfriend. I wanted to be in love. And I still do. It's very hard for me to live alone, and I wanted to have somebody at home. I'd read all the novels in which there were these guys in their great apartments with their cute lovers. It's a tremendously potent fantasy.

PP: In *Angels* you deal with the insufficiency of love, the abandonment of Prior by Louis. How realistic is that?

TK: I think what Louis does is shocking. Realistic? Well, yes, I know two people who walked out on people who were sick. They weren't like Louis—they were actually kind of trashy. I've seen the entire spectrum of behavior in terms of people taking care of people. I've seen people who are just spectacular, incredibly great about it; some who were not so great but who hung in there to the best of their powers; and I've seen people who were there in name only. That's another thing I felt was missing from representations of the health crisis: how tremendously hard it is for people to take care of other people. Some have a genius for it; others don't. It seems to me that one of the ironies of history is that during the age of Reagan while we were being told that incredible selfishness was the key to all truth and goodness, many people who had not been raised in the art of self-sacrifice were being asked to make incredible sacrifices and to overcome their natural tendency to run away from calamity. And Louis was my way of dealing with that. Representing those things is one of the duties of drama. It's what Goethe said about *Young Werther:* you write about it so you don't do it. Louis is not some shit. He isn't oblivious to the consequences of his actions. He knows he's walking from the frying pan into the fire, and in *Perestroika* you know the depths of his guilt. He knows he's made a mistake. And he knows how far he wants to go to pay for it in his own crazy way.

PP: What you've put your finger on is the awesome power of AIDS to transform us.

TK: Yes, I believe that.

PP: Did taking care of friends with AIDS affect the rewriting of *Perestroika*?

TK: It's made it harder. I'll be completely honest with you. The process of rewriting *Perestroika* is so completely and totally overwhelmed by the need to follow *Millennium* that almost any other consideration is nearly obliterated by it. I set myself up. I didn't know that *Millennium* was going to succeed to the extent that it did. But the success of *Millennium* has become a terrible obstacle that has to be overcome. I'm fighting against that and the expectations it raises more than anything else.

Millennium ends with wild fantasy. You don't know if that's the angel of death or the angel of deliverance, but it's gorgeous and it's fun. But *Perestroika* is about everybody finding their way back to reality, which is disappointing and small and hard. I love it when people say about *Millennium,* "It felt like one hour," but *Perestroika* may feel like five hours. It may be five hours! I hope people are grown up about it.

As for AIDS, I feel a lot angrier than I used to. I was always angry about government indifference and the greed of the big pharmaceutical companies, about the way in which society has responded to the plague—I feel very mad about that. But there is a certain kind of anger toward God that has come into *Perestroika* more and more because there are people I have lost, or am perhaps in the process of losing, and I really don't want to let go of them. I've discovered an incredible rage in myself that's worked its way in. *Perestroika* is an uglier, angrier play.

PP: And that rage is directed toward both the government and toward God?

TK: Well, the government is always doing something that makes one angry. I'm not a gay man who got politicized because of a health crisis. The government is always appalling. As much as I despised the Republicans, even I was shocked by the response to AIDS by Reagan and Bush. I couldn't believe that someone as conscious of PR as Reagan could be so blind as to what history is going to make of the way he behaved.

PP: But Reagan was obtuse about history. He said he didn't care because he wasn't going to be around to read it anyway.

TK: Yeah, but he also thought he could rewrite it. I really was astonished in the '80s at the extent to which people believed—and it wasn't only Reagan, though he's culpable because he was elected to be a leader—the way in which society as a whole believed for a long time—believed that we deserved to die because we had sex with each other. This may be changing now, though I don't really know. I still find the depths of homophobia very frightening.

I thought that after the inauguration—as tacky as that might have been—"Well, now the new order has begun, and Clinton is going to do it. We're going to have moved forward a decade in two months. Clinton will be queer-positive and the whole country will have to change." I look back on that now and wonder what I was thinking?

PP: It makes you feel naive?

TK: It does. And there are all these unpleasant surprises like Sam Nunn turning into Jesse Helms. What happened to that guy? I never liked him all that much, but he turned into a raving nutbag.

PP: But the military issue isn't a question of life and death like AIDS.

TK: I don't agree. I believe that one of the major lessons in discrimination today is what Louis says in *Millennium,* "When the shit hits the fan, you realize just how much tolerance is worth." To be tolerated is worth nothing. Because if you're merely tolerated and you get in trouble, you're going to die. Only by having the status of a full citizen, guaranteed by law, are you protected.

PP: And that applies both to the Holocaust and to AIDS?

TK: Yes. The argument is right out of Hannah Arendt. The German Jews made a very big mistake when they accepted a status that was less than German. If you're going to be given a choice between being a pariah and a parvenu, be a pariah because the parvenus are easily dispensed with.

PP: What do you think of Clinton's response to AIDS?

TK: Has there been one? He's given us more money. It's less than he promised but it's something. We now have an AIDS—one would hesitate to call her a czar—I don't know exactly what Kristine Gebbie is. I think Larry Kramer is absolutely right when he says that Clinton's been incredibly bad about appointments and that it's all been too sluggish. I think Clinton's doing what Bush and Reagan did to this extent: I think he's horse-trading with the issue. I think he's not really willing to make it a big deal to start with because he was trying to get the budget through. But, of course, time is of the essence here. And that infuriates me. Is the federal government going to get behind serious safer-sex education? Or can we expect nothing more than the same malignant dicking around that goes on all the time in Congress?

PP: At this point do you think that Clinton is as culpable as Reagan and Bush?

TK: Oh, no. It's hard to give him the time he deserves because he's not a very appealing person, he's too Machiavellian. And we've been deprived for so long—we being the entire populace except for rich, straight, white men—of any expectation of decency from the federal government, so, of course, we're very impatient now. And we have a right to be, and we ought to be, or we'll let Clinton off the hook. He's only going to be dragged into this issue kicking and screaming. I don't think he's an evil man like Bush, but I think he's a rather spineless one.

PP: What's frightening is what is going to happen when the shit hits the fan in the coming decade. It could get uglier.

TK: That's of course scary. I love the way that universal health care—the issue Clinton won on—has now become a way of saving the government money on health care, which is very frightening in terms of AIDS.

PP: Isn't that the most difficult thing about change? Whether you're talking about government or the play or speaking personally. That accommodation to loss?

TK: When I first started writing the second play, I wanted to call it *Perestroika* because I had this wild-eyed notion that Gorbachev was going to make the world a different place and bring about the advent of democratic socialism, which is what makes the most amount of sense to me. And then, of course, things began to go from good to bad to really awful in the former Soviet bloc. There were times I thought I should change the title of the play now because perestroika has not fulfilled its promise.

But actually in its way it has. In one of the clearer moments in his book Gorbachev says that our job is simply to make change irreversible. I believe that change is terribly hard, but I don't believe that it's impossible, and that's the hope in *Perestroika*. And I believe that the worst thing ever is to try and reverse the course of progress, because reaching back to a fantasy past is the hallmark of Reaganism, and the idea of containing change is the ideology of Roy Cohn. And the defeat of these is what we're committed to right now.

PP: Do your characters conquer loss?

TK: They face it. You can't conquer loss. You lose. To suggest otherwise would be to suggest a fantasy. The characters do fantasize to a certain extent: Harper has a speech at the end of *Perestroika* in which she imagines that there is some way in which the losses of the world are working toward some other kind of gain so that, as she says, they're not lost forever. I don't believe that, as human beings, we can do anything other than struggle to face loss with grace, as Harper says, as much as we can.

PP: And the ultimate loss is death.

TK: Yes. And life is about losing. Things are taken from you. People are taken from you. You just have to face it. And let go. Which is the gesture of losing. You have to allow yourself to let go and it's complicated. Because you always run the danger of becoming passive in the face of the agents of loss that should have been resisted, and you don't want to end up doing that, either.

Thinking about Fabulousness

Michael Cunningham

Novelist Michael Cunningham, author of the acclaimed *A Home at the End of the World* and *Flesh and Blood,* interviewed Kushner at the Herbst Theater in San Francisco. Their conversation was part of a yearly series produced by City Arts & Lectures entitled *On Art and Politics.* The programs feature provocative, contemporary writers and artists in dialogue on private, public, political, and artistic issues of the day. The participants and audience were aware that the evening's program, sponsored by—and a benefit for—The Women's Foundation, was being recorded live for possible future radio broadcast on KQED-FM in the Bay area.

MICHAEL CUNNINGHAM: One of the things that most struck me about *Angels in America* is the way it encompasses—it depicts—human evil in its most interesting forms, and then offers forgiveness to almost everybody. There is a man who abandons his lover when the lover gets sick; there's Roy Cohn, arguably the most—certainly in the top five evil figures of the twentieth century. There's a lot of competition for the title. *[Laughter.]* And really the only character who is damned to some extent is a kind of relatively minor Republican functionary. I was wondering, is being an obedient Republican the only unforgivable sin?

TONY KUSHNER: It would certainly classify as an unforgivable sin. Forgiveness is a very complicated thing. It certainly became, as I wrote *Perestroika,* the chief issue because it became a big issue in the world,

From City Arts & Lectures, Inc., Herbst Theater, San Francisco, February 24, 1994. The previously unpublished interview took place before a crowd of more than seven hundred people, each of whom paid $15 per ticket.

starting with perestroika, and all of these sort of democratic revolutions that were going on, not just in Eastern Europe, but also in Latin America for instance, where people really had to ask themselves, "Can you let go of the past?" Can you forgive somebody that's done something really, really terrible to you? It's undertheorized and underdiscussed in the Left. We don't really have a morality that encompasses it, because Christian morality, which is a complete forgiveness, seems emotionally inadequate to most people. It's an act of that kind of forgiveness; it's something that most people aren't capable of doing. And it also seems unjust in a way. I wanted to ask myself questions about forgiveness in the play. I'm not comfortable with the fact that, to a certain degree, Roy is forgiven. He is actually, in the play, only forgiven when he's dead. I think that forgiving dead people is a lot easier *[laughter]* than forgiving live people. But it's not really the central problem. It's complicated. It's also an issue in [Cunningham's] *A Home at the End of the World.* Loss and forgiveness go hand in hand, and it's tricky.

MC: There's been a lot of talk about your high-culture influences—Brecht, Whitman, Marx, and Freud—all of which is obviously true. But I found myself wondering what are your low influences. *[Laughter.]* What kind of garbage, starting with your neckwear . . .

TK: Well, I'm very influenced, as any American ought to be, by garbage. *[Laughter.]* I read the comics. I got liberated from reading the *New York Times* and addicted to reading *Newsday* because it has comics, and the *New York Times* doesn't. I get very cranky if I don't have my comics every day. And there're a lot of TV shows that I really love. I think that *Roseanne* is a sort of a phenomenon. *[Applause.]* It's really sometimes pretty extraordinary. And I love *The Simpsons.* What else do I love? I sort of love David Letterman sometimes even though I know I shouldn't, but he's funny. And that makes it hard. I like listening to rock. . . .

Theater is as much a part of trash culture as it is high art. It always is that. And it's incredibly important for people who are working in theater to always remember that it's show biz and it's sort of sleazy, and a lot of the traditions that you've inherited and a lot of the ways that you have at your disposal for telling a story are ways that were developed by, incredibly, sort of lowbrow, popular entertainment. The theater always has to function as popular entertainment. Or at least the theater that I do, because I don't have the talent for doing anything else, I think, needs to have a real . . . it has to have the jokes and it has to have the feathers and the mirrors and the smoke.

MC: One of the things that just makes me crazy about *Angels* is the way it draws on this incredibly broad, vast, sociopolitical canvas, and it has good jokes.

TK: Yeah, Andrew Sullivan [editor, *New Republic*] called it the West Village answer to Neil Simon. *[Laughter.]*

MC: Ow!

TK: Which I only discovered because he was quoted by John Simon *[New Yorker]*, I think. The distinction between high culture and low culture is—and it's already been said many, many times—an invidious distinction, and I don't think that in point of fact it's really legitimate at all. A great deal of what's produced in the name of high culture here and abroad is quite simply deadly dull and boring, and the perpetual reshaping and refinement of modes of expression that sort of dried up and died before World War I. There's always a great deal of vitality in the art that comes from people living their lives. So it's a fishy distinction.

MC: I live in New York, and fail to take advantage of most of what's there. I sort of hole up in my apartment and torment myself about all that's out there that I'm not seeing and not doing. But every now and then I get very ambitious and roust myself out and go to see a play and congratulate myself for being on the streets after 9:30 P.M. *[laughter]* and almost everything is terrible! Our American theater sucks. I don't know . . . obviously not every single thing. But I'm amazed at how bad most of what people write and perform is.

TK: Probably percentagewise, there's more bad theater done than there is bad novel writing or bad poetry or even bad film. Because a lot of it is sort of excruciatingly inept. I always feel that people who have a certain degree of confidence migrate naturally out of the theater into other media because they can make more money doing other things, and that those of us who are stuck in theater make the best of a bad thing; but one of the reasons that we wind up there is that we can't get our shoes tied in the morning, and so we're not really employable in places where people have a lot of money invested, because they have been watching too closely. *[Laughter.]* And if you don't believe this, a visit to any not-for-profit resident theater will convince you that I'm right. There are a lot of nice people who can't get their shoes tied in the morning, and not being able to dress yourself is in its own way an act of resistance to capitalism. *[Laughter; applause.]* But I think that it's true that there's a lot of bad theater. And maybe not percentagewise there's more bad theater, but simply that a bad play is so much more horrible an experience than a bad film because you're in the theater with all these other people, and then watching these sort of wretched people on stage who know that they're being bad, and you know that they're being bad. There's an excruciating sort of embarrassment that everybody has to share in. You feel not only bored or offended, or homicidally angry—as you can frequently be in a film—but also mortified. It's the risk and the price that you have to pay. The threat of that embarrassment—especially when it isn't realized and the work soars in the face of the possibility that somebody's going to fall on their butt and make a fool of themselves—is what makes theater exciting. But it can also just make it an absolutely gruesome, airless, suffocating experience. As with a bad book, you just throw it across the room.

MC: Do you have any idea why theater in other countries is more alive? Is it just the money thing? Brain drain?

TK: I don't really think that's true. Other countries have a theater culture. In Britain, people see a lot more theater because they do. There's not quite as powerful an electronically reproduced media, so they're not as able to see as much television. You can't really stay at home night after night watching BBC and *The Benny Hill Show*. I mean nobody likes it. It's not just Americans that can't stand it. *[Laughter.]* The British just think they were put here on earth to have a bad time, so they pretend that they like Benny Hill. I hate a lot of theater abroad. A lot of it is just arid and pretentious nonsense. I think there are more exciting playwrights in this country. . . . There's the ethnic and cultural diversity in this country that makes every event on stage edgy and interesting in a way that I think frequently isn't abroad. There's a lot of stuff in Germany that's sort of extraordinary to look at because they still spend a lot of money on it. But it's just, you know, the most gruesome, sort of semifascist, expressionist . . . kitsch. There were a couple of productions of *Angels in America* recently in Germany that got subjected to real Teutonic treatment. So I think this country has the best experimental theater of any place on earth. I mean no other culture has produced a Robert Wilson and a Richard Foreman and an Elizabeth LeCompte and a JoAnne Akalaitis. America is really the breeding ground of great experimental theater work since World War II.

MC: This is both a tricky and an embarrassing question. Here you are, here we are, theater goes along, and some things are good and most things are terrible, and somebody comes along and writes a great play, kind of from . . . almost from out of the blue. Just wham! There it is. Something with scope and vision that entertains and illuminates. And I wonder if you could tell us, where did that come from? So that we can all go home and—if you'll tell us, we can all go home and write epics of our own.

TK: I wrote *Angels* after having written for five or six years. So I don't really feel that *Angels* came out of nowhere. I like *Angels* and I think that it's a good play. It has a lot of problems, and I think it has a lot of things to recommend it, and I think it's entertaining and whatever. It really benefited incredibly by just an accident of timing. It arrived on Broadway at a moment in history when a play about these subjects was going to receive an immense amount of attention and also be the repository in a certain way of a lot of people's hopes.

There are really good things about the play; but I really do believe that I'm an immensely lucky person because the play was ready to go right after this huge shift in public consciousness took place in this country. Around the 1992 election. People finally said, "OK, there are these homosexual people and they really aren't going to go away if we ignore them. They're here, and we have a choice: we can either be polite and well behaved, and sort of decent, pluralistically inclined citizens of a democracy, or we can sound like Pat Buchanan sounded at the [1992] Republican convention." And I think that Americans don't like Nazis, they really don't. That's been one of our saving graces. I don't think we should get too cocky about it and always count on it. But I think that people just listened to him [Buchanan]. What's that great Molly Ivins line about [Buchanan's] speech: "I'm sure it sounded much better in the original German." *[Laughter; applause.]*

I really remember from that summer listening to Jesse Jackson speak at the Democratic convention—although his speech got a little weird toward the end when he was talking about the midget dating the giant. But the beginning of his speech was, as is usually the case with him, absolutely heart-stopping and great. He told the story of that woman in that chicken-processing plant who said [to Jackson], "They call me a lazy bitch." And [Jackson] said, "You ain't lazy and you ain't a bitch." And you listen to that, and I have this really distinct feeling that the country was listening to that. People were hearing it this time and saying, "You know, we really ought to bring this kind of thinking back into Washington." Then, I had a very distinctly similar feeling, watching the Republican convention, when that creep [Buchanan] was up there going around the greatest demonstration of ideological cross-dressing. Even the Republicans weren't really liking it. There had been enough argument before about what was going to go in the platform. It just wasn't going over. And then the minute he was done, everybody trashed him. I mean all of the commentators said, "Well, that was disgusting." I felt, "Something's really changing here." And I think that something did. We are now beginning to be what you call in constitutional law a suspect class, a legitimate minority. That doesn't mean we get our rights, but it means that we have to be taken seriously. *Angels* came along at that moment and got caught up in the whirlwind, and I'm really happy, but it was a lucky break.

MC: Thinking a little bit about being a writer who is gay, I was talking to a friend of mine, one of my best friends who we stay with out here who is a children's librarian in Brentwood City. And we asked her what are the good books for kids and for adolescents about gay kids. And there was a pause, and she said, "Well, there aren't any." There are books for kids about gay adults. But there's no literature for children. In psychological discourse, there is no kind of scholarly or half-scholarly treatment that I know of about a gay childhood that deals with it as anything other than a pathology. And I think it can be a tremendously positive, illuminating thing to be a queer kid. I wonder, what kind of queer kid were you?

TK: Well, neither particularly positive nor illuminated. *[Laughter.]* I was what Dr. Richard Green, in his inestimable wisdom, referred to as a sissy kid. And I was pretty miserable. I mean, weren't you?

MC: Oh, yeah.

TK: We all were. One of the things that's interesting is I've gone back into analysis now because I can pay for it. *[Laughter; applause.]* Not that I have any neuroses that I need to take care of. I just sort of look at it as an intellectual adventure. I keep arguing with my analyst, who is a lesbian, and saying to her that it's really . . . I mean, I still do believe in some of Freud's categories of Oedipus and I don't think that they are quite the way that he described them, but that there are ways in which character structure is formed that . . . From my own experience, I feel that I can identify the way in which I think that my sexuality was traumatized toward homosexuality as opposed to the way that heterosexual sexuality is traumatized toward heterosexuality. I mean all of it is a product of trauma, and I believe that that's true.

But one thing that sort of astonishes me is that I keep finding that, at this point at the age of thirty-seven, surely I've gotten over what I have always imagined to be midlevel injuries sustained as a result of homophobia in my childhood. I was also astonished at how incredibly deep they are. Because I always thought, "Well, I came out of the closet and I dealt with it. I'm proud of being gay, and I really am happy to be gay, and I wouldn't want to be anything else." And I can really say that, and yet there are still issues of shame that are so deeply embedded and it's amazing to me how much damage we do to our children who are lesbian and gay. It's terrifying. And there certainly is no literature. There is nothing out there. And it's because Americans sort of hate their children anyway, whether they're gay or straight.

In terms of theater, you can't get a decent children's theater going anywhere in the United States. I remember somebody told me that they had written a children's play that was going to be performed by a bunch of Catholic schools, and that the word "zit" was in the play. It was for high school students. And the nuns made them take the word "zit" out because they thought it was . . .

MC: The word "zit"?

TK: . . . yes, because it would upset the high school students. As a culture, [we] all sort of understand that if we can destroy the minds of our children before they are eighteen, they won't find the society completely intolerable and desperately in need of change. *[Laughter.]* So any attempt to make any social policy corrective to education is horrendously difficult.

MC: Do you ever think about having a kid?

TK: Yeah. I was just in Louisville, and we had to audition . . . I actually wrote a part for a kid in this little one-act play that I've just written *[Slavs!]*. And we had to audition eight-year-old girls. They were so great—and they're eight years old! I can't remember what I was like at eight. But I imagine it wasn't anything terribly impressive. These speeches that I wrote for them have these impossibly long words, like "communality" and "heterodoxy" and "ideology," and they just plowed right through them, and they stood there, and they were so . . . and I thought, "God, that would be great to really be able to say I raised a child who really had her shit together at the age of eight like that." And I sort of loved them.

It's funny, you know, maybe [it's] the only thing that I really envy straight couples. It's hard to be straight; it's hard to be gay; it's hard all over the place. I would love to be able to just let this happen. I would love to be able to just get pregnant. *[Laughter.]* Because, as two gay men, it's like deciding to buy a six-bedroom house in the Hamptons with no money. It's such a huge undertaking. It's so enormously impractical. You can't raise a child. They cost a fortune. You'll probably mess them up. . . . I would always want to choose. But I'd like to be able to just say, "Okay, let's go off birth control and just do it," rather than having to fill out forms and put that kind of will, that kind of push out into the world.

MC: This may be a little tired, but I'm still interested in it. Do you have any problem with the idea of being a gay writer, or do you think there is such a thing—the whole idea of yourself as someone who is this kind of writer as opposed to just a plain old writer?

TK: We've all sort of decided that, haven't we? I don't think it's at this point so tired to say, "Well, I just want to be a writer and I don't want to be categorized." Who needs that? No, I want to be thought of as a gay writer. What worries me is that when I write plays that don't have gay people in them, I want to be thought of as a gay writer as much because I still think it's coming from a gay sensibility, a homo sensibility, and you know, I think that people should know that when they're going in to see [the plays]. But I hope that I'll be allowed to be a gay writer even when there aren't gay people, or obviously gay people and openly declared gay people, in my plays. It's great to be part of a community. I want to be thought of as a Jewish writer. I want to be thought of as a gay writer—mostly as a gay writer, because I experience in my life a lot more homophobia than I do anti-Semitism. There may come a time when I feel that it's more important to be thought of as a Jew than as a gay person. And I want to be thought of as an American writer, and even a Southern American writer. I just think you situate yourself in communities that nourished you, that you are sort of still fighting with and struggling with and in love with. . . . Do you consider yourself a gay writer?

MC: Yep. Guilty as charged.

TK: It's also exciting because we can think of ourselves now as actually building collectively a culture. I can think of myself as being one of a group of playwrights like David Greenspan, Holly Hughes, Tim Miller, and Suzan-Lori Parks, who are writing a new kind of gay theater. And I think that that's exciting. I wouldn't want to be, you know, denuded of that so that I could be part of the same club as David Mamet or something like that.

MC: Well, I don't think straight white male writers will ever amount to anything anyway. [Laughter.] What have they done?

You've said that you oppose the whole idea, the myth of the individual in the culture, and then more specifically in art. I've heard you say that this whole rampant culture of the individual has led us to Reagan and Bush, and the inability to pass even simple gun-control laws, and an inability to educate our children decently. More specifically, in the realm of playwriting, you said that *Angels in America* is what it is because over two dozen people were intimately involved with it, and that it was, in many ways, a collaboration. And yet, you're sitting up here, your name's on the playbill, you're the one who gets famous. How does that feel?

TK: Well, it's problematic. The myth of the individual is sort of a big, grand-sounding category. I believe in individuals. I believe that people are individuated. I believe that people have lots of very particular characteristics, and that everybody is the ongoing and developmentally progressive accumulation of a lot of very, very complicated history so that people turn out very, very different. I love the fact that people are different. And I don't think that socialism is really about sort of turning everybody into automatons.

One of the grim ironies of history is that the aspect of Leninism that developed ultimately into Stalinism, that really began to think of people as interchangeable parts in a machine, came to Lenin from Ford and Taylorism in this country, and the mass-production ideal. I don't think that socialism has ever been about denying that people are individuals. I just think that it's about beginning to struggle in a really, really powerful way with why economic justice and equality are so incredibly uncomfortable for us, and why we still define our worth by how much money we individually can make at the expense of other people, and why we find sharing and collective enterprise and motivations that are not competitive so phenomenally difficult. It's a tremendously difficult struggle that one has to undertake. It has to do with unlearning privilege; it has to do with examining what sort of events and activities make you feel worthwhile as a human being. But I really believe that the world is doomed unless we can re-create ourselves as social beings as opposed to little ego-anarchists.

Of course, I'm compromised. I live in a capitalist society. I own these plays. I did the lion's share of the work on them so I can sort of justify it to myself in that regard. I have this woman I was telling you about at dinner who writes me furious letters. She actually lives around the block from me in New York; she doesn't know it because I don't tell her what my address is. She really hates me, and she writes me these really furious letters demanding to know how my income is divided up, because she can tell that I'm a bad socialist. This is one of the lessons that we learned from the collapse of the socialist experiment in the Soviet Union—in a world in which the global economy is capitalist, you can't really carve out a niche of socialist endeavor. I can't say that I've tried to, except to be as scrupulous as I can be about where the money goes. But most of it goes to me, so I don't know.

MC: Is it fun being famous?

TK: Sometimes it is, and sometimes it's a drag, and it has a weird effect. You feel that you have to create this personality that can get up and do unnatural things like what we're doing right now *[laughter]*, and this personality that can deal with journalists, and this personality that can be on live television and stuff. And you have to make yourself into this person. The real trick is to try and not become that person, because it's a fiction, it's an artifice. You meet a lot of people, especially in New York, who have completely forgotten the distinction between what they really are and what they've sort of projected themselves into *[laughter]* and, you know, it's scary. This kind of phony self that you create can't write a play or a novel, or paint a painting. It can pretend that it's done those things, and talk about what that was like, but it can't really do that kind of work. So I admire writers who really just sort of retreat from the public eye, although politically that's problematic, because sometimes you can use celebrity for political aims. And of course, I mean it's trashy fun. It's fun to be approached on the street, and somebody say, "Oh, I loved your play." It makes you feel good. So, it's like being the popular person in high school, which I never was.

MC: What are we doing in New York? Why do we live there and not here? Do you have any idea?

TK: Because there are earthquakes here, and *[laughter]* because New York is important. San Francisco, there is no question, is infinitely more civilized and beautiful. But [in] New York all the problems of modern civilization are there in your face twenty-four hours a day, and it was for a long time the city of the birth of modernism, and then it became the city of the crisis of modernism, and now it's the city of the apocalypse, and it's a magical place, even if the magic is sometimes pernicious. And we're both New York junkies. I expect to live there until I die, although I'd like to have a house here or something, an apartment, to escape to . . .

MC: Well, me too. If anyone has a cheap place to rent . . . *[Laughter]*. There is a question I feel like I need to ask on behalf of some activist friends of mine. One of the things that was thrilling to me about *Angels in America*—I saw it on Broadway—my lover and I were sitting next to this couple who [were] obviously from someplace out of town, you know, New Jersey or Connecticut, and were rattling candy papers and speculating not too quietly to one another about what was a dream and what was real. These are people who don't go to the theater. In the last five years, they'd probably been to *Cats*, *Phantom of the Opera*, and *Miss Saigon*, and *Angels in America*. And here they were seeing this thing. I loved it for that. Though some people I know have been carrying on a bit about the fact that what these people are seeing as their one direct experience of gay people living with AIDS is a central character who collapses in the face of his lover's disease and bails out. Do you have any problem about showing the public something that's sort of questionable PR?

TK: Well, I'm not in the PR business. Those people should go see *Philadelphia. [Laughter.]* I liked *Philadelphia* but a lot of it is a public service announcement, and that's not what I do. I mean, in your novel *[A Home at the End of the World]*, the gay men are very, very complicated, difficult people. They wind up at the end in a pretty grim, I mean very moving, and I think in many complicated ways, hope producing, but difficult circumstance at the end of the world.

I hate that [criticism]. I've actually heard very little of that kind of criticism of the play, and I think it's sort of bullshit. There are very, very few gay men probably who have walked out on lovers who have had AIDS. I don't actually know anyone who has. I wanted to write what I wrote in *Angels* because I felt that it was something that a lot of people were afraid of, and that a lot of people weren't talking about. It's very, very hard, I think especially for men, given the way that the male psyche is constructed in this society, to take care of other people and people who are in the midst of a catastrophic or terminal illness. A lot of time, with the best intention in the world, the willingness to help flags. Or a fear of death takes over and you want to run. I've seen people who have stayed, but who have fled in the spirit; and I've seen people who have stayed, but at tremendous cost to themselves. And I wanted to honor the courage of those people. But there were all these plays out about people with AIDS at the time that I wrote *Angels* where it wasn't even discussed as a problem. Immediately, we all knew what to do, and we all sort of knew how to take care of each other because we're just, you know, these swell guys. That's not true of me, and I felt that that wasn't true of a lot of people. I saw it producing tremendous stress, not just among gay men, but anybody who has to take care of somebody who has Alzheimer's, somebody who has to take care of somebody with cancer. Everybody's getting sick now from something or another, so it's becoming like health care, both institutional and personal, has become the central issue of our times. Or one of the central issues of our times. I thought it was really important to write about it.

And, you know, I think the gay people in *Angels,* they're my friends. They're based on my friends, they're based on me, they're based on people that I like. I admire them. I think Prior is a great person. I think Belize is a great person. I think Louis is a great person. I mean Louis goes through hell, but he works his way back to being a decent and moral man, and struggles terribly with his choices, and dares to do the unspeakable to see what happens when you do it, and finds out that what happens when you do it is that you're incredibly, incredibly unhappy. I just don't know what those people want to see, because activism and the coming to power, I think, is very, very hard to depict in art. Maybe you can do it in film because you can show big crowds. But it's a long time since *Waiting for Lefty* and I don't even know that "Strike, Strike, Strike" really worked all that well back then, because it didn't make people strike, strike, strike; it just made them leave the theater yelling "Strike, strike, strike." *[Laughter.]*

We come to the theater, and we also come to novels and even film, in the way we come to our dreams. The guarantee that you have when you come to a theater is that nothing is going to happen to you that will actually produce bodily harm. You won't have to do anything while you're watching the theater except maybe be bored or irritated or embarrassed, but you're not going to be hurt. Consequently, you can allow yourself to be open to a variety of experiences that if you had to experience them on the street might actually wind up in your death or dismemberment. So you're afraid of them in real life, as you probably should be; but in theater, you can come and watch them, which is one of the reasons probably that we dream the things that we dream. It can tell you things that you couldn't face knowing when you're conscious and acting in the world. Then hopefully you take the world that you see in the theater and take it out into the real world if it moved you. That's what it should do. I think that that's really what art should be. It's the pessimism of the intellect, and the optimism of the will is something you have to provide, you know, by seeing how bad things have been, then, when you go out in the world, what you have to do to keep things from continuing like that. *[Applause.]*

MC: Toward the end of *Angels in America*, there is, what was for me, a great moment. One of the characters turns and speaks to the audience for the first and only time and says, "You are fabulous creatures, each and every one. And I bless you: *More Life.*" By that time, I was a mess. I was weeping, and I looked over at that couple next to me, and I thought, "Well, my God, you know. So we're all fabulous! Even if your hairdo is grounds for criminal prosecution, and you voted for Bush both times, and you're really just sitting there thinking about how you're going to get your car out of traffic and back to New Jersey before the rush really starts. We're all forgiven. And you are next to me, and I am [to you]." It was a wonderful moment. Since then, I've been wondering, did you really mean it? Are we all really fabulous?

TK: I've been thinking a lot about fabulousness. *[Laughter.]* If the great antecedent form of gay theater was theater of the ridiculous, then the new theater that . . . all of us who are lesbian and gay and working in theater now are creating is something that I'm calling "theater of the fabulous." I could go on for a really long time about that and I won't. But one of the things about fabulousness is that there's an issue of investiture, that you become powerful because you believe yourself to be. In a certain sense, the people in the theater are all fabulous at the moment that Prior, who has become invested by the audience with a moral authority and a kind of a prophetic voice, blesses everybody—they're fabulous, whether they want to be or not. A lot of people in the audience don't want to be fabulous. And when they go out in the world, they have to then decide whether they're going to earn it or not. Probably many of them will fail to do so. Nobody can be fabulous all the time. I mean a lot of people are awful, terrible people, and anybody that voted for Bush should be chucked in the river. I mean, you have to live with yourself if you did it, and I really honestly don't know how people do.

Americans are very, very big-hearted as a people. I think that's really true, most of us are, or 40 percent of us are *[laughter]*, which is a lot of people for one country. Which doesn't mean that we're smart or that we do the right thing. But I think that there is a kind of a generosity. There's also a kind of relativism and a real willingness to forgive. Some people feel that Roy is forgiven in *Millennium* when Ethel calls the ambulance, which she, I think, does only because she doesn't want him to die until he's been disbarred. *[Laughter; applause.]* I think that forgiveness only counts if it's really something that you struggle with. And I don't think that we should be quick. I don't forgive Ronald Reagan; I don't forgive George Bush; I don't forgive Ed Koch. I don't forgive these people. I can't yet. You have to wrestle with it because you also don't want what's happening now in Bosnia to be the model for human interaction, where one group's complaints against another group produce, you know, holocaust, and people can't forgive until the fifth generation. But it's really, really hard.

MC: Why don't we take some questions from the audience. . . . The question is, "Please talk a little more about gay sensibility. Everyone talks about gay sensibility in the arts, but no one really defines it. What is it?"

TK: You first. *[Laughter.]*

MC: No, your name's on the ticket, honey. Well, really, what would you say? *[Pause.]*

Oh God. It's certainly . . . we were talking at dinner about our therapists. We both see women therapists. And I very consciously set out to find a woman because I wanted to be talking to somebody who had actual personal experience with being marginalized and taken less than seriously and kind of shunted aside, even though I think a woman's experience is very different from a gay man's. I would have been happy to see a gay male shrink as well, but I didn't want to talk to a straight man and be worried that he wasn't going to get it, that he had been so much at the center, he'd been the one that the products were for and the messages were for. And I think that has its own sort of disfiguring effects. I wanted to talk to somebody who understood that some of what I went through was paranoia and delusion and some of it was real. I think that, to me, is a big part of gay sensibility. That's what I feel makes me different from a straight male writer, you know. You see more of the underbelly, you see more of the back of the hand. And I think that's a revelation, and you can do things with it. How about you?

TK: Yeah, I think that's true. There's a really great book out by Wayne Koestenbaum called *The Queen's Throat*. He talks about the diva or the opera queen as being an instance of retaliatory self-invention when the rejected or despised self is adored because it believes itself to be adored, and that exacts a kind of revenge on the culture that rejected it by becoming this sort of fabulous thing. There's an amazing thing that all oppressed peoples do, whether they're victims of racism or misogyny or homophobia or anti-Semitism. I think that there is a way in which people take hatred and transform it into some kind of a style that is profoundly moving to me because it shows people's enormous capacity, or the enormous power of the imagination to transform suffering into something powerful and great. For Jews, it's called menschlikeit and for African Americans it used to be called soul and now I think for younger African Americans it's called badness, and for gay people it's fabulousness. There's a quality. And I think you're right. It comes from suffering and having survived the worst that the world can throw at you. And also, of course, we sleep with people who are our own genders and form our most intensely, erotically cathectic relationships, at least, with people of our own genders. In *At Home at the End of the World* you do a great job of exploring the way in which sometimes the most intense relationships are not the ones that are erotically cathected but . . . and I don't know what that does as opposed to being, you know, in a hetero-sexual relationship. It's got to do something. I mean it's got to mean something, but I wouldn't want to characterize.

MC: The [next audience] question is about [Jonathan Tolins's] *Twilight of the Golds,* which did really well here, died in New York. It lasted only about five weeks—I guess New York audiences [are] appar-ently reasonably tougher. What do you think about that? What do you think about the play?

TK: It's not New York audiences; it's New York critics, and they're not the same thing. I didn't actually see *Twilight of the Golds* because it opened and closed while we were in previews for *Perestroika,* which is the most mind-bendingly difficult period of my life. It really was. I couldn't do anything except think about *Perestroika,* so I didn't see any plays.

I'm a big fan of *The Kentucky Cycle,* which opened and closed in clouds of journalistic nonsense, and sort of angry Kentuckians who felt that he [Robert Schenkkan] didn't quite get the accent right or something . . . I mean, I thought it was a marvelous and important play. [Tug Yourgrau's] *The Song of Jacob Zulu,* which was a really power-ful piece about apartheid with amazing musicians, Ladysmith Black Mambazo, opened and closed in no time. That's why Broadway is doomed. You really can't keep anything that's interesting going. You would think the critics would understand that and understand that it's their job, that if anything even marginally interesting gets to Broad-way, they should sweat bullets trying to get people into the theater. But they are unaware of their fundamentally parasitic existence *[laugh-ter]* and constantly kill the host. So, I got really, really lucky, and I had a stamp of British approval which protected me a lot.

MC: You're all fabulous *[laughter]* and we bless you. *[Applause.]*

The Oddest Phenomena
in Modern History

Bruce McLeod

Bruce McLeod, scholar and playwright (coauthor of *In the Sweat* with Naomi Wallace), interviewed Kushner for the *Iowa Journal of Cultural Studies* at the Holiday Inn in Iowa City on March 19, 1994.

BRUCE MCLEOD: I wanted to talk about *A Bright Room Called Day*, which, post-*Angels*, some have been known to call "the flop." I'm interested to know why you think it wasn't well received and also, more specifically, I want to know more about the character of Zillah . . .

TONY KUSHNER: That's why it was a flop . . .

BMCL: Well, that was what I was hinting at: was Zillah too much in your face and, connecting her with *Angels*, is she similar to Belize, who for me is the one character who prevents us from feeling that we are all part of a ghastly trial and one happy and unhappy family in the U.S.? Do Belize and Zillah represent a similar defamiliarizing voice?

TK: Yeah, that's interesting about Belize and I do think that is a problem with *Angels*. That aspect of the American myth is very seductive to me and the play probably ultimately—it's virtually impossible to discuss a problematics of forgiveness without getting an audience— people have such a deep need for forgiveness or try to understand forgiveness, so that they sort of leap at it, and false consciousness makes it so easy to believe that forgiveness is there for everyone; it's just appalling. The play is probably problematic in that regard.

When I wrote *Bright Room* I really wanted with Zillah to explore for myself why it was that as a political playwright in America I felt the

From *Iowa Journal of Cultural Studies* 14, no. 1 (spring 1995): 143–53.

need to cadge my politics so thoroughly—so that everything had to be hidden and you have to try to find a way to write political theater that wasn't overtly political. It's like Valéry's gunshot in the chamber concert: that you commit some kind of rudeness by having something that is unapologetically political discourse sound in a theatrical event. And I didn't, and I still don't completely understand what thing it is in us that has succeeded in making political argument, which is ontologically no different than any other kind of discourse, so anathema in aesthetic events—so I wanted to try with Zillah to just have it there on the stage, and she's got a character, it's not as if she stands up and reads a diatribe. In a way it is what Tolstoy did in *War and Peace,* with its alternating chapters that go back and forth, or with Melville, who is my favorite writer, and the interweaving of scientific speculation; it's something that novelists seem able to do and get away with. And also, rather than make a sort of coy metaphor [between the Third Reich and Reagan era U.S.] and saying watch out it could happen here, the point of *Bright Room* is that the Holocaust is only useful as a standard of evil if you're actually willing to apply it, and if you don't apply it, if it's set up as a unique metaphysical event that has no peer, then those people really died for nothing. And it makes critics berserk . . .

BMCL: About Zillah? I mean if you'd taken Zillah out . . .

TK: I don't know what they would do. A little company in New York asked me if they could do a production without Zillah before I agreed to have it done at the Public, and I thought because of the reception it had gotten at the Bush [in London]—I'd already been beaten up very, very badly for it—well, OK let's try it and see what happens, and it was a very small company so I thought no one is really going to review it, and then about midway through those negotiations, when I suggested it to a friend who wanted to do it at the Public he was horrified, and I thought "he's right, it should have her in it." The critics see it as if there were no play there, as if they had sat through one long, demented monologue comparing Reagan to Adolf Hitler.

Times change too. When the play was clobbered it was on in New York when the bombs started falling on Baghdad. Even a year later John Frohnmayer, the former head of the NEA, was getting up in front of the National Press Club and saying we're on the road to fascism—and in the last years of Bush things had gotten so bad, so scary that people were beginning to say there is nothing that guarantees America won't eventually lapse into fascism.

BMCL: There is a quote from *Perestroika* that I wanted to throw at you: Louis says "You can't wait around for theory. The sprawl of life,

78

the weird . . ." and Hannah finishes with "Interconnectedness . . ." One of the more compelling things about the play is that sense of connectedness. Is there a danger that if that is taken too far an audience can sort of sit back and say: yeah, we're all in this together, we're all oppressed? Especially with the dominant strain of identity politics within academia, there is that tendency to feed the personal guilt/blame game and discover all sorts of ways one has been oppressed (rather than exploited, which seems to me very different). Does the sprawl of life that you set up, with all its contradictions, allow people to identify with the messy, problematic family of the U.S., and the question becomes one of working out personal relationships and not how we are complicit with the workings of a social system?

TK: The play's politics, I hope, to an uncertain degree are the politics of identity and there is always the oppression olympics that everybody falls very easily into, but I hope there is enough in the play that complicates—the big democracy-in-America argument between Louis and Belize and Belize's journey through Part Two—so that most audiences would not get that from the play. I certainly try as a writer to be very specific about the kinds of oppression that people experience. The one unifying factor is that everybody experiences a tremendous amount of pain if they have a lived experience of oppression, and gay and lesbian pain is not different in a certain sense from African American pain, although the consequences probably of homophobia are in some ways less disorganizing and terrible than the consequences of 250 years of African American history. And the consequences of having been born into a Jewish family in America with a history of anti-Semitism that's very much with us to the present day is clearly a very different sense of oppression—and a lot of Jews in America have lost contact with it actually or lost the lesson of it and have gone way off to the Right. It's hard. I've tried to be as specific as I possibly can be. It's an interesting question for [Naomi Wallace's] *In the Heart of America* also: whenever you are describing evils on stage you have to be careful that they are not weighing in too similarly in the balance.

BMCL: Let's return to Belize for a moment: he seems to be the character who is most on top of things and appears to be dealing with what's going on fairly well. He embodies both compassion and critique but seems to be curiously free-floating. Why don't we get more of his background, or is that to come?

TK: That is certainly something I would want to deal with in Part Three. But, background—you learn a little bit about his background:

I had a monologue where he, in a scene with Roy [Cohn], told his life's story and I tried it in about ninety different places and it just never fit. The characters don't talk a lot about their backgrounds, you learn little dribs and drabs, you learn that Belize has a boyfriend uptown and that he used to do drag . . . everybody has one or two things, but I don't think the play lets anybody luxuriate in that very much. When I was writing this part I was wrestling, and I'm still wrestling, with the whole question of representation and the rights of representing different people's experience. The issue of a white writer writing a black character is so loaded. And I made mistakes when I started the play in 1988 and if I were doing it over again I probably wouldn't make him a nurse; having read Toni Morrison's *Playing in the Dark* I would have avoided that. I didn't feel tremendously comfortable with the fact that I was writing a contemporary black character and I think some of that discomfort is embedded in the text of the play. But I also think—my favorite painter Vermeer (I'm writing a play about him) always shoves pieces of furniture between you and the women you're watching and they're not really available to you in the way that they are in even say Rembrandt, where the women are not only objects, but are made accessible to you, the presumably male viewer. Vermeer is always shoving things, frequently with lion-headed finials, in-between you and these women as if to say: look but you can't touch, they don't belong to you. They don't belong to the painter either because the painter is always very specifically positioned, and the women are aware of the painter. There is a way in which Belize refuses to let you in and doesn't give away very much and that just became part of who he was. I wanted him to be the ideological counterweight to Roy, that there were two people in the play who were not lost and inert and swimming around deeply confused. I wanted there to be two people, one of the Left and one of the Right, who had a very clear moral compass and knew exactly where they were in the universe at all times, and who were not in theoretical, ethical crises. And Roy wasn't. He had a perfectly functioning reactionary ideology that got him magnificently through a host of contradictions and gave him a wonderful life until he got sick. And Belize also is somebody who knows where he is at—of course being confused is part of being Left and that's probably something that I need to work on. I'm going to do it in the film a little bit more. There are things that I can address that maybe the play didn't.

You know it's sort of like you're writing it and then you think, "Oh this shouldn't be this way or there should be more dykes in the play, and there should be this or that," and then you start to fix it and it begins to feel like tokenism. I wrote it, and it doesn't pretend to any omniscience or perfectly democratic view—it's a Jewish fag play. That's the starting point for it.

BMCL: In a number of reviews of *Angels* the character of Harper has been described as a sort of pill-popping . . .

TK: Insane . . .

BMCL: And flaky woman—sort of stereotypically flighty, dizzy, and given to escapist fantasies. She never seems to quite come down to earth. She also appears to be rather asexual in a very sexy play. In other words, she seems less able to deal with her hang-ups and remains afloat as it were. Have you had trouble with characterizing Harper or . . . ?

TK: No. I reject all criticisms of Harper . . .

BMCL: So there have been other criticisms of her?

TK: I don't think there—perhaps I shouldn't say this in print, but I don't think the part has been played properly yet. While one might have expected a play about gay men to run into homophobia from straight actors or straight directors, I think much more the play has run into an issue of sexism with its interpreters up to this point. I don't think Harper is crazy, she certainly isn't flaky, and I don't think she has any issues really with reality. She has an incredibly powerful imagination and one of the thematic valences in the play is the question of imagination, the question of where in the absence of—where does the new come from? Is there anything new or is it all recycled? Is there any leap possible and if there isn't a leap possible then is history cyclical and just repeating itself over and over again? She is the person that carries that theme through the two plays. I think of her as having a tremendously healthy sexual appetite, she's just married to a man who doesn't have any interest in her. She thinks about sex, she talks about sex . . .

BMCL: But she still wants her husband after the point at which we might wish to see a woman appear less dependent or derailed (even if imaginatively powerful): I mean the whole bit "I still miss his penis" and begging Joe to look at her, that whole narrow fixation on him . . .

TK: Well, she's in love with him. Her tragedy that she has been avoiding and the thing that she has to face, and does face finally in a very brave way—although it takes her, it takes everyone a long time to face their stuff—is that she is somebody who loves very deeply and has fallen very deeply in love with the wrong person and is shattered by the loss of this person. The play is about, in terms of Harper's story, the devastation and a willingness to keep moving in the face of devastation. I feel that that's really important. Harper like Prior has to deal a lot with loss and what you do when you've lost someone that you'll never be able to really let go of, someone who's completely, absolutely, and totally worked into the fiber of your being. Like forgiveness I think that loss is underrepresented in the theoretics of the Left. People are seriously deformed by what they lose and troubled to the end of their lives. The poet Thomas McGrath writes magnificently about it. It's not even right to call it loss in a sense because you don't lose it, it just isn't there anymore, it's an absence that's unbearable and I think that's what Harper is dealing with. Again I tried to have a scene where she met somebody and it's sort of sad, as Marsha Gay Harden said, that she's married to a gay man and in her usual way she decides to leave and start a new life by going off to San Francisco where there are no straight men. *[Laughter.]* But I suspect that also will be in Part Three.

It's frustrating to me because this is where you're really dependent upon—but people start with the assumption of a kind of abjection and weakness in her that I think is absolutely not in the writing. It's just a part that hasn't found its interpreter yet.

BMCL: Do you perceive yourself as part of a left-wing Jewish tradition? Do you consciously position yourself that way?

TK: Yeah. I feel that I'm very much a product of what I consider the most important tradition—I'm not a religious Jew and I think the Diasporan Jewish culture has a magnificent history of progressive involvement with the cultures that Jews have found themselves in and interacting with. It's very much a part of who I am. So yes.

It's a very distressing thing to me that American Jews have lost contact with the traditions of socialism and humanism—I don't consider myself a humanist but I probably am—but there are important progressive and radical European traditions that arrived with Jews in the U.S. from Germany to Russia that really informed American Jewish consciousness all the way up to the 1950s, and Roy's generation is really the generation that succeeded in beginning the severance of that. It still continued in a very lively way which manifested itself most obviously in Jewish support for the Civil Rights movement, but at the same time that that was happening there was this tremendous support for Israel and that's been part of this calamity—it's driven international Jewish culture from its progressive basis. I don't know what's to be done about it, what recourse progressive Jews have to call . . . I'm sort of floundering for words because I don't know what to call us at this point. I mean we're not a religion, it makes everyone uneasy to think of us as a race, including Jews, it's very odd; we've wound up being the oddest phenomena in modern history.

BMCL: I found it intriguing that right at the end of *Perestroika*, in the epilogue, there is an invocation of Jerusalem as a place of healing, then there is a brief undercutting of that invocation via the exchange between Belize and Louis about Israel and its occupation of the West Bank and Gaza Strip, but when real-world issues about the Israeli-Palestinian conflict, and specifically Palestinian rights to the occupied territories, are introduced, Jerusalem does not reappear. It is raised metaphorically and somewhat literally but absented from realistic discussion. Is Jerusalem a problem for you, and thus when you evoked it you immediately absented it?

TK: Well, that's quite deliberate in the same way that when the angel crashes through the ceiling at the end of Part One the line about Steven Spielberg undercuts—my intention there is to undercut the mythical and the magical aspects of the moment with an invocation of contemporary culture and the real world, and [I am] hoping to situate at least part of what's going on on the stage at that moment within a Spielbergian expectation: the way in which Spielberg, and Spielberg as front-runner for the Reagan counterrevolution, has co-opted our sense of millennial yearning as being something to do with salvation from above. At the end of the play this myth, which is again part of the millennial and apocalyptic tradition that the play is feeding off of, both Jewish and Christian, invokes this wonderful healing, hopeful myth and then reminds us that there is this tremendously difficult political specific to it that is absolutely worked into the fabric of it. You can't dissolve yourself in myth and mythic hopefulness and that's what I think is good about *Perestroika* in that, unlike *Millennium*, it ends in a very real place. You have to have utopian visions, I believe that, to be able to go on in life, but the utopian—it's the Ernst Bloch thing—has to be concrete-knowing hope, it has to be hope that has been filtered through the most lamentable conditions of real existence and I think that is basically what the ending is doing.

Jerusalem is . . . it's very, very hard. It's hard every Passover. Jews all over the world for the last 2,000 years say: next year in Jerusalem, and that's both literal and nonliteral. A lot of progressives get rid of it because of the obvious Zionist, imperialist implications of it. It's tremendously complicated—I really believe that the Israel lobby has pulled American Jews into bed with some really awful people is undeniably the case. The biggest supporters of Israel are the most repulsive members of the American Jewish community and Israel itself has got this disgraceful record . . . but anti-Semitism is alive and well and Jews do occupy a very precarious position in the world. For all of the wealth and cultural clout that they have accumulated in this country I still believe that we are a definable target and as such . . . I don't know what I'm trying to say except that I feel incapable of unambivalently rejecting a Jewish yearning for a homeland, although I can unambivalently say that I think that it's a terrible historical problem that modern Israel came into existence.

When I was in Israel and you go to the Holocaust Museum—you were talking about public spaces earlier—the entire museum is very subtly built on a ramp that leads you through the whole history of anti-Semitism and Jewish persecution, and it leads you up this ramp without you noticing that you are going uphill until you've gone up five stories and you are on this balcony overlooking modern Jerusalem: this is sort of the end point, the logical conclusion, this is what all that suffering was for, so that we could be—of course not looking toward East Jerusalem—the occupiers of this land again. And that's appalling, and you can look at that and go, "Oh for God's sake," and no matter how moved you are by some of the things in Yad Vashem you feel sort of sick at it. But then I went to the Wailing Wall and it *is* astonishing, you can't not feel as a Jew tremendously moved by a Jewish presence at the Wall. And above the Wall on the Temple Square is a six-branch menorah, each light representing one of the six million that died in the Holocaust, and more than anything else that I saw, the presence of that menorah made it feel like—that was the refutation of the success of the European attempt at genocide. But that sounds horrible too! Most Palestinians would probably hate me for saying that. The progressive Israelis that I met would describe a vision of what Israel ought to be and it sounded exactly like the position the Jews occupied in the ghettoes in Europe in the Middle Ages— a kind of buffer zone, a sort of financial hub—we'll handle the money between the Arab world and the West. Well, if that didn't work in the Middle Ages it isn't going to work here. And they don't need that buffer zone now, nobody wants it, it's all in computers and it will happen in nanoseconds—it's a fantasy and it's a fantasy of ultimate powerlessness because Israel is a creation of the U.S., bought and paid for. There are lots of beautiful little orange groves and olive groves which the Palestinians had before the Jews were there, and some very attractive European-looking cities, but there's no real country there. I don't know.

Liza Gets Another Tony

Liza Minnelli

"Liza and I first got together at the Russian Tea Room [on May 4, 1994]," recalls Kushner. "I brought along my best girlfriend, Michael Mayer [director of the acclaimed national tour of *Angels in America*], because he knows a lot about songs and singers and he is *seriously* into Judy, and because I was nervous about doing the interview. We had caviar and a very nice time with Liza, and the tape recorder didn't pick up a word of our conversation. So I met Liza for a second encounter at Caffé Rafaella in New York's Greenwich Village" in late May.

TONY KUSHNER: I liked talking politics with you the other day, and I wanted to drag you back into that.

LIZA MINNELLI: I'm so unauthorized to speak about politics. Let me preface everything by that.

TK: OK. So having prefaced it, I thought it was interesting what you were saying about Clinton and lesbians and gays in the military.

LM: I thought that the gesture was absolutely right. And I thought the thought was absolutely right, and the concept is absolutely right. But to do it so that it won't work didn't seem right to me. It was just too haphazard, there wasn't a detailed plan of how to proceed. I asked Jeane Kirkpatrick, and her opinion was that to get one case reversed would have made the snowball start in such a way that it couldn't be stopped.

TK: What do you think about sexual preference, though? Is it a biological thing? Or . . .

From *OUT* 13 (July/August 1994): 62–64, 144–45.

LM: It's so private and so personal, and everybody's talking about it all the time. I just think, "Wow." All right. Everybody's got the right to do, and be, whatever makes them happy, and whatever gives them peace of mind and dignity and self-esteem. I just think life is difficult now. You have to set your own rules, in a way, because there aren't any clear-cut rules for any of us anymore.

TK: You give me the impression of being somebody who's conquered her demons. But we were talking earlier about singing and suffering, and it seems to me that there's a complicated energy in your performance, that it's predicated to a certain degree on a feeling of pain, a kind of darkness and unhappiness. I was wondering if it's an ongoing struggle for you.

LM: I don't think anything is accomplished through negative energy. It defeats you. So I've always tried to be positive. I've always found the humorous side of it, always. And now the fight to find the humorous side is so lessened. It's so much easier now. It's just clearer.

TK: What made it easier?

LM: I think we all grow up thinking happy endings. "When am I going to land? Where is the happy ending?" There's no such thing. It's, "Did I have a good time today? Did I laugh today? Did I get it done today?"

TK: But what do you think about pain?

LM: I think it's a shared emotion. It's the one thing that we all have in common. And if anybody gets too high falutin', or too fancy for their own britches, their pain is the same as anybody else's. But there's a shared, common pain that we all have that I find is a good thing to sing about.

TK: Why would pain be different, in that regard, from joy, for instance? Is joy more individuated, less of a recognizable feeling, or . . .

LM: You can get to the joy. But you've got to go through the pain first. I'm more prone to joy. But I think if I just went sailing out, happy all the time, people would hit me right in the mouth.

TK: I like that expression. So you feel you're prone to joy?

LM: I really am.

TK: Your mother was clearly a very unhappy person.

LM: No, I don't think that's as true as people think it is. But I gave up trying to fight that rumor.

TK: Talk to me about her.

LM: We all have our own memories. No.

TK: No?

LM: I can't anymore.

TK: Really?

LM: It's not worth it. What I'm proud about—and I'm not changing the subject because I'm changing the subject, but in thinking about
her, and about this whole celebration [Stonewall 25]—it's massively
cool to me. It almost brings tears to your eyes, your observation that
Stonewall happened right around the time that she died. [Judy Garland's funeral was the day of the Stonewall riot.] And then all of these
years later, I'm singing, "We'll get through it," and fighting for the
same thing. And it gives me faith that certain things continue, in
different forms. Maybe there's a tradition of oppression, and I guess,
in her own, in our own silly way, it's freedom fighting.

TK: I think it's interesting that you say "in a silly way." When those
drag queens started throwing bricks at the police . . .

LM: Well, "freedom fighter" sounds like I'm taking myself too
seriously. But if anything anybody does artistically inspires somebody
to fight and stand up for themselves, to take one step forward, and not
be afraid, to think, "There's one person, even if it's a woman I never
met, this singer I never met, who understands how I feel. I'm not by
myself."

TK: But "silliness" is a fascinating thing about the Stonewall uprising . . .

LM: I was trying to be repulsively humble, and it didn't work.

TK: No. But I think you made a very important point, because the
fact that the death of this great movie star sort of sparked this street-
queen uprising, makes the whole thing sound kind of camp and
silly . . .

LM: But it's not. When somebody has been pushed around and
pushed around and told, "You're a fool, and you don't count, and
you're silly," all those words that just make you feel so awful, and you
can't stand up for yourself, because you don't know how to—and
maybe there's not enough reason to—but then something happens to
somebody you care about. And suddenly you say, "I don't give a shit if
you think I'm silly. You can't push me around anymore. Because I
care about this other person." That's a common thread of every revolution in the world. That's the storming the Bastille, in a funny kind of
way. "You can't push us off the street anymore and into the mud while
the carriages go by. I don't care if we look dirty. We're going to fight
back." So the underlying emotion of picking up a brick—even if

you're wearing a dress—it may seem silly, but a brick hurts. It's serious. A brick is serious. Maybe if there was a frivolity involved, it was still the first time they defended themselves. And I'm proud of them.

TK: Let's talk about the relationship of gay men to your mother's art, and also to your art.

LM: It's always been like that. I grew up watching her concerts. And there was always a large portion of the audience that was gay. But they were such a good audience, the best audience in the world.

TK: What do you think they came there for?

LM: Relief. And for fun. And for music. And then again, that vulnerability [of Garland's]. I mean, look, every real diva liked her. But the real glamorous stuff, like Marlene Dietrich—her audience, to me, was much more gay than my mom's. My mother's audience seemed to be very intense—like, on the edge of their seats.

TK: And what was the Marlene audience like?

LM: Just more "Oh, isn't she divine!" More vocal, I think. Because she wasn't. She wasn't singing, so they were singing.

TK: What was Dietrich like?

LM: Oh, she was wonderful. But she was very sort of, "Now, ven you are making de soup, you put . . ." One side of her was like a grandmother. It was so mad to just sit and listen. You think, "I'm sitting and talking to Marlene Dietrich, and she's talking about soup. Far out." You know? She was from that wonderful era when a woman sits down at a makeup table and creates.

TK: Did your mother do that sort of facial composition?

LM: No, she couldn't be bothered. She was too funny to do it. Please. *[Laughs.]*

TK: But I guess, for you, the style also is to just . . .

LM: I'm more into fashion than my mom was. Halston taught me everything. He was the best. He said, "The costume is your dancing partner. It's got to go with you."

TK: Do you mind if I ask you about [your late ex-husband] Peter Allen? I guess talking about Halston triggered the question. Were you close to Peter at the time that he got sick? Did you know that he . . .

LM: No, I didn't know about it for a long time. I saw him quite often. I noticed one day at Radio City that he was getting thin. You know, there's that jawline. I said, "I'm frightened." He said it was throat cancer. You don't want to intrude. Our friendship was so great, because we had boundaries of respect with each other. So I didn't ever really say anything, until finally . . . He was going through all of these treatments, and I would see him in the evenings, and we would go out.

I'd say, "You have to go with me. We have to go to this place, I need somebody to take me." And he'd say, "Oh, darling, you don't have to look through the papers to find something to get me out of the house." And I said, "Yeah, I do." Because he was just going to come here [to New York] and not see anyone. Finally, toward the end, I said, "Peter, we're not just talking about throat cancer, are we?" And he said, "No, love, we're not." And that was it. That was the only time we ever talked about it. He was very private, and he had enormous dignity. I think it was that simple thing of not wanting anybody to feel sorry for him—that thing of not wanting to be pitied is enormous with this plague, I find.

TK: You said that when you guys first met, you didn't realize that he was gay.

LM: I don't think he did, either. You know, we were so young. We were babies.

TK: How old were you?

LM: Eighteen, nineteen. I met him because he and his partner—they called themselves the Allen Brothers, and they were really talented and good—they were playing someplace, and Mama saw them, and hired them to open for her. She was crazy about the two of them, and they were so funny. Peter, of course, was the funniest, and the hippest. And the closest to me. He became, like, wonderful. I remember once my mom yelled at me about something, and he said, "Don't talk to her like that."

TK: Wow.

LM: Nobody had ever stood up to my mother, you know.

TK: What happened?

LM: I married him. *[Laughs.]*

TK: Right on the spot.

LM: He was completely . . . on my side. And we adored him.

TK: You said about three weeks into the marriage you found out he was gay.

LM: Yeah. But we worked our way through that. It was amazing, for two kids. But we cared about each other so much, we tried to make it work, and then it just didn't. I just got scared. And also, you don't want to keep anybody in a bind. Everybody should do what they need to do.

TK: Your father [director Vincente Minnelli] died in 1986. Were you very close to him?

LM: Very, yeah. He was wonderful. He was very funny. A terrific father. He really did give me this sense of wonder, of possibility. And for all the practicality that my mom drilled into me, he would give me this, "Anything you want can be accomplished."

TK: How old were you when they divorced?

LM: Six.

TK: Was it acrimonious?

LM: I never saw any fighting. And they never spoke badly about each other. Never. And I appreciated it. To this day, I think of that.

TK: How much time did you spend with her, and how much of it . . .

LM: Mostly with her. But I spent as much time as I could with my dad. I wanted to spend more time with him, because he was more lenient, you know.

TK: Do you believe in God?

LM: Yes, I do.

TK: Like in an organized sense, or . . .

LM: No. Just in the way that looks, that plant. *[Points to a large potted ficus.]*

TK: Do you believe in the Devil?

LM: No, I don't believe in the Devil. But I think that the human side of us that gets overcome and drawn into that darkness is hell. I think depression is hell. What we struggle through and pull ourselves out of, you know, and get to the other side—you can never tell until you can look back and go, "That was hard. But, OK, I made it this far. Far out. Now where am I going? What's going to happen now?" I think the greatest spirituality you can ever feel is when you're grateful.

TK: Hmm. That's nice.

LM: When your gratitude's in place, you're in place, I think.

TK: Grateful to other people? Or to God, for being alive?

LM: Just for just sitting here and being able to talk to each other. We're not scared. We can say anything we want to. I guess that the feeling, chemically, the greatest feeling in the brain, and for the body, is being in love. So I think everybody's always trying to feel like they feel when they're in love. When you fall in love, it's, "The sun is shining. Oh, God, isn't it great? It's raining. Oh, God, isn't it great? Oh, look, the taxi just splashed. Oh, God, isn't it . . . "

TK: Are you a roller-coastery kind of a person?

LM: I'm not a drama queen. I'm not attracted to pain. I don't go toward it. I think people think, especially when you're really young, that living is being in pain and suffering. Which is fine, except you get a little older, and you think, "Well, that's enough of that, thank you very much. I'd like a comfortable chair, and I'd like to put my feet up. I've suffered, thanks. Now what do I want to do?" I really like the middle of the road, that just "fine" is good enough now.

TK: If you were president of the United States . . .

LM: Oh, my nerves. We'd all be in trouble.

TK: Apart from AIDS, what kind of transformations do you think ultimately need to be effected to make the world a better place?

LM: If I had a wish? It would be to have more education. To rob kids of their dreams is the worst thing. The best ad I ever saw was, "A mind is a terrible thing to waste." That's always impressed me. Education would heal up a lot of us, you know? . . . And as for AIDS, if I ever can tell anybody about an exciting time that I lived through, admiring and watching, and feeling proud to be a part of it, it was watching the integrity and the community of the gay community taking on AIDS. I've never seen anything like it.

TK: Yeah. It's a remarkable thing.

LM: It just *kills* me.

After our talk, Liza and I headed to Stonewall Place for the photo shoot. Liza's appearance on Sheridan Square made a big impression. One man, a dancer who said his name was Miss Andre, had her sign his hand. Kevin [an onlooker] accidentally stepped on her foot.

MISS ANDRE: I live for Liza; she's the only one. I mean, there's many of them—I live for Michael Jackson and Madonna and them all, but she's the one in my book too.

TK: Why do you feel that way?

MISS A.: Because she's fabulous, she's clever, she's accepting. I'm gay. She'll accept everybody for who they are. She's not judgmental, she's just herself, and she'll treat you the same way.

TK: Do you like her music?

MISS A.: Sure. It's lovely, totally awesome, really. I couldn't put it better 'less I lied.

TK: Do you do drag, or . . .

MISS A.: Drag. Can't you tell? *God!* Let me use no fantasy language. Damn. Of course I do. I'm Miss Andre. My real name is Andrew. It's the *Village,* give me a break.

KEVIN: I lived in what my friend told me was Liza Minnelli's mother's apartment, Judy Garland's, on Central Park West, on Seventy-second Street.

MISS A.: Tell Liza to call me.

Kevin then sang a song about home, which he says Stephanie Mills sang in The
Wiz. *He dedicated his rendition to Liza. Louis [another onlooker] joined us.*

LOUIS: That was Liza for real?

TK: Yeah, that was her for real.

LOUIS: 'Cause, you know, they have fake imitations.

KEVIN: That's the real Liza.

LOUIS: She is beautiful, right? She's a very nice person, very edu-
cated.

MISS A.: She's very nice.

LOUIS: She has love, and her love shines in her personality toward
society. That's why society, the United States, loves her. Good job, girl.
Good job, sweetheart. God bless you all.

The Gay Rights Movement—
Twenty-Five Years

Charlie Rose, Andrew Sullivan,
Donna Minkowitz, and Bruce Bawer

In an effort to explore twenty-five years of the gay rights movement and the legacy of the Stonewall riots of June 28, 1969, television host and commentator Charlie Rose invited notable gays and lesbians to discuss the topic during Gay Pride Week in New York. The first discussion included historian Martin Duberman (author of *Stonewall*), Jim Fouratt (a contributing editor at *Spin* magazine and a cofounder of ACT UP), Barbara Smith (cofounder and publisher of Kitchen Table/Women of Color Press and editor of *Home Girls*), and Sir Ian McKellen, the British actor whose solo performance, *A Knight Out,* was the current hit on Broadway.

Most of the program was devoted to a discussion among four prominent young gays and lesbians, who remain active and vocal about current gay and lesbian rights issues. The panel, moderated by Charlie Rose, included Donna Minkowitz, Bruce Bawer, Andrew Sullivan, and Tony Kushner.

CHARLIE ROSE: To continue our discussion of Stonewall and the modern gay movement are Pulitzer Award–winner playwright Tony Kushner; Andrew Sullivan, editor of the *New Republic* magazine; Bruce Bawer,

From the *Charlie Rose Show,* WNET-TV (Channel 13), New York. This previously unpublished interview was aired on June 24, 1994, and was viewed by approximately three million of the Public Broadcasting Service viewers in the United States and Canada. Courtesy of Charlie Rose Show/Rose Communications, PBS.

author of *A Place at the Table;* and *Village Voice* writer and lesbian activist Donna Minkowitz.

There is strong disagreement at this table. Andrew, what is the essential disagreement in terms of where the movement is right now, and what it ought to be emphasizing or not emphasizing, and what is the conflict within the movement?

ANDREW SULLIVAN: Well, I don't want to put words into other people's mouths. The movement is about affirming the equal dignity of human beings who happen to be born and grow up loving someone of the same sex and finding a way for our society to recognize that emotional integrity and that human dignity. It doesn't have to be about a whole range of other issues which are hung over from the new Left of the late 1960s and the accidents of how the gay movement collided with that in the late 1960s. It's about affirming that we are like everybody else, that we are human beings, worthy of respect and love, that can have real relationships and real jobs and be part of our society. That we are assimilated: we grew up in straight families, we have straight friends. We are part of America.

CR: Are you saying that those who emphasize differences, differences that might come out in gay pride parades and other places, are destructive to . . .

AS: No.

CR: . . . achieving the goals of the gay movement?

AS: The key issue is distinguishing culture and politics. I'm in favor of a flourishing and a wider diversity of activities, people, lifestyles, and cultures as imaginable. But when you actually address the politics of a country like America, you have to get serious. You have to start talking about things that actually can be negotiated, things that actually can be held in common with other people, rather than constantly harping on what sets us apart. And harping is what sets us apart. It victimizes gay kids across the country or in regular families that want to leave, to lead regular lives.

CR: Tony.

TONY KUSHNER: There's a distinction that you're making between culture and politics that I don't think holds up. The dividing line you make works because what you have to do in order to make that division is to basically say that politics is a small service event that serves to cover up and correct limited wrongs, and that somehow then there's this giant sea of human phenomenon called culture that isn't part of political activism. As a playwright . . .

94

AS: I don't want to see politics . . .

TK: . . . I have to say I completely disagree with that.

AS: I don't want to see politics enforcing culture. That's what the religious Right wants . . . to use politics to enforce a cultural view of the way people should be. And what the Left wants . . .

TK: But they don't want to use politics. What they want to do is to use government to enforce religious differen——

AS: Well, the same thing. What you want . . .

TK: No, it's not.

AS: . . . to do is use government to enforce it as well, for a different kind of . . .

TK: No, I don't. No. I want to use government to guarantee individual dignity and guarantee hu——

AS: Well then, we are in agreement to that point, but . . .

DONNA MINKOWITZ: The question is what kind of politics. The main disagreement, as I see it, is whether the gay movement should align itself with other groups that are also disenfranchised—with the poor, with women, with people of color. In *A Place at the Table*, Bruce has said that we need a place at the table, but in fact what we need to do is overturn the table. The table isn't serving lots and lots of other groups. Everyone is underneath the table scrambling for crumbs. What we need to do is build a new table, and I would also argue . . .

CR: Stop, stop, stop. Let Bruce jump in because everybody else has had a chance to speak, and since we brought in his view, we ought to have him speak to it.

BRUCE BAWER: Thank you. You mentioned the word "diversity," Charlie, and the thing that strikes me as one of the ironies in this whole situation is that the gay Left talk so much about diversity, but they use this word "solidarity" as this ideal of what they want, and what they mean is solidarity according to their own politics. Gay people are supposed to all agree with the gay Left politics, but gay people are diverse. The gay population in this country is as diverse as the straight population in this country. The huge majority of gay people do not share the exact political agendas that Tony Kushner and Donna Minkowitz, or for that matter, me and Andrew.

AS: Somebody's article used the word "capitalism" as a dirty word—I mean, Tony and Donna are from the extreme Left in this country. And there's no reason why someone, because they fall in love with someone of their own sex, should adhere to the view that capitalism and a free-market democracy are flawed.

TK: You guys set up a number of paper tigers, and one of them is the politics of the Left, as though there's one politics of the Left. I had only met Donna today. I like her work very much, but I'm sure that we diverge on many, many issues. The politics of the Left is a very complicated thing. One thing that the Left asks is that people don't stop asking questions, and that you keep exploring what the implications of your own situation are in the world at large. I don't think that the politics that you're espousing is doing that. There is no requirement . . .

AS: How does it stop people from asking questions?

TK: I don't think it stops people asking questions.

AS: The liberal society I support . . .

TK: It keeps them approaching it from a police point of view, which is very odd.

AS: . . . is all about asking questions. It's questioning the dogmas that you have, as well as . . .

TK: Right, but I think you stop asking . . .

AS: . . . the dogmas that I have.

TK: . . . questions at a very critical point. You go to where you can see the immediate gains that could be made by a kind of consolidation of lesbian and gay politics at this point if we cast ourselves off from other people who are struggling for their own liberation. You think that we are weighing ourselves down by concerning ourselves with things that are not . . .

AS: These struggles are very different struggles.

TK: I don't agree with that.

AS: They have very different trajectories.

TK: You call it an accident that Stonewall happened in 1969. Stonewall could not have happened at any other point in American history except 1969. The three people that were on here before us [Jim Fouratt, Barbara Smith, and Martin Duberman] gave eloquent testimony to that. It isn't an accident of history.

AS: But they also gave eloquent testimony to a tradition of argument about homosexuality and protest about homosexuality in this country before that force—for like a century and a half. It's not as if the argument about who gay people are began in 1969 at all.

TK: But nobody's saying that.

DM: Well, I'm glad you brought that up because one question is, When did gay people begin? You talk about gay people being born, and it being an accident of birth, but in fact historians, gay and lesbian historians like Martin Duberman, believe very strongly that the homosexual as we know it only came into being in the nineteenth century, that in ancient Greece and . . .

AS: Do you agree with the religious Right, Donna?

DM: No. I'm going to finish. And in their . . . well, in some ways I do.

AS: You do? You believe it's choice.

DM: And in the Middle Ages . . . Let me finish.

AS: You and Jerry Falwell have a lot in common.

DM: In many other cultures . . .

AS: You need each other.

DM: In many other cultures and most of history before the nineteenth century, there were not homosexual persons. There were certain acts like sodomy. In Puritan America, your straight grandmother might be considered as likely to commit an act of homosexual sodomy as anyone else.

AS: Historians are divided about this, Donna.

DM: It's also . . .

AS: There are many historians that argue . . .

CR: Andrew, let her finish.

DM: The mainstream of gay and lesbian history believes this. It's also significant that most of the people who take your viewpoint—that it's very bad to discuss choice as a possibility in becoming gay or lesbian—are men, because many lesbians believe that they have chosen a way of life that allows them not to be subservient to them.

AS: And good for them. I have no . . .

DM: In the 1970s, many, many lesbians chose a lesbian lifestyle, and it's important to say that. It doesn't mean that everyone chooses, but I don't think it's harming anything to say that sexuality is fluid . . .

CR: For my benefit, when you say "chose a lesbian, gay/lesbian lifestyle," what do you mean, in terms of "chose to have," "chose not"? With free choice at a certain age, they preferred a gay/lesbian lifestyle? Is that what you mean? And what do you mean by lifestyle?

DM: Yes. I mean with a fairly free choice. Many women are in heterosexual marriages because, to them, it felt like a heterosexual choice. They could feel an attraction to men; they could feel an attraction to women. They decided to live a lesbian lifestyle. I hate the word "lifestyle" actually.

TK: Lifestyle is different from orientation.

DM: I don't agree that each of us has a natural sexual identity, a fundamental thing . . .

BB: The huge majority of gay people feel very strongly that their homosexuality is something that is innate, natural, constitutive.

DM: I disagree. Talk to some lesbians.

BB: The people who agree with you on this are completely political. They're people who have a certain Left politics and their homosexuality is an aspect of their politics.

TK: When you say they have "certain Left politics," you sound like somebody from the McCarthy period. I'm sorry, but you do.

BB: No.

TK: It's this demonizing thing. No? "They . . ."

AS: It's ridiculous.

TK: It isn't ridiculous.

AS: You're stuck in the McCarthy period.

TK: "A certain Left . . ."

AS: You can't actually think again of what the possibilities for gay people are in the 1990s. You're just stuck in the late 1960s.

TK: I think that that's . . . *[Crosstalk.]*

BB: You're trying to define . . .

TK: Your sense of what possibilities are for the 1990s is if someday we can get married like heterosexual people as though all gay people want a monogamous . . .

BB: This is a matter of wanting all of the same rights as straight people.

AS: Yes, a lot of gay people want it and nobody opposes . . . right?

DM: A radical gay movement can give straight people things they do not already have. The gay and lesbian liberation movement could liberate straight people, too, like from gender norms, from sexual repression.

BB: The more you bring in these other things, the more gay people are going to be alienated from and aren't going to be part of this movement, which should properly be seen as a move——

TK: When you hear Barbara [Smith] talking about Betty Friedan saying [that] at one point the feminist leader said, "Lesbians are a danger to feminism," aren't you worried that in twenty years people are going to be saying that about the two of you? You're asking us to say, "At this point, it's too dangerous to include other struggles in our struggle."

AS: Not dangerous *[crosstalk]* for different issues. It's just categorically different.

98

TK: And you're saying that . . . [Crosstalk.]

AS: I had no objection to a variety of lifestyles. The gay rights movement is about making sure that nothing is forbidden us that is given to heterosexuals.

TK: I think that you wrote very movingly in your article about racism. Really terrifically. I'm not saying that you're racist; I do think that you're being somewhat disingenuous when you say that you don't think it's a danger. When you said earlier, before the cameras were rolling, that we haven't gained anything because we've been too . . . and you say in your article that the Left is always sort of losing its energy because it's casting its glance in too many directions.

AS: It is.

TK: That is to say it's a danger to clash . . . to cast your glance in every direction.

AS: It's failing not because of different directions; it fails because it mistakes—to make this point again—politics for culture. And so it's a politics of theater. It's not a politics of argument, and until you have a politics of argument, you will not get the basic gains for gay men and lesbians who really want to live equal lives with others in this country.

BB: In your piece in the *Nation,* you [Kushner] quoted Oscar Wilde to the effect that a politics that does not include utopia in its map is the kind of map that is not even worth looking at. The whole problem with gay politics is that it's been guided for too long in too many cases by people who were going by a map with utopia as the goal. We need to turn this politics around so that we're using a real map of the real world.

DM: A real map as though a real map could never . . . you're shortening your imagination. You're not asking for enough.

BB: My imagination includes what's possible in this world.

DM: You also have to think about who is gay. Gay people are poor people; gay people are people of color. There's a fourteen-year-old lesbian who lives in the Bronx who writes to me, "You know, it's supposed to be OK. Everything's supposed to be OK with me now that K.D. Lang is out, but it's not OK, and I'm still suicidal."

AS: But, Donna, there are lots of disagreements, just to be fair, about how one helps the poor, how one . . .

BB: Exactly.

AS: . . . deals with race. It is not simply a question of whether you're for them or against them. There are many different arguments about how we might help the underclass, how we might deal with

99

sexism. Just accept that it's not either you're for all these people or against these people.

BB: No.

AS: There's just a disagreement about what we can do.

DM: But there's also a moral issue here. I believe that it's morally bankrupt to say, "Give me my rights, but not theirs, not theirs, and not theirs."

BB: It's not a matter of saying that.

AS: But I'm not saying that, and no one's saying that. It's a terrible calumny to say that we are.

BB: It's a matter of saying . . .

AS: We're saying, "These are these issues. These are *these* issues. Let us see the differences. Let us be intelligent about it, instead of believing we're . . ."

DM: But if you weren't . . .

AS: ". . . we're stuck in 1969, and we have a summer of love."

DM: . . . weren't male you might not be able to separate those aspects of yourself so easily. If you weren't white, you might not be able to think about, "OK, now I'm going to think as a black man. Now I'm going to think as a homosexual." You might not be able to draw that kind of a line down yourself and decide . . .

AS: It's not that . . . no.

DM: "OK, well the gay rights movement part of me will do this, and the black part of me will do that."

BB: You're looking at the politics as this thing where all the right answers are on this side, and all the wrong answers are on that side, and that we all have to buy into this one column A here. And it doesn't work that way. Each of us as individuals should look at each issue separately and see which we think is the best route . . .

CR: Let me bring Tony in and then come back to you.

TK: Something's being stood on its head here. The Left is constantly being represented as incredibly monofocal, single-issue, and demanding a certain kind of thought. What we're asking for is an expansion of thought, not a limitation of thought. You're talking . . .

BB: You're talking monolithic thinking, not monofocal.

TK: . . . about a real politics. I agree with Donna that it's morally bankrupt. I also agree that—in terms of pragmatics—it's bankrupt because we're not going to get . . .

CR: What's bankrupt?

TK: To simply say that short-term strategizing around what Andrew calls eliminating proactive discrimination, which is gays in the military and the ban on marriages, is not enough. It's very important, but it's not enough. If we only get those things, we will still be, as gay people, suffering terribly. When I say that "capitalism" is a dirty word—well, maybe you don't agree that "capitalism" is a dirty word—but something is truly . . .

AS: Hardly anybody does in this country, Tony. *[Crosstalk.]* If you want to be pragmatic, you've got to start engaging America . . .

TK: No, I think that's actually hurting . . .

AS: . . . not engaging the West Village.

TK: . . . the twenty million people who live on the streets in this country who think that capitalism is a problem. Maybe they don't know the word "capitalism." Some of them do; some of them don't. But they think that it's a problem.

AS: You try getting elected president arguing "capitalism" is a dirty word.

TK: I do know that . . .

AS: Just get, get . . .

TK: I do know that if AIDS . . .

AS: . . . get real.

TK: . . . , for instance, has environmental cofactors, and if the environment is crumbling, and if there is a reason for the environmental disintegration that's going on, it is my concern as a gay man as well as a human being that the environment is collapsing, and I have to be able to think that large to be able to think small. What are you aiming for? What are you going for? That we have . . . *[Crosstalk.]*

AS: Many, many, gay people, for example, are quite religious. When you ask them what are they going for, they talk about their religious faith, and they understand that religious faith is separate than politics. For many people from the 1960s, for many people from that period, politics is religion, and they cannot see that a whole new generation has a different view of the world. They're not right-wingers; they're just people who exist in a different world and a different climate, and they are the people who are trying to reclaim . . .

TK: What is the dividing line between culture and politics?

AS: . . . the gay movement forum.

TK: But where is that divider? Donna, you were going to say something.

DM: I want to get back to what Tony was saying about the practical reason to not divide, to not have a narrow conception of the gay rights movement. Look at what the religious Right is doing. They've organized an amazing, well-funded campaign against us. Ten states will have antigay ballot initiatives on the ballot in 1994.

AS: By being extremely focused.

DM: Well, in fact, they're able to organize . . .

AS: And you want us to dissipate our energies . . .

DM: . . . in the black community and among poor people because the gay movement, for the most part, nationwide, has ignored those communities because the gay movement has bought onto the image of us as, "oh, we're all rich; oh, gay people should get rights because we're affluent, because we can afford them, because you will sell things to us." Therefore the Christian . . . *[Crosstalk.]*

No, excuse me. Excuse me. The Gay Games took an ad in *Advertising Age* magazine that said, "The Gay Games: The way to reach the affluent gay market." Now, what affluent gay market? What about the nonaffluent gay people? And, the religious Right used that issue in Colorado. That is why they won in Colorado, because they painted gay people as wealthier and more privileged than everyone else.

AS: But how do you deal with the fact, for example, that levels of disapproval of homosexuality are far higher among black Americans by every poll than among white Americans? How do you bridge your coalition when you find that, in fact, racially some of the biggest enemies of the gay rights movement are among minority populations? Or they're just suffering from false consciousness.

DM: I'm not familiar with those polls. I wouldn't say they were suffering from false consciousness.

AS: They agree with the religious Right.

DM: There also are polls in which black people favor gay rights. But the way to do is not by ignoring the needs of the black community . . .

AS: I don't want to ignore the needs of the black community.

DM: Or to ignore the parts of the black community that are lesbian or gay.

AS: I want to see black gay leaders. I see nothing wrong with that at all.

BB: There's no reason why a handful of leftists should be formulating a whole menu of . . .

TK: Talking about a handful of leftists? I mean, *Hello?* Sorry.

BB: Well, maybe you don't hear that in the circles you move in. But most gay people in America will listen to the things that you two are saying and really not identify with any of it.

TK: That's actually not true. I would imagine Donna Minkowitz has a much larger readership than you do, and I think that more people have come to see *Angels in America* than will buy *A Place at the Table*. I don't want to get . . .

CR: No, I don't want you to, either. That's unbecoming, Tony.

TK: No, no, but what he's doing though is pushing us into the margins and saying, "This is a minority viewpoint," and it's not.

CR: All right . . .

BB: *Angels in America* is among those very affluent gay people that Donna Minkowitz looks down on.

DM: In fact, gay historian John D'Emilio has said there are more of us, more lesbians and gay men than there used to be, and there will continue to be more of us. And if our numbers grow, we don't have to think of ourselves as this fixed group that you seem to be referring to.

CR: Having listened to all this, is the bottom line that you want to speak to issues of liberation and equality without necessarily assuming you have the same political views on other issues that Tony does and Donna does?

AS: Yeah, I want formal equality for gay people and lesbians, and that's what the gay movement should be about. I have no problem with people in the culture at large expressing themselves in whatever way they want. That's the glory, I think, of a free-market, liberal democracy. It's no accident that one of the least left-wing countries in the world has one of the strongest gay movements, because the market in a free society allows for individuals to find their own destiny the way they want. That's what America's about; that's what I think the gay movement should be about.

CR: All right, Tony, last word in terms of what you have learned and listened [to] here today, what you go away with from this.

TK: Again, the people that are claiming that there's been this leftist domination are also the people that are now saying, "This is what the gay movement should be about," which is not putting words in your mouth—in fact, it's what you just said. "The gay movement should be about whatever gay people and lesbian people are about."

CR: In all of their diversity.

TK: And it reflects an immense diversity, and that diversity will inevitably move us in all sorts of directions.

BB: "Diversity" is an important word to me. The gay population in this country is incredibly diverse, including the politically diverse. Gay people have the same political range that straight people have from conservative to very Left. The more we try to tie gay politics, gay equal rights, to a very Left-leaning agenda, the more gay people are going to be alienated from it and the less effective it can be.

DM: The gay movement is not just about sexuality. It's also about gender. The gay movement is about men who are feminine and women who are masculine and creating space for that. That's why the gay movement can be liberating for everyone, including straight people who don't want to be bound by gender norms.

CR: Thank you all. Pleasure.

I Always Go Back to Brecht

Carl Weber

Conversations between mentor and student can be treasures, especially when the student has gone on to mentor other artists. After receiving his B.A. in medieval history from Columbia University, Tony Kushner advanced his studies at New York University's Tisch School of the Arts, where he received an M.F.A. in directing. At NYU, Kushner studied with renowned theater practitioner and Brecht scholar Carl Weber, whose genius and artistry Kushner acknowledges as seminal influences in his own development. Weber interviewed Kushner by telephone from Stanford, California, with the latter at his home in Brooklyn, New York.

CARL WEBER: Tony, in articles and interviews you have frequently commented on the impact which Brecht's theater has had on your own work. When did your first encounter with Brecht's work actually happen, and what brought it about?

TONY KUSHNER: It was in the second semester of my freshman year at Columbia University. I took a modern drama survey course. We read Dürrenmatt and everybody else, Ionesco, Beckett, etc. And I believe, if I remember correctly, we read *The Good Person of Sezuan* and *Threepenny Opera*. I was intrigued by *Threepenny Opera,* although not terribly impressed with it. I thought that *Sezuan* was complicated and interesting but I don't remember having much more of a reaction than that. If I'm remembering correctly, two things happened simultaneously the next semester when I was a sophomore. I had a professor

From *Brecht Yearbook/Das Brecht-Jahrbuch,* vol. 25 (Madison: The International Brecht Society, 1995), 67–88. This interview took place in November 1994.

who was teaching my Western humanities class, a sort of survey course in classics of Western political, ethical, and philosophical thought. He was a Latin American Marxist, and he gave me Ernst Fischer's *The Necessity of Art* to read. I was very disturbed and upset, challenged and excited by Fischer. That started me reading Marx. At the same time, Richard Foreman was doing *The Threepenny Opera* at the Public Theater at Lincoln Center. I was seeing a great deal of theater in New York at the time, almost all of it on Broadway, and Foreman's *Threepenny Opera* . . . I was absolutely devastated by it. I thought it was the most exciting theater I had ever seen. I went back to see it six or seven times and I became very interested in Brecht from that point on.

I took another modern drama course that had a heavier amount of Brecht in it and I read the *Short Organum*, which is the point at which I fell completely in love with Brecht. I read all of *Brecht on Theater*. The *Short Organum* was a kind of revelation for me. It was the first time I believed that people who are seriously committed political intellectuals could have a home in the theater, the first time that I believed theater, really good theater, had the potential for radical intervention, for effectual analysis. The things that were exciting me about Marx, specifically dialectics, I discovered in Brecht, in a wonderful witty and provocative form. I became very, very excited about doing theater as a result of reading Brecht.

cw: What was it that immediately captured you in Brecht's writings?

tk: I think in all of German literature there is, for Jewish people, a certain recognition. The history of Jewish literature and the history of German literature are fairly inextricable. Even in translation there is a kind of a diction and sensibility that is recognizable. I've always felt myself very deeply drawn to German literature.

cw: What do you actually mean when you talk of a certain kind of diction?

tk: It probably is the Latinate structure of the sentences. Also, the folk idioms that are very similar to the idioms of Yiddish.

cw: Of course, a lot of Yiddish idioms crept into the German over the centuries. A lot of German sayings are Yiddish sayings, and vice versa.

tk: German-Jewish culture is sort of the *Hoch* culture of Jewish society. It is—what's the term?—*plumpes Denken*, it's a kind of "fat" thinking. It is Benjamin's term, I think.

cw: *Plumpes Denken?*

tk: Yes, the idea of "fat" thought. It is a very cause-and-effect kind of thinking, a very grainy sort of thinking. It isn't French . . . I'm doing a bad job of describing it.

cw: You mean a specifically dialectical kind of thinking?

tk: Well, it is very dialectical and firmly rooted in the Enlightenment and in a kind of rationality, a belief in the recoverability of ultimate causes. It is ethical and not obfuscating or obscurantist.

cw: If you think of Heidegger, for instance, there is lot of obscurantist German thinking.

tk: There is certainly also a great deal of obscurantist writing in Jewish mystical traditions. But this is another sort of thinking, like Spinoza, or Bloch, or Hannah Arendt, or Goethe. There is a very domestic sort of clarity about it.

cw: And you found that in Brecht?

tk: Yes, I did. I think of it as a diction that is also intrinsic and rather grim, and that I find in Brecht. I think there is a Jewish-German connection.

cw: Absolutely, a connection and a long tradition that started with Lessing and Moses Mendelssohn, and maybe even earlier.

tk: Yes, I guess that's it.

cw: Now, when was it that you decided to study directing? And at what time did you begin to think about becoming a playwright?

tk: I didn't really think about becoming a playwright. Being a playwright is what I always wanted to be. But I was too intimidated by it, and I felt that, if I couldn't write *Mother Courage,* I shouldn't write any play at all. Also, when I studied Brecht, I studied Shakespeare, and I studied Shakespeare with a man named Edward Taylor. I don't think I remember that he actually spoke about dialectics, but his approach to analyzing Shakespeare was entirely a matter of analyzing the dialectics and paradoxes in Shakespeare. Reading Brecht and Shakespeare at the same time was wonderful because I was discovering what a dialectical method was and finding it was a critical tool for understanding the two playwrights whose work I admired the most. I was also very much drawn in Brecht to the epic form, to the chronicle play. It was almost immediately as soon as I read *Mother Courage* that it became my favorite Brecht. I loved the multifocal, the multiple perspective of it. You know, Brecht talks about it when he writes about Breughel and the lack of a single point of perspective, the complexity of signs, and the physical conflict in a terribly grandiose prism. I liked this sort of sprawl of the big epic plays in Brecht.

cw: That essay on Breughel reflects very much Brecht's directorial approach. When did you decide to explore directing?

TK: I think that I wanted to be a playwright and that I wanted to be a playwright very much like Brecht. But I was afraid to try that, so I thought, well, maybe I could be a person who directed Brecht. It felt to me that it was a reasonably good way at least to start to explore how to make theater. And that if writing was going to happen, it would happen alongside it, which is pretty much exactly what happened. I had read an article in *Yale Theater* about you and R. G. Davis. In the absolutely most violent flash of my Brecht fixation I was just reading everything about him that I could find. *Yale Theater* published in one of its first issues . . .

CW: Yes, they published a piece about Epic West in Berkeley.

TK: Right. And you were working on *Calendar Tales* . . .

CW: No, Ronnie was. I was working on *The Baden Play for Learning* and on *Messingkauf.*

TK: Right. I read it and I thought you sounded great. I wanted to fly right out to San Francisco and work with you. It seemed this was the kind of stuff that I should be doing. I had also read Ronnie Davis's book about the San Francisco Mime Troupe, which is a really wonderful book.

CW: It is, I agree.

TK: He talks about Brecht with a very strong American sensibility. Also, one thing I've never really mentioned is that I did study to be an artist for a brief while. Not exclusively to be an artist, but I took painting and drawing.

CW: You are actually very talented in that way, as I know from all the drawings you did while you were at NYU. I remember especially a New Year's card you made and gave me after Brezhnev's death, a cartoon-like drawing that somehow seemed to anticipate *Perestroika* and its results, at least in retrospect.

TK: I also used to make masks, and the idea that Brecht's was a theater that had room for things like half masks, that it incorporated popular forms of theater like *Commedia,* felt exciting to me. In fact, one of the very first experiences that I had at NYU when I was thinking about applying there . . . maybe I called you and asked about meeting you, and you didn't have time to meet with me but you said that I should come and see one of the projects. Someone had just finished directing the first half of *We Won't Pay We Won't Pay,* and I had never even heard of Dario Fo before. As I remember it, it was presented in one of the studios on Seventh Street, and it was a rather good, lively performance, and I loved the play. I believe it was directed by Bob Bresnick.

CW: Yes, I think it was.

TK: He was supposed to do the whole thing and felt they only had enough time to do the first half, and that was all they were going to present. But it was actually very good and it introduced me to Dario Fo. At any rate, that's how I think I decided I would direct instead of simply writing. I already had written a couple of things that were heavily influenced by Brecht. A children's play, based on a Grimm fairy tale and in twenty-four scenes, that was completely epic, though I had no idea what I was doing.

CW: That was before Columbia or while you were there?

TK: That was in my last year at Columbia. And then I went to NYU.

CW: Why did you pick that particular Brecht one-act play that you auditioned with?

TK: Well, I had read the Methuen volume with the Brecht one acts. I needed something short, and I thought I'd like to do Brecht. *The Beggar, or the Dead Dog* was small. It was a very strange little play, and I was moved by it. I also liked some of the visual ideas that I had had about it. It had the possibility of using masks, which I was determined to do.

CW: I also remember very well the backdrop you had painted for it.

TK: Yes, it was based on an Inigo Jones drawing. It was sort of black, and it had a lot of death imagery which was very important to me at the time. *[Laughs.]* And I think that I had absolutely no idea what I was doing and I had absolutely no idea what the play meant.

CW: During your time with our program and the further work on Brecht that you did when you were at NYU, and while we worked together on *Happy End* and other things, did your earlier perception of Brecht change, or not? And if so, in what way?

TK: It's weird to be talking to you about this directly because it has so much to do with you. From that first interview with you, I felt that getting the chance to work with you was going to be a chance to work with a live connection to the Brechtian tradition. I didn't really know very much about you when I showed up at NYU, I didn't know that you were also someone who had worked with Handke, and with Heiner Müller, and Ed Bullins, and people like that. So, I was unprepared for the extent to which you had been a figure in the American avant-garde. And as I told you, I think, when we were all graduating, and you were leaving NYU, that was an incredibly important part of our work together, establishing the connection between two key radical traditions in the theater.

Your main pedagogical tool, the fable, taught me a great deal about the way in which content, narrative, and meaning function together, and the kind of rigorousness that is necessary to make a successful play. That forced me to reconsider the Brecht that I had read and to look at it more thoroughly, and it gave me a new appreciation of how intricately and carefully worked the texts are, and how incredibly economical they are. Especially the scripts where Brecht had a chance to hone them through rehearsal, there is nothing wasted at all. Even in *Sezuan,* which he didn't really have the chance to trim, everything is in the service of the fable and everything is important. I don't know if I'm making myself clear, but there is a sort of marriage of the narrative drive, the emotional life of the play, the psychological life of the play, and the political meaning, the *Inhalt.* It's all so beautifully and intricately interwoven. And also the necessity of having a deep understanding of history, a political understanding of history. And having an overtly ideological historical narrative that one uses in a sophisticated way was something I got from working with you. I think of an instance of when you were demonstrating . . . somebody had brought in a scene from the *White Devil* or *Duchess of Malfi* to the directing seminar, and you were sort of acting for us. You did it again when we were doing *Happy End.* And I felt that I was watching a way of doing things, and a way of rehearsing, that was a direct example of what Brecht means. I don't think Brecht is actually very good in describing what he expects actors to do.

cw: When writing about the theater, he never concerned himself very much with what particular method an actor would employ and how an actor should work. He basically wrote about the results he wanted to see in performance.

tk: Right. It was fascinating to watch you perform. I understood something about what Brecht wanted in acting from watching you, in terms of creating moments that are deeply invested and also clearly observed by the performer.

cw: Isn't it actually Brecht's concept of gestus that you are talking about now?

tk: Yes. But "gestus" is one of those promiscuous terms, I think. I understand it as having several possible applications.

cw: Brecht was never very consistent in writing about it and in defining it clearly.

tk: Particularly in what it meant.

cw: Probably, in his own mind, he was at times also quite ambiguous about it, about what it was supposed to be. When you saw him at work, however, you really understood it.

TK: When you work on one of his plays, you understand the usefulness of finding the visual motif that will help to string ideas together for an audience that run through the play and appear at various points, a visual motif that will privilege those moments.

CW: Did your directing experience—at NYU as well as during the various off-off-Broadway productions that you directed while you were still a student and shortly after—did these experiences change your way of appropriating Brecht's methods? In my memory, your production of *The Heavenly Theater* was a striking example of a young director who is writing plays and who is beginning to bring both things together.

TK: Yes, I think I was. Although your critique of *Heavenly Theater*—that it was in a sense too rational, that what I was trying to describe, which is this extraordinary historical phenomenon of a revolution that takes place during a carnival, that it was too mired in a kind of "Marxist-Leninist" or even Brechtian dramaturgy, and that the carnivalesque was not really happening—was absolutely true.

CW: But it was probably a necessary phase to go through for you.

TK: Right. In many ways that was really my first play. And I didn't have the tools or the skills to take it where you suggested that I should take it. It was a lesson in terms of finding the right model for the subject at hand. The real, deliberate attempt to write a "Brecht play" was *A Bright Room Called Day.* You and I had a discussion about Brecht writing various plays as answers to other plays that he was impressed or disturbed by, and about the way in which Brecht or Shakespeare incorporated or used previous material and tried to write a dialectical response to it. I took a Brecht play that I have very little respect for, which is *Fear and Misery of the Third Reich,* and attempted when I started out to write *Bright Room* to do a sort of Reagan-era version of it.

CW: Did you say you have little respect for it?

TK: I have very little respect for it. The scenes are fairly mediocre. They have a lot of interesting moments because they are Brecht's but they are not terribly impressive. The whole thing, when it is strung together, has certainly never been one of my favorite Brecht plays, especially not for its dramaturgy.

CW: Well, that is an opinion you share with Heiner Müller.

TK: In terms of its response to what was going on in Germany at the time it simply failed. The play that really impresses in that regard is *Mother Courage,* which I think is very much Brecht's response to Hitler, and then of course *Arturo Ui,* which I have gained a great deal of respect for in recent years. I still think of *Mother Courage* as a sort of a Trotskyite piece. It is consonant with Trotsky's analysis of what was going on in Germany in the years before, which allowed Trotsky to prophesy the rise of Hitler. The petty bourgeois run amuck. The perilous socioeconomic position of the petty bourgeois in Germany resulted in their manipulability and turning to Hitler. *Mother Courage* still is a tragedy which is appropriate to the history that Brecht had been watching.

CW: You said that *Bright Room* was kind of an answer to *Fear and Misery.*

TK: It was a necessary thing to do for me. It was an attempt to deal with Brecht, with German subject matter, with Germany . . . probably with you. In fact, definitely with you, which is why I wrote in the introduction that the play is about exile. I don't want to get "Bloomy" (as in Harold Bloom) about it, but there is something to the idea that, when one is a writer, one is profoundly influenced by a very great writer the way I was profoundly influenced by Brecht. That one does have to engage in a struggle, you may call it an Oedipal struggle or not, depending on your views of Oedipus and Freud, but it is certainly a struggle of someone who is fighting to find his or her own voice and persona as a writer, and to wrest an independent persona from a progenitor. There was a way in which I used *A Bright Room Called Day* to do that with Brecht. I did many other things for myself with that play but I made an attempt in direct imitation, to—in a certain sense—get it out of my system. And also to find a way in which I was indebted to and also diverged from Brecht in terms of handling political material, in terms of a style and a diction, while recognizing the impact that other writers, including writers who were not necessarily dramatic writers, like Wallace Stevens and Pound, had had on my sense of how to use language. I think that I was working on all of that, and with Brecht. And I was also dealing directly with German subject matter, dealing with you as another father figure, and, struggling with that, using a kind of a fable. *Bright Room* was the first play that I basically outlined and wrote a fable for, doing the fable scene by scene by scene.

CW: You didn't do that for *Angels,* did you?

TK: No, I didn't. I tried very hard, but in *Angels* something else happened. The play took over and went off in a direction I had never foreseen. When I was plotting the play, I started with a fable that I had to discard because the play went off in a direction I didn't anticipate, including being seven hours long. Then I returned, by the time I was working on *Perestroika*, to a fable, just because the plot was so complicated that I needed to lay it all out or I wouldn't have known what the hell I was doing. And I still do use outline in form but I discovered that sometimes a play just has to take off and run on its own.

cw: Well, that could happen to Brecht too. Look at his journals, for instance, when he writes about wrestling with certain plays.

tk: In *Szechwan* his characters certainly took him by surprise.

cw: You wrote a couple of years ago an article for *American Theater* where you argued for an "American" Brecht, an Americanization of Brecht, so to speak. Do you still see things the way you wrote about them at the time or have you changed your mind?

tk: What I was writing about in that article, if I remember it correctly, was what I'm describing now. Which is the necessity of making any writer one's own, or one's country's own, if the writer is not of one's own country.

cw: Or one's culture, if one is living in a country with a multitude of cultures, like the U.S.

tk: Yes. I have become very depressed about the way Brecht is done in this country. And I also think the failure that the theater practice in this country has had in coming to terms with Brecht points to all the things that are deeply problematical with our theater practice in general.

cw: Nevertheless, he still is one of the four most frequently performed playwrights in translation in the country.

tk: I am sure that is true. But what depresses me about the way he is done is the complete lack of intellectual rigor. People simply don't have the intellectual tools to understand him.

cw: Sometimes they don't even seem to care.

tk: That is completely true. They are steeped in a set of images and of notions about what Brecht is supposed to be. And there is a desire to be apostate about a tradition about which one knows nothing, and apostasy by uninformed heretics is really uninteresting. It is senseless to stand Brecht on his head if it is done by people who don't understand whose head it is.

cw: And who don't even know where his feet are.

tk: *[Laughs.]* Right. Basically, what one winds up with is a kind of carnival, an unintelligent, bourgeois production. The best productions of Brecht that I have seen—not surprisingly—have been by a Rumanian.

cw: By Andrei Serban?

Yang Sun (Lou Diamond Phillips), a pilot, and Shen Te (Charlayne Woodard), the "good person," fall in love in a scene from *The Good Person of Sezuan,* Kushner's adaptation from Brecht's play. Production directed by Lisa Peterson at La Jolla Playhouse (La Jolla, CA, July–August 1994). (*Photo by Ken Howard.*)

TK: Serban's *Good Person of Sezuan,* and by Foreman. I have not seen a lot else, but most of the stuff I have seen was just gruesome.

CW: How was the production of your version of *Good Person of Sezuan?*

TK: The problem is, first of all, that the American theater allows for four weeks of rehearsal. I am convinced that it is absolutely impossible to do a play of the length and complexity of any of the great Brecht plays in that amount of time. It is especially impossible with Brecht because you must learn something before you approach him. You can't understand *The Good Person of Sezuan* without understanding the historical process that the play is describing, in terms of the beginning of modernization in a country that is premodern but becoming modern in a very ugly and a rapid fashion, and the devouring of the country by the city. You really have to understand the disintegration or, rather, the destruction of the craftsmen and the family, the cottage industry, by the factory, to know what is happening to these people in the play. People have to understand it, and they also have to care about it. You can't do *Sezuan,* you can't do *Mother Courage,* unless you care about money and where the money goes. American actors don't care about those things, and American directors don't, and American designers don't. They don't want to bother with them too much. Economics seems unworthy as a subject.

CW: Which is particularly absurd in a country where money really is the most important thing in most people's mind.

TK: Yes, absolutely. And of course it is always the way that the people most obsessed with money are the people who, like the British, go on and on and on, in their sort of mildly anti-Semitic way, about Jews and money. But there are no people on earth, except maybe Americans, who are more obsessed with money.

CW: Well, meanwhile the Germans are also obsessed with money, I dare say. And the Chinese, I'm afraid.

TK: There is, maybe, another German-Jewish similarity. I find that Germans and Jews are at least willing to talk about money, and willing to talk about haggling, which is after all an activity in which most human beings spend an outrageous proportion of their life. I mean, people haggle, that is how you get through.

CW: Many Germans actually don't like to hear about haggling and think that it is bad manners.

TK: Yes, but there is a lot of it. Look at *Faust.* It is all haggling about money and about contracts.

CW: Of course, it is going on all over the place. But they ignore it, they suppress it. They don't want to know about it, or they pretend, at least, that they don't know about it.

Let's go on to another topic, a very timely topic: The recent historical changes, and also some scholarly investigations into Brecht's private life, have caused a sharply critical reevaluation of Brecht's achievement. What do you think about this phenomenon? Is it valid? Is it just a fad? Is it overblown or is there some justification?

TK: Well, my friend Brian Kulick said, and I think he is right, that one of the manifestations of the poverty of American intellectual life is that we frequently only turn our attention to important writers and thinkers and artists when we discover a scandal or ostensible scandal about them that will enable us to justify the fact that we don't know anything about them. So, we become interested in Freud at the point at which Jeffrey Masson has shown up to tell us that Freud covered up important information about the extent to which his female patients were being sexually abused and not just hysterically fantasizing sexual abuse. And even though Masson's discoveries in that regard, if they are actually discoveries, are incredibly important, it has enabled a new generation of lefty-type intellectuals to decide that Freud is not worth coming to terms with. Or the discovery that Marx had illegitimate children means that we don't have to bother with Marx anymore. Or the discovery that Paul de Man was a Nazi sympathizer or that Heidegger was a Nazi means we don't have to bother with Heidegger anymore. Or if Hitler gave Elisabeth Forster-Nietzsche a bouquet of roses, that means that we don't have to worry about Nietzsche anymore. John Fuegi's book on Brecht is, it seems to me, an appropriation of feminism for the purpose of commie bashing, and really tremendously unimportant. The great tragedy of it is that it is the only major biography of Brecht that has come out in a very long time, and there desperately needs to be a good, responsible, serious, in-depth biography of Brecht in English, a new one.

CW: There isn't one even in German.

TK: Yes, and it is appalling. This is definitely not it. It seems to be sensationalistic, and the parts of it that I have read at least seem to be kind of nuts. It is just an outrageous overstatement that I find deeply offensive. The man is all but saying that Brecht is a villain equivalent to Adolf Hitler or Joseph Stalin. That is insane, completely insane. And this endless carping after the issue of ownership of ideas and the actual authorship of the plays and poems is suspect in the extreme, although a great deal needs to be written about Brecht's collaborators, especially the women. It is unquestionably the case that were he not someone who had this penchant to work with really brilliant women collaborators, he probably wouldn't have written such great female characters. I simply think that he was a very, very great writer. I don't know if Margarete Steffin was as great a writer, I don't really know.

CW: Well, you have occasion to read about Steffin's collaboration with Brecht, and also some of her writings, in the last issue of the *Brecht Yearbook.*

TK: Oh, that is great.

CW: There is a play of hers, a children's play which is quite nice, but it is miles away from the level of Brecht's own writing.

TK: I don't think that even Fuegi claims that the journals were written by someone other than Brecht.

CW: I don't think so, no.

TK: There are passages in the journals that, in the case that everything else that Brecht had ever written were lost, would certainly make you sit up and take note and say this was some kind of writer. And the *Organum* and a lot of the theoretical writings and a great deal of the poetry will certainly secure for him one of the most prominent seats in the pantheon of twentieth-century literature. Even if you want to believe that Steffin wrote *Mother Courage,* and I don't believe it . . .

CW: But Fuegi doesn't claim that, only that she had a part in it.

TK: Well, that she had a part in it. And that, after she died, he didn't write any more great plays.

CW: That is especially stupid, of course.

TK: I think it is a shame. It is an offensive book by somebody, as you pointed out, who really doesn't know the first thing about creating theater. He also is somebody who has absolutely no idea of what Brecht was trying to do theatrically.

CW: Now, what about the recent historical changes, the collapse of socialism and all that. Does that, do you think, necessitate a reviewing of Brecht and a reevaluation of what he did? I think I know the answer but I'd like to hear it from you.

TK: The answer is yes. Simply because of the collapse of the Soviet empire, the necessity is there to examine what the passage of time and history has done to any writer's understanding of his trade. At this point it is wonderful to have Heiner Müller as well as Brecht because I think that Müller has already done a great deal in terms of considering Brecht in the light of the passage of the last fifty years. Müller points us back to the *Lehrstück,* which I think is very important.

CW: Why do you think that?

TK: In my reading of it—which may be idiosyncratic or completely insupportable in terms of scholarship—it really does seem to me that Brecht is in the *Lehrstück* wrestling with a phenomenon that Fuegi never admits Brecht wrestled with, which is the question of the individual ego and the question how one marries a historical, social construct like the individual ego to a theory, and what is the practice of that. What is the way in which the individual, which is a sort of glorious and immensely destructive creation of hundreds and hundreds of years of Western civilization, how does the individual become a socialist subject? How are we to remake ourselves into people who are fit to remake the world? And what becomes of the individual when the individual encounters the necessity to collectivize, in the sort of struggles unto death that the protagonists or antagonists in the *Lehrstück* suffer? I think of the construction/deconstruction of the flyer, or the young student on the road, or the revolutionary. The capacity for collectivity is profoundly interesting.

CW: You are talking of the Young Comrade?

TK: Right, in *The Measures Taken*. It is a form of death and it leads Brecht into some very interesting poetry and some very powerful writing.

CW: But it is actual death, of course.

TK: It is actually death, although it is death with a kind of resurrection. Although, in some cases there is not a resurrection, in some cases it is death and oblivion. But look at *The Baden Play of Learning* and the use of Chinese poetry, not just in terms of the sound of it but also quite literally in the use of Buddhism and Confucianism, of Lao-tse. It is fascinating, and I think he asks very important questions. The plays are extraordinarily radical, both in terms of their content and also in terms of their problems. I am very excited by them, and many of the questions raised by a play like *The Baden Play of Learning* are of immense applicability to the examination of the ruins of the Soviet system and the socialist experiment in Russia. Was it Peymann or was it Wolfgang Bauer? Who was it who said you may carp and criticize about Brecht but in times of crisis you'll reach for him?

CW: That was Claus Peymann, in the late seventies.

TK: And it is true.

CW: Actually Dan Sullivan, the artistic director of the Seattle Repertory Theater, said something quite similar to me once: "In times of political crisis you either play Brecht or Shakespeare, that is, certain plays by Shakespeare."

TK: Well, there you go.

cw: You already answered to some extent the next question I jotted down: which of Brecht's works do you believe are today the most timely ones? Certainly the *Lehrstücke,* in your opinion, are among them.

TK: Yes. I had a wonderful time staging the *Baden Play* and would love to do it again. I think that *Mother Courage* is always going to be first and foremost for me, because I think it is simply the greatest play written in the twentieth century.

cw: How about *Good Person of Sezuan,* which you just recently translated and adapted?

TK: I think *Sezuan* is almost as good. It simply moves me less strongly than *Courage.* I really do believe that in *Courage* we see the influence of Benjamin or, at least, the ground on which Brecht and Benjamin really understood one another. *Courage* is really a Benjaminian vision of history.

cw: *Courage* was begun at a time when he saw a lot of Benjamin; they did spend quite some time together in Denmark.

TK: Exactly. It is truly history as the accumulation of catastrophes and calamity. It is so tremendously dark and incredibly powerful in a way that, I have to admit, I personally don't find in *Sezuan. Sezuan* is a purer thing in a way, it is very much what pure epic theater is supposed to be. In *Courage,* as in *Galileo,* he strays a bit here and there from the absolute template to create the most powerful work that he can. But there is something very pure about *Sezuan* that is enormously challenging. Although, I don't know what the goodness of Shen Te is. That is the mystery for me, and I would like to crack that. We talked about it a great deal when we were working on it in La Jolla. I don't know what her goodness is. One should be careful that it doesn't become a kind of Forrest Gumpism. It must not be essentialism, she must not be "essentially" good. She has a very strange poem in the trial scene that ends with something like "For your great deeds, oh Gods, this poor mortal . . ."

cw: It is the long apologetic speech to the Gods when she tries to defend her invention of Shui Ta.

TK: Yes, it goes all over the place and it is very, very odd. I suspect it needs badly to be newly translated, because I didn't trust it in the process of working on my adaptation of *Sezuan* from a literal translation. I was also looking very closely at every other translation which I could get my hands on in terms of finding out how to understand that speech. No one translated it satisfactorily. It has got some very strange things about it as, for instance, "My mother washed me with gutter water. . . ." It almost seems to be heading toward a kind of psychological explanation. Why is this person a "good person"? We get the point that good people in general don't succeed. But what is it about Shen Te that is different from, let's say, the water seller Wang? It is an odd thing in the play that I am not entirely clear about. I don't have any such problems with *Mother Courage.*

cw: How do you feel about the early plays, like *Baal* and *In the Jungle of the Cities?*

tk: They are incredibly beautiful because they are written by a genius. Despite what I guess Mr. Fuegi says, that Bie Banholzer wrote *Baal.* They are very powerful and very disturbing, and they would be wonderful to stage. I have never been terribly interested in them beyond that because they are too close to Expressionism.

cw: They are actually not, they are really a response to Expressionism. They refute nearly everything that Expressionism believed in or postulated. I just have directed *In the Jungle of the Cities,* and it worked extremely well, it is a wonderful play. It worked much better, frankly, than I expected when I started exploring it.

tk: It was the first time you did it?

cw: Yes, the first time that I did it and that I did a real analysis of it. It is an incredibly demanding play and very timely, I think, in its harsh view of a market-based society. My feeling is that several of Brecht's plays that describe or comment on capitalist society might become very interesting again, plays that for a long time were thought of as old hat and that appeared to be obsolete. But I don't think they are now.

tk: Certainly, with the kind of freedom he had before he became, how shall I say, more responsible. The freedom to explore issues of sexuality, which to a certain extent he edges away from or homogenizes in the epic plays. *Baal* is fascinating in that respect. Sexuality is just an anarchic principle in *Baal* and it is dangerous. I think that the visitation of various kinds of political discipline that Marxism brought to Brecht made the difference between him being a very interesting, early twentieth-century writer and the writer of transcending importance that he became. He would always have been inasmuch more interesting than Stefan Zweig. But it is important, that, had it not been for Marxism and his commitment to a political movement, he might very easily have gotten lost in the same thickets of psychology and sexuality that others did. But still, I agree with you, those are very interesting plays.

cw: In this context, to what extent do you expect the recent changes in American politics, and specifically their consequences for the arts, will influence the American reception of Brecht?

TK: Of course, since there won't be an NEA [National Endowment for the Arts] in the next year, nobody will be able to afford to do Brecht plays, they are all too big, except for *The Beggar, or the Dead Dog*.

CW: Yes, you were very prophetic way back in 1981.

TK: *[Laughs.]* Well, I think that is going to be a big problem. It seems to me that the successes of the Right frequently happen in periods when nobody wants to hear of any kind of oppositional thinking or art, which are then followed by a worsening of circumstances, which are then followed by an interest in oppositional or alternative vision. But it may be slow in coming, I am feeling very, very nervous for my own skin, respectively speaking.

CW: How do you feel about your own position right now?

TK: Well, I really don't know.

CW: Did this change your interest in certain topics? Have certain topics become more important to your mind than they were before, or not?

TK: I don't know what last Tuesday means [the elections on November 8, 1994]. I am confused by it in a way that I have never been confused by any political phenomenon in my own lifetime. I don't get why it happened, exactly. There are some subjects that are becoming extremely interesting to me, for instance the question of labor.

The *New York Times* had an interesting article on the front page of Sunday's *Week in Review* asking: why isn't there class conflict, why aren't all these people recognizing they have class interests that are being betrayed, lethally betrayed, by Big Business, and why now do people blame government instead of blaming business, and why is the boss never really seen as being the enemy and is rather being seen as a fellow victim? The article laid out in political and sociological terms how much the Right has won and how much the elimination not even so much of the Soviet system as an alternative—because it never really has been an alternative for us—but of an ideological space marked "alternative," how the elimination of that has absolutely forced people into simply accepting as a given all the things that are contrary to their own self-interest. You won't blame the boss because blaming the boss means developing a critique of capitalism as a system and, of course, we all know now that capitalism is the only conceivable system. Look at the destruction of the trade unions, the idea that everybody is downscaling and everybody is being put out of work. No one is getting angry at these corporations anymore because it is simply assumed they will maximize profits at the expense of human beings, and that this is the way that it has to be. There is no notion of any sort of redistribution of wealth. The only thing currently acceptable with respect to redistributing wealth is the capital gains tax so that we can send more money to the people who already have enough of it.

CW: Do you think that Brecht's work, plays or whatever, could have any impact on this situation at all? If it would be performed, that is.

TK: I think there is one thing. It is like the hope of the desperate and the weak and the perilous. It is incredibly important, especially now, to state publicly that socialism once existed and is still being thought of, and thought enough of to be mentioned. In other words, there are times so reactionary that the best one can do is to serve as a marker for the possibility of alternatives. As a marker for the antithesis, and I think that Brecht serves that function. In doing *The Good Person of Sezuan* at La Jolla, California, for incredibly wealthy people who finished eating their toasted Brie with almonds and came to their seats, you know, the audience is completely white . . .

CW: How did they react?

TK: With a certain amount of condescension, and a certain amount of subdued enjoyment, and a certain amount of discomfort and dismissal, and all the things that one would expect. I have nothing astonishing to report. Except that I felt that it was enormously important that this important cultural institution was devoting this kind of money and human energy and space to the statement that the play makes. When Shen Te says "You miserable people, look at what you're doing!" it is in some way the most obvious, corny thing in the world, and it is also immensely powerful. She takes the child and she says: "Look at this dirty mouth. Are you so debased that you can't even take care of your own children?" Nothing could be more relevant. When I staged *Mother Courage* at the University of New Hampshire, in the shadow of a giant nuclear power plant out there, the whole town of Hanover worked in that plant. The whole time that we were doing *Courage*—this was in the dark years of Reagan—there was a radio ad running which we actually used during the intermission where an engineer says—and you hear children playing in the background— "People are always saying they are afraid of the nuclear reactor, but I am a safety engineer and I know that this reactor is safe." And then he says: "I have to know because my children and I live a mile from the reactor." You know, this man *is* Mother Courage. And so, on one level, it seems like a corny little bromide when she says: "If you want the war to work for you . . ." But on the other hand, it is the simple truth, it is the great motto: "The very simplest words must be enough. . . ." It is incredibly important to keep doing it, to remind people that reality is to be interpreted and is not just what it seems. Which is a radical concept in these days.

CW: We have covered a lot of ground. Just one final thing: In what way do you feel Brecht is important for your work in this particular historical moment? It is a sort of corny question, I know, but also a kind of capping question.

TK: Important in terms of my work? I guess that there is a personal as well as an aesthetic answer to that. Personally, when I go back to Brecht, which I do constantly and I just did it in a very extensive way for *Sezuan* and also reading the journals, there is an issue of redoing one's commitment. Look at those wonderful little nips he takes at those who he is talking about in the journal when he refers to the kind of writers—and he is talking about some of the émigré writers in Hollywood—who didn't like capitalism because, unlike themselves, capitalism isn't harmless. He also talked about a writer who is a petty bourgeois and who has acquired the propensity for ethical thinking. Brecht had a great contempt for a certain kind of writer who sounds politically engaged and yet really isn't, who is essentially content with things remaining as they are. Through everything in Brecht there is an absolutely serious desire to see the world change *now*, as they say in *Sezuan*: "Now, Now, Now." The urgency of that "Now" is something that I go back to Brecht for. So I remind and then I chastise myself if I feel that I am slipping because it is very hard to maintain the commitment. He is incredibly important to me as an origin and also as a goal. In terms of the specifics, after having written a different kind of epic with *Angels*, where I went off in new directions for me in terms of creating an epic play, I am interested in going back and in reexamining in the next play that I am writing the epic form in a more traditional way, a more classically Brechtian sense.

CW: Which play is that?

TK: It *[Henry Box Brown or The Mirror of Slavery]* is a play about the relationship between the textile industry in Britain and American slavery that has a more conventionally epic form. And then *Dutch Masters,* a play about Vermeer, which is huge and sprawling. I have been thinking a great deal recently about epic theater and what the epic actually is, what the large form is, since it seems to be the form I am going to spend my life with. Even *Slavs!,* a one-act play, became three acts and an epilogue. It seems to be the form that I am wedded to. So, I am thinking about what it means and if it is something that I should simply accept. Is it a form that I am suited to, or is it something that I should try and wean myself from.

cw: How is your present production going? After all, it is your first foray into directing in a long time.

tk: I find I am directing like a writer now. I stage a little of it, and I go back and I restage it, and I do a little bit more and then I restage the whole thing.

cw: That is the way Brecht worked as a director.

tk: Because he was a writer, I think. That is the way most writers write. The problem is you need to give the actors more space. What is frustrating is that I have put the whole thing up now, and I like the flow of it and the look of it, I'd just wish I now had two or three weeks to really let the actors take it over and run with it. But I don't, it is frustrating. Remembering how hard it is for actors to get to perform it is staggering. I usually come to the first reading and then I go away.

cw: It's been a long time since you have directed.

tk: Yes, it really is.

cw: It's good for you, believe me. It will help you a lot as a writer.

tk: Yes, I think it does, it's very good to do it, at least once in a while.

cw: For Brecht, writing and directing were always two sides of the same coin. Tony, I thank you for a most inspiring conversation.

The Proust Questionnaire

Charlotte Stoudt

As part of a study guide for Baltimore's Center Stage production of *Slavs!* (January 6–February 18, 1995), Charlotte Stoudt, then dramaturgy intern and now literary associate under James Magruder, asked Kushner to fill out "The Proust Questionnaire." Created by French novelist Marcel Proust, this questionnaire is used "to discover the preferences, passions, and regrets of artists." Kushner's responses to the questionnaire, it was hoped, would provide the students and adults attending the production of *Slavs!* a more intimate insight into the likes and dislikes—hence, into the mind, spirit, and tastes—of the playwright whose work they were about to see performed. Kushner responded by E-mail on November 24, 1994.

My chief characteristic: My absolute inability to give simple, unqualified answers to questions like these.

The quality I prefer in a man: Femininity.

The quality I prefer in a woman: Fabulousness, industry.

What I appreciate most in my friends: Their fanatically ardent devotion to me.

The talent I would most like to possess: To be able to write poetry.

My main flaw: Laziness, meanness, or cowardice, depending on the occasion.

My favorite occupation: Writing plays.

My idea of happiness: Reading that Jesse Helms, Newt Gingrich, and

From *The Next Stage at Center Stage* 1, no. 3: 16–17.

Trent Lott have been abducted by aliens and taken to a far-off galaxy for study and experimentation.

My idea of misery: Reading that the aforementioned persons have become leaders of the majority party in Congress.

What I would like to be: The author of at least five important plays, and many minor ones.

The country I prefer to live in: The upper west side of Manhattan.

The color I prefer: Joseph Cornell blue, which can only be found in glass.

The flower I prefer: Giant white mums, which florists in this country call "stadium" mums, but which I call Sarah Bernhardts, because they were her favorites, too.

The creature I prefer: One-year-old children, or dogs.

My favorite writers in prose: Herman Melville, Tolstoy, Dostoevsky, Virginia Woolf, Abraham Lincoln, Anton Chekhov, Tennessee Williams, Zora Neale Hurston, Raymond Williams, Ernst Bloch, Martin Luther King, Jr., Bertolt Brecht, Emerson, Alfred Doblin, Italo Calvino, C. L. R. James, Trollope, Dickens, Wodehouse, Lewis Carroll, Trotsky, Marx, Freud, Benjamin, Marguerite Yourcenar, etc.

My favorite poets: Shakespeare, Brecht, Wallace Stevens, Whitman, W. C. Williams, Pound, Robert Duncan, Mandelshtam, Akhmatova, Tsvetayevna, Adrienne Rich, Audre Lorde, Stanley Kunitz, Elizabeth Bishop, Marianne Moore, Thom Gunn, Thomas McGrath, Li-Young Lee, Wordsworth, Dickinson, Charles Olson, etc.

My favorite fictional characters: The narrator of *Bartleby the Scrivener,* Blanche DuBois, Sonya in *Uncle Vanya,* Mother Courage, Rosalind in *As You Like It,* Ivan Illich (Tolstoy's).

My favorite composers: Mozart, Shostakovitch, Elvis Costello, Cole Porter, Gershwin, Harold Arlen, Duke Ellington, Beethoven, Mahler, Schubert, Tchaikovsky, Verdi.

My favorite painters: Vermeer, Rembrandt, Franz Hals, Pieter Sanraedam, Brueghel, Odilon Redon, Picasso, Cezanne, Van Gogh, Tintoretto, Michelangelo, Hokusai, Sue Coe, Maurice Sendak, and my sister, Lesley Kushner.

Which fictitious male characters attract you: Well, I would most want to sleep with Pierre Bezukhov, Konstantin Levin, Nathanael in Marguerite Yourcenar's *An Obscure Man,* Colette's Chéri, and Wodehouse's Pongo Twistleton (nephew of Frederick, fifth earl of Ickenham). And I have always harbored a thing for the young Phineas Finn.

Which fictitious female characters most attract you: Dorothea Brooks, Maggie Tulliver, Anna Karenina, Gudrun Osvif's daughter in *The*

Laxdaela Saga, the narrator of Marilynne Robinson's *Housekeeping,* Natasha in *War and Peace,* Sethe in Toni Morrison's *Beloved,* Mrs. Dalloway.

My heroes in real life: At the moment, Kenzaburo Oe, for refusing to accept the Emperor's Imperial Arts Medal; Paul Monette, Cornel West.

My heroines in real life: At the moment, the Lesbian Avengers who went to Idaho to help organize that state to defeat an anti-lesbian and anti-gay referendum; Barbara Smith, who runs Kitchen Table/Women of Color Press; Toni Morrison; Caryl Churchill; my sister; my best friend, Kimberly Flynn.

My favorite names: For boys, Mendl; for girls, Rose Marie.

What I hate most of all: Homophobia, racism, sexism, anti-Semitism, arrogance, privilege, mean-spiritedness, dishonesty, xenophobia, deliberate stupidity, greed, bellicosity—in brief, conservative politics.

Characters in history that I most dislike: The list is endless. Recent figures would include Nixon, Kissinger, Reagan, Bush, and the Republican legislators aforementioned.

The military action I most admire: The defeat of Hitler, apart from acts of barbarism committed by the Allies.

The reform I praise most: I suppose, currently, the new South African Constitution.

My favorite food and drink: From my sinful past, fried chicken and Coca-Cola; from my new, healthy present, red beans and rice and Coca-Cola.

How I would like to die: Very old; in my own bedroom; in bed; working, reading or talking on the phone, praying or having sex; in spring or early fall; immediately after the arrival of some very good news.

My present state of mind: Amazed, depressed, confused, enraged, appalled.

The faults for which I have the most toleration: Those which I myself possess.

The season and weather I like best: All seasons in San Francisco, as long as the sun is out; otherwise, early fall in New York. All weather is good except rain.

My motto: Currently, "A day's work every day now. Now, now, now!"—Glenway Wescott.

A Conversation with Tony Kushner and Robert Altman

Gordon Davidson

Sotheby's, the two-hundred-and-fifty-year-old New York art auction institution, sponsors a prestigious annual series of dialogues that "explore the creative process in politics, music, art, sports, film, theater, literature, and journalism" (Sotheby's audience program, December 5, 1994). This particular occasion, which was a benefit for the Lenox Hill Neighborhood House, was an unexpected convergence of personal and professional synchronicity for the evening's guests, Robert Altman and Tony Kushner. Altman's production of *Mrs. Parker and the Vicious Circle* had just opened, and his long-awaited *Prêt-à-Porter* (marketed in the United States as *Ready to Wear*), which Altman directed, was to open the next day. Kushner's play *Angels in America* had closed on Broadway the night before, and his *Slavs!* would have its eagerly awaited New York premiere at New York Theater Workshop within days of the Sotheby's event.

The pairing of Altman and Kushner also brought together the director and the screenwriter of the anticipated film version of *Angels in America*. Altman was the only American director that Kushner would accept to direct the screen adaptation of his play. However, since that time, Altman has dropped out of the project and Australian director P. J. Hogan (*Muriel's Wedding* and *My Best Friend's Wedding*) has signed on.

From *Conversations at Sotheby's*, Sotheby's Main Sales Room, New York, December 5, 1994. This previously unpublished interview took place before five hundred spectators, each paying $25 a ticket. © 1994 Sotheby's, Inc.

The moderator for the program was Gordon Davidson, producer and for thirty years artistic director of the Mark Taper Forum in Los Angeles, one of America's most influential resident theaters. Davidson produced the first complete production of *Angels in America, Parts One and Two,* at the Mark Taper Forum in November 1992.

GORDON DAVIDSON: How do you define what you do?

ROBERT ALTMAN: I play in the sandpile. I deal in theater, really, basically whether it's on film, or on a stage, or off the stage or whatever. And it always has to do with the presentation of ideas and emotions through performers. Through actors. I don't do much. The actors do the work. That's what I do.

GD: Did you always want to be a filmmaker? Did you start with that?

RA: Well, I wanted to be, first I wanted to be really good-looking! *[Laughter.]*

GD: And you accomplished that. Then what did you do?

RA: Then I wanted to be rich. I failed at all of the ordinary jobs, real jobs. And so I fell into this thing of theater and . . .

GD: And Bob has actually done it all. I mean, if everyone could take your résumé and say, "This is what I've . . ." You have done film and theater and opera. And you've crossed all kinds of boundaries and reinvented the art form, too. How about you, Tony?

TONY KUSHNER: I write plays. That's essentially what I want most in the world to do, in terms of an occupation. My ambition is to just write better and better plays. I think it's a terribly difficult and strange form to work in. And I feel that I'm just at the beginning of understanding how it works. I hope I live a reasonably long time, and that in the course of that I sort of hang onto my marbles. Which is asking a lot these days. *[Laughter.]* I was just reading a biography of Eugene O'Neill, who, unlike most American playwrights, actually got better and better and better as he progressed through life, and lived long enough to be able to write at least two or three great plays instead of writing one or two great plays at the beginning of his career and then spending the rest of his life declining. I think that's really admirable. That's what I would like. That's what I'd like to be when I grow up.

GD: All right, so then how do you go about doing that?

TK: Good-looking, too, would have been nice, but . . .

GD: What's the process?

TK: Of writing? Oh, my God! Well, I don't know. It's mostly sort of avoiding writing as long as I possibly can. And then when the play is really ready to come out, taking dictation. That's what it feels like. I used to feel that I was a terribly bad person and a procrastinator because it took me so long to get started writing something. But I've come to realize that that delaying process is an integral part. A lot of it is research and a lot of it is hard thinking. And then some of it is just completely ineffable, and I don't know what goes on in the delay. But it usually takes about a year for a play to come together for me.

GD: Do you pick a subject first, or . . .

TK: Yes, I pick a subject. It usually comes with a title. And then I start reading around it and talking to people about it and thinking about it.

GD: Do you like to do research?

TK: Yeah. I do a lot of research.

RA: I think [there's] this gestation period that we go through, whether it's stalling and avoiding just starting, and we're working all the time. So one half of me [is] the half [in] which I serve my own ego, when I put things off and I wait until the last minute to get it done. And I feel, "Well, my subconscious is working and I'm gathering material together, and I'm beginning to write." And the other side of me— and it's probably more truthful—is just plain old fear and procrastination. [One is] afraid that what might happen is that whatever system you used when you first succeeded or you smelled success, you tend to try to re-create those circumstances . . . It's scary. But do you think that habit has anything to do with this?

TK: Fear definitely has a great deal to do with it. Complete, unadulterated terror.

One of the things about your career that's remarkable is that you have worked basically from film to film to film at an astonishing rate. You haven't really stopped making movies since you started. When we got together for the first time to work in Paris, I was amazed. You were in the middle of preproduction, I guess, for *Prêt-à-Porter* and working very long days and sort of running all over Paris looking for locations. And I really wanted to hide in my hotel room and not go anywhere near you, because I was terrified . . . we were beginning to do the treatment for *Angels in America* and I was shamed by the degree to which you were just willing to dive in and start working.

RA: That's all fear.

TK: Yeah.

RA: It's like Little Eva going across those ice cubes, those dogs snappin' at your ass, and you just keep running. *[Laughter.]*

TK: Do you work on more than one thing at a time, or do you have to really kind of line it up?

RA: I work on more than one thing at a time. But there comes a time when I have to deal with the one thing. But the other things are stirring all the time. Tony and I have been working for, what, a year now, on trying to bring these two films, *Angels in America,* to film, and I don't have an answer to this yet. There's a big problem with it because he used a lot of film technique in his play, and in the stagecraft, and it's done that way. So when it's translated back to film, if I just used that, I think we'd just have an ordinary film. So there's all kinds of fear and wondering how are we really going to present this thing, because I don't think there's any one person who knows. There's not a book you can open that says it should be done this way or this way. We're always afraid of failure all the time, aren't we?

GD: Soon after [the Mark Taper Forum] opened *Millennium,* a deal was struck with Bob Altman to do the film version, and they've begun talking about it all this time, and still talking and still writing.

TK: I've actually written some.

GD: And I see Bob already gave us a hint that he thinks of it as two films rather than two parts of . . .

RA: I think it has to be two films. To try to condense it into one film is . . . it's like reading a novel in *Readers' Digest.* For a lot of reasons it should be two films. Just on a commercial standpoint, which we have to consider, these things cost so much to make. If people don't come to see them, where are you? My vision is that we could, when *Angels* opens . . . it is linear, the two parts are linear so you can't see Part Two first really satisfactorily. So we will open the first part in theaters, and then maybe three weeks later, maybe two weeks, maybe six—I don't know . . . that will be a research thing to do—we'll open the second one, maybe in twin theaters, because now the cinemas have all these various screens. Suddenly we have the audience set up so that you can see . . . I don't remember which is first.

TK: *Millennium, Millennium, Millennium.*

GD: You can see *Millennium* and you can come out the door and you can go next door and go right back in with a new bag of popcorn and see *[laughter] Perestroika.*

TK: That's the way we should have done it on Broadway! *[Laughter.]*

RA: Assuming that you like these things, or the audience likes them, you can, after seeing *Perestroika,* you'll turn back and say, "God, I've got to see that other one again." *[Laughter.]*

TK: You spend the rest of your life doing it! *[Laughter.]* Figuring out how to get out of the movie theater!

GD: We had kind of planned to do that, you know, on Broadway. When I did it at the Taper in Los Angeles we did open the two plays back-to-back. But when we came to Broadway—[because of] partly timing and partly the amount of work that Tony wanted to do on *Perestroika* before we opened it and complications of union production situations on Broadway—we [only] opened *Millennium.* It wasn't until the following fall that we opened *Perestroika.* And as you know, it just closed last night after eighty-three performances, and we're both proud and sad, and . . .

TK: Eighty-four *weeks* of performances!

GD: Eighty-four weeks! Eighty-four weeks.

TK: Eight a week. *[Laughter.]*

GD: I just reduced the royalties by a lot. *[Laughter.]* How do you feel about the closing? What was yesterday like?

TK: Yesterday was kind of amazing. I felt very sad about it. I wanted it to run, you know, for eight years. And I'm sorry that it didn't. On the other hand, I feel that there's been a lot of press. Frank Rich wrote in the *New York Times* yesterday that as of the close of *Angels in America* last night, for the first time in American theatrical history, there are no serious dramas running on Broadway. And that is alarming for a number of reasons. *Angels* has been positioned incorrectly as being the sink-or-swim model for serious drama on Broadway. It ignores the facts that the play is seven hours long, that it cost two hundred and fifty thousand dollars a week to run it on Broadway, that at the point that it closed it was still pulling in around a hundred and fifty thousand a week, which could have kept any normal, you know, straight play running. I use the word "straight"—if I can use the word—you know what I mean. *[Laughter.]* The thing is somewhat anomalous and should be considered that way. Basically, I'm very proud of it.

GD: Well you should be.

One of the things that drives me crazy is, of course, the way the press, especially today, and it applies to movies, too, the news is box office, news is cost of production, news is . . . success is measured in dollars and in no other terms. The news about *Angels,* rather than celebrating this extraordinary run of a very complex and challenging piece—the first of its kind, really, I think in modern history—is about how much did it lose. And, of course, then they kept getting the amount of money wrong. In fact, [the show] probably has not recouped some six hundred thousand dollars of over three million dollars in what it took to mount and run. That money will probably get returned to the investors through the road company and movie sale, and all of that. [The press does not say,] "Wow, what a bargain we got! We got this extraordinary piece."

RA: That's the press that we have today, which is really at the low—all of them. The *New York Times*, whatever's considered the best, they're all in the gutter. *[Laughter; applause.]* It's because they're trying to fight television. They're trying to fight these short bites on television. It's distressing and it's discouraging, and it's destructive. I don't see anything in the press that is supportive of anything that has to do with the arts at all. It's all negative.

TK: And in film it's really frightening, because one thing I've noticed is, about two or three years ago, there was a moment around the time *[Angels]* opened when *Crying Game*, which I had problems with, was a success and an independent feature. There was a sort of a reawakening of interest in movies that weren't these giant, megalithic studio productions. That lasted for about twenty seconds. Now there's been this incredible backlash where the only thing that seems to count this year in terms of getting any kind of notice or attention is how much money you make in the first week of gross. Suddenly films are making two hundred and nineteen—I mean, *Forrest Gump* . . .

RA: Well, that's the intellect. That represents the intellect of the average reporter who reports this. *[Laughter.]*

TK: So they don't feel too challenged by Tom Hanks's character. But it's the amount of money that these things are pulling in, which is very depressing because film has such extraordinary potential. But in this country it's constantly being . . .

GD: This is a complex issue, because it's very easy to bash the press just the way we feel we've been bashed. I'd love to try to get to the heart of what is the difference now. Certainly on some level you [Kushner] are supported tremendously by the press. And it's nice to be on that side of the wind. And you [Altman] have, too, in your time. Yet overall there seems to be just a lowering of . . .

RA: They're fighting for their lives. They're in competition with Channel Blah-Blah, or whatever it is.

GD: So you think it's a newspaper problem?

RA: Absolutely.

GD: A readership problem.

RA: Absolutely.

GD: And then rather than elevating the dialogue about the medium and the art form, they reduce it to a common denominator.

RA: They are finding their competition. And their competition is Channel . . .

GD: And they're more interested in gossip.

. . .

RA: I was having breakfast Saturday morning, and Jami Bernard, a film critic for the *Daily News*, is on some show with a couple of hosts and they were talking about films. It got my attention because they talked about *Mrs. Parker and the Vicious Circle*, which is a film I produced. Alan Rudolf's film, which is doing very well. People really like it, although the reviews have been tepid. And they were saying how much they liked it, and that got my ear. Then they started talking about future films, and they said, "Well," to Jami Bernard, "what do you think, what about *Prêt-à-Porter*?" She said, "Well, I haven't seen it." Now this is a critic. She said, "I haven't seen it yet, but I hear it's not so good!" *[Laughter.]* And I dropped my oatmeal! *[Laughter.]* What is this? We called her today and she said, "Oh, I guess I shouldn't have said that, but that's what I hear." You just give up. There's no way to fight that. Next time around with a film I'm not going to show it to the press, no matter how favorable they seem to be. They're all looking for something negative to say, because that's what gets the attention . . . it sells papers.

GD: You [Kushner] once said on an interview that you were worried that you were becoming a media whore.

TK: Did I say that?

GD: *[Laughs.]* Do you think that there's a danger in that? That as the spotlight, you know, is put on you, you find yourself interview after interview . . . both of you have been exposed to that.

RA: It's like you're assisting in your own execution. Your press people say, "You've got to go talk to these people because they're the ones that are going to write about you." "I know, but I know they don't like this." Because they've already expressed themselves. It's like you're going to go to the guillotine and the guy that's setting up takes a liking to you. And he says, "Listen, kid, stretch your neck a little bit like this, and that way the knife will go right through, because if you tighten up it may stop, and we have to do it twice!" *[Laughter.]* So you say, "Oh! OK, I'll help!" *[Laughter.]* I figure if they want to kill ya', let 'em; let 'em use up more bullets. *[Laughter.]*

GD: While we're clearing the air, you [Kushner] had an incident the other day. *[Laughter.]* In the *New York Post* there was a, what do they call it, "Page Six?"

TK: "Page Six." There was a lead story on "Page Six" on Wednesday of last week [stating] that the reason that my new play—which is a little one-act I wrote for the Actors' Theater of Louisville last year, *Slavs!*—was in New York Theater Workshop (where I used to be associate artistic director) and not at the Public (where George Wolfe is the producer and he also directed *Angels in America*) was that George had read the script and, in the words of the *Post*, "smelled a flop" and decided not to do the play. As a result, he and I had had a screaming fight and were no longer speaking to each other, and I had vowed never to work with him again, and had had to give the play to this smaller theater because nobody else wanted it. This is, of course, a complete word-to-word fabrication; it has absolutely nothing to do with the truth. And the fact of the matter is that we had given the play to the Workshop before it was even written because I wanted to do something at the Workshop, and that George had, in fact, asked to do the play. George and I are very good friends and we're working on a new project together, all of which they could have easily found out, but they didn't want to mess up their story with facts or reportage. *[Laughter.]* I actually called the *Post* and screamed. The guy said exactly what you just said, Bob, which is, "Well, we've got to sell papers." As I was saying backstage, it was Roy Cohn's favorite part of the *Post*. *[Laughter.]*

There used to be sixteen daily newspapers in New York City, and most people read three or four. Now there are four and two of them are dying, and one of them is sort of dying and only the *Times* seems to be surviving. They now know that when people stop reading a newspaper or when it goes out of print, those readers don't go to another newspaper. They simply stop reading newspapers. So, newspaper readership is becoming extinct under these people's feet. They're panicked and terrified, and they will say a lot to sell a paper, even making stuff up.

RA: It's become the ethic of the business. You don't look at the truth of the matter, how good or bad a piece is, or what your job of reporting is. Your reporting job is now to do something that will be sensational and will sell papers.

TK: It may be even worse for arts reportage. Most people who write about the arts don't believe that they matter very much. They don't feel bound by the same journalistic ethics that one would hope a regular reporter is bound by.

GD: All right, we've taken care of the press *[laughter]*, right?

RA: Don't read!

GD: *[Laughs.]* One assumes that reviews can hurt, right? Yet, this whole question of process is very important to me. Many years ago I stage-managed Martha Graham and I had the privilege of working with her. She said: "This thing about intuition. A little light bulb doesn't go off, like they do in the comic books, and suddenly you say, 'Eureka! $E = mc^2$!' You really are preparing your intuition all the time, and it's a long process. And you can't even know how it's cooking. But when it's ready, it then does come out in some kind of forward motion that you make." Take me back for a minute [Tony] to even Lake Charles. How did all of that life there feed into what you have come to do? You were born into a family that was very involved in music, and you liked to read a lot.

TK: Yeah. That certainly helped. Everybody in my family is in the arts, so it's clearly something that was bred in the bone. I grew up in a very small town in Louisiana, which I think was a good place to grow up. I learned things about language from living in the South, because I think the Southerners have a very lively and rich relationship to American English.

RA: You have affinity for the Southern writers?

TK: I do. Sometimes they make me crazy because they sound too much like the people I grew up with. *[Laughter.]* But I do. My favorite playwright is Tennessee Williams, and he's a very, very Southern writer, and I'm very much influenced by him.

Part of the work of creating something is like exercising a muscle. If you don't do it a lot all the time, it becomes stale and it gets very hard to do. And if you stay with it and don't let yourself get fallow, which is a thing that I'm struggling with a lot right now in my life, because I like to do anything better than writing, and I have to force myself to write. When I write a lot, I write better. But then there are always these *ideas.* The best ideas that I've had, I don't know where they came from, and I don't know what made them, and I don't think it was just force of will and discipline. And that's frightening. When you talk about the fear that artists have, that's truly terrifying. That there is this place . . . like the idea for *Nashville*. I don't know if you know where that came from, or if . . .

RA: Well, I think these things just arrive from a combination of calculations in your mind that are not conscious, and the elimination, and suddenly one thing fits the pattern. It's like grinding a key until it fits. And when that fits you think, "Oh, this is it!" But I don't think anybody can tell you what the genesis of it was, where it came from. Afterwards we can make up and invent reasons of why, and justify why we did what we did. But I think that's all justification.

GD: But you're about to make a film before you do *Angels, Kansas City*—does that come from your own youth?

RA: Not really. The emotion of it does. I mean, I grew up there. This film is about 1934. I was eleven years old then. But it's the world that I romanticized through my father and jazz and politics and gangsters, and that sort of stuff. And that's a colorful historical period. But as I look at it now, there's nothing in there that's really about me . . . I've determined it's not really about me. And if it is, it would be invalid because it comes from false memories, I think.

GD: I care about both of you in this beginning journey that you're on. My image of you, Bob, is one which I saw etched in my mind when I saw you at the Lincoln Center Film Society Award that they gave you a year ago. It was of a group of actors—you, surrounded by a group of actors so in love with you and so grateful for the way you work and the way you respond to them, and the freedom that you give them without structure and without rules. And I think of Tony, in my experience with him as a playwright, and the attention and the care to words and to having the words achieved in a certain way in the theater. Two very different mediums, motion pictures and the stage. And there are clichés about that, which you like to destroy, too. One is about language and one is about pictures. But a great language can be in film and great images can be on the stage. How do you feel about screenwriters?

RA: Every one of them is different. I did a production, a film of *The Caine Mutiny Court Martial*. I've done . . .

GD: Quite a few plays.

RA: I did *Streamers. Secret Honor,* and there was never a screenplay. I just took the book. It was in my hip pocket and that's what we went by. I remember in doing *The Caine Mutiny*, Herman Wouk came, and I said, "I'm doing this last scene very differently, and I hope that you approve of it, and hope you like it." And he said, "What are you changing?" And I said, "I'm not changing anything. I'm just doing it differently. Instead of making it this last speech where the man stands up there and talks and everybody's quiet, I've got him . . . one guy in a roomful of drunk sailors partying. And I've got the one guy following the other one through the place trying to get his attention and saying all these same words, but you don't necessarily hear them all directly." In the end, he said, "Well, it was great! It worked terrific." So there, we were using his words. The actors would come up to me in that production and say, "I don't like saying this. Can I change this?" And I said, "No, you cannot change this." And they said, "Why?" Because they worked with me before and I don't usually care about the dialogue, because mainly I've written it *[laughter]* and I know that it's different in different cases. But in *The Caine Mutiny Court Martial*, I said, "You are not speaking. It doesn't make any difference whether you speak, because you're on trial. You're sitting in a chair and there's an audience and a bunch of judges that are listening to you. So you are not speaking in your natural way of speaking. So forget it! Force those things. Find a way to say them." Because, I think that's what this particular thing is about.

We come to another, *Angels in America*. I'm not going to pick this piece and get it on the set and start saying, "Let's change this," or let the actors change this and change that. The reason I did it was because it existed in this way. I don't see myself changing that. In *Nashville* or in *Prêt-à-Porter*, the dialogue, in most cases, doesn't make any difference *[laughter]* as long as their behavior is correct. But there are some cases where it's very, very important. So I just think to make a black and a white out of *[Angels]* is incorrect. When I did *Streamers*, David Rabe, in his contract with me, said, "You can change anything you want." I said, "Well, I don't intend to change very much. I really don't. Maybe there's some cutting to be done . . . if I can get the camera in close on somebody's face, I don't have to say those words that have to be said on stage."

TK: Right, right.

RA: And he said, "But there's one section at the end, Cokes's speech, that can't be tampered with." And I said, "Fine." We shot it, of course that went in, and at the end of the editing period, I had Cokes's speech the full length, the way it was, and I said, "Come in and look at it." And he said, "Well, it's terrible." I said, "Well, cut it." And we did cut pieces of it. But that's a real black-and-white area that never exists. There're always shady gray areas and crossovers.

GD: When you start listing the plays that you have actually filmed, you certainly have had that kind of relationship to that writing.

RA: And the operas that I've done, I certainly didn't change those. Let them change the dialogue there!

GD: Tony, did you once refer to screenwriting as blueprinting?

TK: I've referred to it as a lot of things. I don't think it has anything to do with playwriting. It's a phenomenon to me that I think bears closer examination: that most playwrights don't write as well after they've tried writing screenplays. The more time they spend writing screenplays, the less they develop as playwrights. They're very different forms.

One thing that I'm discovering as I work on the screenplay is that when you write a play, every single thing that you write you have complete responsibility for. And it's going to be read either as a text or by actors. I think a writer's responsibility is that every word matters. A lot of what you write in a screenplay doesn't matter at all, except insofar as it describes or attempts to persuade other people to try something one way or another. It's an incredibly difficult form, but I think it's very different. I have always said that I think it's closer to novel writing than playwriting, because it's more to do with narrative than with dialogics, which is what I think the theater is all about. For many reasons, I approached Bob to do *Angels,* and one of the reasons that he was the only, I mean, quite literally, the only director that I would want to do this film, is that I actually wanted a lot of changing to happen. And I still, I don't believe him, really. I think that they're going to change things when they get on the set. *[Laughter.]* And I want that, because I want the play to have a separate existence. I don't want the film to be in any way sort of a faithful recording.

RA: Well I think it will. When we get to the verb and really they're there, things will self-evident themselves. At least that's been my experience with writers. I have a terrible reputation, and have for years, as far as writers are concerned. Screenwriters have said terrible things, that I don't respect their work, which is not really true. In most cases when I need the screenwriter the most is when I'm shooting the film. And you can't find them then because they've got another job and they're working in some other studio doing something else at that time.

GD: Partly the system encourages that, in a way.

RA: Yeah. If somebody doesn't want their work changed, it's very simple just to make that a condition. If I say "I want to change it," and they say "You can't change it," then I'm simply not the right person to do it.

. . .

GD: Tony and I were down at the Public Theater on the day we made the decision [to produce *Angels* on Broadway], still wondering whether this was not the best place, fewer seats to sell. Maybe it would run forever instead of just running only eighty-four weeks, which is a tremendous achievement. There were physical problems. Where would we bring the angel from? Where would they be able to go in the trap? So [there were] a lot of questions that finally led it to where it did [run], on Broadway. I think it was right that it played there, and it did help change things. A lot of clones of *Angels in America*, in a good sense . . . I think some playwrights had been given the freedom, or the permission, as it were, to try things on the stage that they might not have done before.

RA: It was a grand achievement. I mean there's no question about that.

GD: You, certainly, in your work have not been afraid to look at the society and tell the truth as you see it. And I think that this is a terrific marriage. But I'd love you to talk a little bit about the things that are on your mind in that area.

RA: Maybe instead of meeting next week, we can just do it now.

GD: *[Laughs.]* Tony?

TK: We only had a couple words about it upstairs, I mean [we're] both in varying degrees of profound despair over the results of the recent election . . . I feel that I was profoundly influenced by your work, from the time that I'd been a moviegoing person.

RA: Say it, an adult!

TK: An adult. *[Laughter.]* No, earlier than that, actually. Even earlier than that. I was only twelve, you know, when *Nashville* came out. But, I think that we have very different political traditions that we're heir to, and don't have the same . . . I mean, I don't actually know. We've never really discussed this fully. But I feel that politically we're very close on the spectrum. I've always found your work to be incredibly thrilling from a political standpoint; I think that it's political in a way that I have found useful and incredibly instructive because it isn't pedantic, it isn't dogmatic. It avoids the pitfalls that a lot of political art can easily slip into. It's enormously complicated and human and funny, but it's also epic. Some of the movies that you've made that I love the most are some of the smaller ones, like *Thieves Like Us. Three Women*. Movies that on the surface maybe don't appear to be political, but I think actually always speak to the political moment.

GD: A connection is there, but [is] *Angels in America* the film going to exist in a slightly different time zone than *Angels* the play?

TK: There are a number of movies that are going to be coming out soon about AIDS. There are a number of movies about gay men coming out. Most of them are drag queen movies because apparently it's OK to show gay men now on screen as long as they're wearing dresses *[laughter]*, which is progress apparently.

RA: I did that in *Prêt-à-Porter*.

TK: But one thing that we [Altman and Kushner] agreed . . . , since that conversation, which was before this holocaustically frightening election, [was] that *Angels* is to a certain degree a play about the Reagan era, which apparently is a lot livelier than we had realized. I want to make this big sort of gay movie, and I'm very excited about that, and I want the film to be about AIDS.

RA: The realistic problem that we face, and I don't even know if we've had this discussion, is that your play used so many cinematic antecedents. You used the technique. You had cross-cutting, people talking at the same. It's cinema. On the stage, it became a new way of looking at theater. But then, when we translate that back to film, is that going to be ordinary?

TK: Well, that's what we're avoiding right now and I think that when the . . .

RA: And so, I keep thinking, "Well, how do we keep what happened to the audience receiving the information in theater? How do we keep that same excitement and education, and emotion? How do we do that in the film?" It cannot just be a literally graphic translation. And I don't have the slightest idea of what our solution is going to be. I truly don't.

TK: But I know you'll think of something! *[Laughter.]* I have complete confidence.

RA: I know we will solve it, because it's a problem that must be solved, or else it doesn't exist. I mean, the piece doesn't exist. So it will be solvable. We will do it. But I don't know what it's going to be, and I don't think we're going to know, until the pigeon is released.

[When] we're in production and we can't stop. But we're going to have to find something like that, and I trust, just from my own history and experience, that those things occur to you. They present themselves eventually.

TK: The other problem is that it's not only structured like a movie. It's actually literally structured like an Altman movie. *[Laughter.]* . . . The form is stolen from *Nashville.* So I think it's going to be *[laughter]* . . . it's going to seem like an incredible retread unless we come up with something new.

GD: But you were very concerned as we were, you know, finishing in L.A. and trying to get it to New York, that somehow time would run out on the play. Do you still feel that?

TK: No, I don't.

GD: What's different?

TK: Well, now that the GOP is in control of Washington the play's got a whole new lease on life, as far as I'm concerned. *[Laughter.]* And I think that that's unfortunate. I don't know. It's weathered well. Nobody knows.

RA: It's a better play than you think it is.

TK: Well . . .

GD: Maybe we can hear from the audience.

AUDIENCE MEMBER: Can you say something about what's happening to Broadway with Neil Simon's play? With Simon taking his next play *[London Suite]* off-Broadway, is Broadway going to be limited to these giant musical extravaganzas?

TK: Well, I hope not. That's a very big, complicated question. The thing that worries me the most at the moment is that I'm afraid that the business of making Broadway affordable again, for making the kind of budgets that you need to produce serious drama on Broadway, that there's a great deal of union busting that's implicit in that. And I'm very worried about that, because the people that worked backstage at *Angels* who cost us a fortune . . . I mean, it was incredibly expensive, but none of these people are millionaires. They don't have estates, you know, in Levittown. *[Laughter.]* But they're very hardworking guys. They do an incredibly difficult job, and they're incredibly skilled. I don't begrudge them any of the money they made, and they made a lot of money. They used to call the production "The Money Store," because they had so much overtime. I'm worried about that.

Broadway must be saved primarily because those theaters are the most beautiful, dramatic houses in this country. The Booth and the Walter Kerr are two of the most beautiful theaters in the world. They need to be saved, and they need to be preserved for serious plays. The only way to do that is to quintuple the size of the NEA and have the federal government subsidize it. *[Applause.]* That should be our national theater—twelve Broadway houses that are kept subsidized so that we can have a repertoire of really serious plays going on there, and you can go and see them for twenty-five bucks or less. That will save Broadway. Otherwise, it's simply doomed. What's happening now, which is truly horrifying, is that you have these kind of simul-opera musicals like *Beauty and the Beast,* which are basically amusement park rides. They install them; they stay there forever. They're basically an excuse for selling souvenirs. They're incredibly destructive to the theater. But without federal subsidy, which, of course, you know, this month doesn't look too likely *[laughter],* we're going to wind up with this kind of horrifying little, sort of phony Broadway where you can come and you go to Mama Leone's and you see the little phony Mickey Mouse musical, and then you go home with your mug and your T-shirt and your CD. That's what this will be.

GD: The other problem is that the announcement that Neil Simon was looking for an off-Broadway theater is a bit of a smokescreen. All of those problems have been coming for a long time. The announcements that Neil was going to do it are actually catch-up stories. They contain a lot of old information. The truth of the matter is he's going to have trouble finding the right theater. They're occupied and it is true that off-Broadway is enjoying a very productive time now. People are enjoying going to see a wide range of plays. Off-Broadway used to be the experimental arm of Broadway, and it's become Little Broadway. And off-off-Broadway was more like, oh, you know. So everything gets kicked down the line.

You're absolutely right that the good workers in the theater who happen to be union are good workers, and they deserve everything. There are work rules that could be improved. There are tremendous costs that could be reduced. But [nothing will change] until Broadway, which is the Broadway producers and theater owners, really get serious about the depth of the problem. Which I think is happening, if all of this news and talk about it actually can bring about some change. But it's the kind of change that needs dynamite, not little baby steps. And it would be very serious.

I've worked for thirty years now in the nonprofit theater in Los

Angeles, but my feeling is that a healthy theater includes commercial theater and nonprofit theater. It's the equivalent almost of trying to figure out how to make good independent films, how to create good independent theater in the proper houses.

AUDIENCE MEMBER: European playwrights, 95 percent [of them], understand socialism, and feel socialism, and write socialist plays. How come in America such a limited number of playwrights, like Arthur Miller, David Mamet, and you, are in that frame of mind?

TK: David Mamet? *[Laughter.]* Well, I think for the same reason that every other country on earth reads the vast body of socialist theory and history and considers it simply part of a decent, well-rounded education, and in this country nobody reads it or knows anything about it, including the part of American history that is socialist and progressive. Many of our playwrights are simply completely unfamiliar with the tradition and believe the Right when it tells us that simply because the Soviet Union fell apart we now no longer have to consider a political project that's been eight hundred years in the making, and that still remains at least one of the only alternatives to the present form of social and economic organizations.

Also, [and] this has been said by a lot of people, since the McCarthy era, which had very, very profound effects, it's hard to write political theater that more than just scares people away because of a fear of blacklisting or being called up before HUAC [House Un-American Activities Committee]. The real success of the Right . . . and we're seeing this now with the Dan Quayle–*Murphy Brown* war, which he theoretically lost, but, of course, obviously won very big, because then Bill Clinton, who's supposed to be progressive, gets up and says the exact same things that Dan Quayle was saying. What we don't understand is the profound impact that the Right has culturally. And the Right of the fifties, Roy Cohn's generation, won very big in terms of making people feel that Communism was not so much an evil as an immaturity, and not of real interest to people who were sophisticated, and that a reductive psychology was actually the grounds for contestation and not political thinking. That's been very, very hard to overcome. I think it's starting to change. There are a number of writers of my generation who are writing more and more overtly politically, [Robert Schenkkan's] *The Kentucky Cycle*, Anna Deavere Smith. There are a whole lot of American playwrights now who are getting aggressively political.

AUDIENCE MEMBER: Who do you feel is out there, whether it be new, old, if you excuse the expression "old"—their voices not being heard. As you said, "fluff"—*Beauty and the Beast*—has taken a lot of the publicity away from some of the smaller plays that should be seen, or maybe filmmakers are out there that have something to say [but] they're being overrun by some of the bigger blockbusters that are just taking the business away from them. Who do you feel is out there that maybe should be heard that you admire?

RA: Well, they're in an embryonic stage. There are millions of them! But they're getting lopped off like this. *[Snaps his fingers.]* Their heads don't get up above and they're destroyed. There's no growth that's going on. To name anybody individually . . . we all have acquaintances and people that we know whose work we respect that can't get to first base, strike or no strike. *[Laughter.]* But primarily it's the garden that is the problem. In other words, the person that is going to be the greatest playwright of all time, overshadow Tony Kushner, is somewhere out there and probably eleven years old now. We don't know. But will he mature? One, he may get hit by a car, or he may get hit by crack, or he may get hit by AIDS. And that'll wipe him out. But the other thing is he just may never survive the system that allows him to be recognized. We're looking for just a few people who manage to break through. What we're all talking about is giving more room, a space for this kind of talent to develop and to show itself.

TK: I actually do have one name I just want to throw out. I think that gender plays a big part in this. I have to say that. Women have a much harder time as playwrights getting produced, and also getting the kind of attention that they deserve. In my opinion the best playwright in the country today, and she's quite young, is a young black woman named Suzan-Lori Parks, whose work has been done at the Public. It's not narrative, and it's challenging, although I don't think it's difficult. She's really the best writer for the stage that this country has had since Tennessee Williams. She may prove to be better. She's not even a particularly close friend of mine, so there's no hidden agenda in this. She's completely extraordinary. I'm insanely jealous of her, and I think that people should see her work.

GD: The issue is a nurturing issue, and an issue of how you move through the system. As things close down, as it's harder to get to a certain point, then people begin to lose courage. But I can tell you that the talent is there, and the potential is there, and it's tremendous. One who works in the theater is concerned that sometimes one thinks one is working as a dinosaur in a situation—in a cultural situation—which is so loaded with media and all forms of electronic competition. But we also know that when a play like *Angels* comes along, and other plays, that the immediacy of the experience, the experience in this room and the kind of communication, can never be replaced, and that's the excitement of it.

AUDIENCE MEMBER: Doesn't talent really survive systems, whatever the system?

RA: Talent, yes. Talent survives—will survive—all systems. But for how long? There's a pocket of people who discover and nourish and embrace those things. But this band of television saturation that we have that's defining countries now . . . nations are no longer defined by land mass, or I think soon won't be. It's AT&T and IT&B and DB&C. And there's no chance to get through. There's too much alternative stuff [that] is fed them. People sit around and they can't find the audience. With all this access, the artist can't find the audiences anymore.

GD: But Tony said, [when] I asked him on this day after the closing of *Angels* how he felt, he said, "Scared." And I said, "In what ways?" One has to do with creativeness and the other has to do with income. *[Laughter.]*

TK: It's a very interesting question. I think that there are a lot of things in the system that we have now [that are] clearly doing very badly. People live with an absolutely insupportable level of stress. The environment is collapsing. There's much too much homelessness; I mean, any homelessness is too much. There's poverty, there are kids walking around with guns. Everybody is frightened by the world that we've created, so the system is failing us. It would be nice if people cared enough about art that they would also realize that another impetus to change is that the system that we have now is survivable by a few. But if the system wasn't so hard, then we would have many, many more than we've got.

I've known so many people that have fallen by the wayside who had great talent, who just couldn't survive the rigors of trying to make a career. I've been incredibly lucky, and I know a lot of people who are as talented as I am, or more talented than I am, who have not been as lucky. Several writers who I think are much better than me who have simply not succeeded because they didn't have the break, they didn't get lucky. Luck shouldn't play as big a part of it. Also the education system kills a lot of artists . . . because it doesn't expose kids to art, it doesn't teach kids the tools to analyze art. And whenever you have a society that's undereducating or de-educating its population the way America is, the arts are going to suffer both in terms of audience and creators. A part of the system that I'm particularly terrified about is the way that schools are falling apart right now.

RA: The universities right now are dropping, the big universities, they're dropping their arts departments, totally! They're totally becoming trade schools. And how do you fight that?

The Road to Optimism

William Harris

Days after *Angels in America* had closed on Broadway and before *Slavs! (Thinking About the Longstanding Problems of Virtue and Happiness)* would have its premiere at the New York Theatre Workshop (December 12, 1994), journalist William Harris spoke to Kushner. They met at a "greasy spoon diner, somewhere around Ninth Avenue and Twenty-third Street." Among the topics explored, Harris was particularly interested in hearing Kushner "talk about the role of artists in society, and about the future."

TONY KUSHNER: One has to have a complicated kind of optimism. You can't refuse to look at how horrible things are. If *Perestroika* [the second part of *Angels in America*] has any power, if its optimism has any power, it is in part because the play drags the audience through a lot of very painful things on the road to that optimism. You have to be willing to admit that the world is sort of horrendous. Otherwise, you're sort of a fool, or a Republican, which is redundant.

As artists, whatever personal successes we may be able to claim as a group, individually we are all dreadful failures. We haven't addressed the right issues. We must remember the role that art played in the early part of the century, the role that artists of the WPA [Works Progress Administration] played in shaping a support for a progressive agenda, and that many artists played in the birth of the Great Society programs of the 1960s.

From *Dance Ink* 6, no. 1 (spring 1995): 28–29. The interview took place in December 1994.

Outside the Chamber of Deputies in the Kremlin, (clockwise) Ippo-
lite Ippopolitovich Poplitipov (Lee Wilkof), Yegor Tremens Rodent
(Christopher McCann), and Serge Esmereldovich Upgobkin (James
Greene) react to the death of Aleksii Antedilluvianovich Prelapsarianov (Ronny Graham) in *Slavs! (Thinking about the Longstanding Problems of Virtue and Happiness)*. Coproduced in January–March 1995
by Center Stage (Baltimore) and Yale Repertory Company (New
Haven, CT), directed by Lisa Peterson. (*Photo by Richard Anderson.*)

We're not doing that. We had a few good years of resistance to Reagan toward the end of the Reagan/Bush era, and then we settled down and got confused or lazy or both during Clinton. I think one should want one's work to respond to the needs of the time, to take up the burden of the time. I take that responsibility very seriously. The point is not to say things that we think audiences want to hear, but to make sure that we make more noise so that they do hear what we have to say. I think most artists in this country are progressive and have progressive things to say.

My favorite book from my days as a medieval-studies major at Columbia is *The Cloud of Unknowing*, this great tone poem about the inscrutability of God and the impenetrability of the cloud of unknowing that surrounds certainty, which could make faith not faith anymore but iron conviction.

The road that theory is supposed to lay down for us is that in the place of blind religious faith, theory gives us the belief that there is a way of understanding history, so that the steps we take have a certain direction and a certain design. When a very great theory, and Marxism is a very great theory, suffers the outrages of history, as it has—as well as having caused a few outrages of history—then we're left reexamining what that was, why that happened, and what we're going to do now. There are some lessons that the collapse of the socialist experiment in the Soviet Union needs to teach us.

As the two scrub ladies are saying at the beginning of *Slavs!*, we do have to ask questions twice. Is the concept of a revolutionary avant-garde always going to be a precondition for some sort of authoritarianism or fascism, a dictatorship of the proletariat? That's a completely legitimate question, and it was a question being asked in the early days of the revolution by people like Rosa Luxemburg, and it's a question that we have to go back to now. If you take away the incentive and the competition, do people create as well? I don't know what the answer is now. And that's a big thing for somebody who calls himself a socialist to admit. But it may be the case that profit or some sort of profit motive is necessary.

And what does that mean in terms of our possibilities for societies that are not competitive but cooperative? Do we give up on that idea? And if we do give up on that idea, do we simply give up on the idea that human society is capable of being made better than what it is? Do we just step over the bodies in the streets and say, "This is nature; this is the way we are, and we can't do anything about it, and maybe when these people die, they'll go to a better place"? Or do we say, "That's not acceptable, that has to be changed"? These are the fundamental questions that people have to ask now.

On Art, Angels, and
"Postmodern Fascism"

Michael Lowenthal

Shortly before Kushner was to give the opening keynote address at the fifth annual OutWrite Conference in Boston (March 3, 1995), he was interviewed by writer and editor Michael Lowenthal (editor of *Gay Men at the Millennium*). Lowenthal conducted the interview over the phone from Boston; Kushner was in New York.

MICHAEL LOWENTHAL: You've said that being a writer and being a leader require opposing qualities. Yet some of our movement's most prominent leaders have been creative writers—from pioneers like Edward Carpenter to contemporaries like Larry Kramer and Sarah Schulman. What do you see as the political role for writers in the lesbian and gay movement?

TONY KUSHNER: I don't know what Sarah or Larry would say, but I think it's hideously problematic. The production of any art, in the way that people are constructed by this society, is an activity that takes immense amounts of time, energy, and solitude—as well as a certain healthy interaction with the world. I have literally written a third in the past year of what I had written in previous years, simply because of the amount of public speaking that I've been doing. I've suddenly turned into a fund-raiser; it's work that I hate. But we're all running out of money. So I feel like it's an important thing to do. But for somebody like me, for whom writing is difficult, it's kind of disastrous.

In most progressive movements in history, artists have tended to

From *Harvard Gay and Lesbian Review* 2, no. 2 (spring 1995): 10–12. The interview took place on January 26, 1995.

be prominent and sometimes even the leaders. There's [Vaclav] Havel, and the Munich republic of 1918. There are many instances where poets actually wind up becoming presidents. I think it's a great thing when you have the arts and the political world sharing and talking and deeply involved with one another. But it's a dilemma. We wind up losing a lot of really great art because our artists wind up having to be too removed from the isolation necessary to produce good art. But then maybe that's a trade-off worth making. We need people who can write a good speech, and sometimes that's writers.

ML: As the movement has progressed, how has this affected the trajectory of gay writing for the theater, from somebody like Tennessee Williams, who was very gay but it's all in subtext, to Edward Albee, whose work touches on some gay themes but who has remained semicloseted in his public life, to you, who are completely out in your work and your life?

TK: I'm part of a progress that's been made. Tennessee wasn't out, but he sort of outed sexuality in general without outing himself, which would have been virtually impossible [at the time]. Gay men and lesbians have always been in the forefront of causing American society to confront sexuality. Whether we had to disguise it as heterosexual sex or not, we're part of that. As the movement has progressed and made a space for people like me to come into existence, we've come into existence. So I'm totally in a continuum with these guys.

ML: Can you project where it is going in the future, with still younger writers who have come of age seeing *your* plays?

TK: I would hope that in some way the success of *Angels* has made a slight foot in the door for lesbian writers, because there hasn't been nearly enough of that.

Also, there's a greater degree of formal experimentation, because one thing that's been happening is that gay and lesbian audiences are becoming more sophisticated in terms of their aesthetic. We're farther and farther away from the gay sitcom play. There's a certain degree of experimentation that's now acceptable and even expected. The body of our work is developing and maturing.

ML: Are there limits to the new openness?

TK: There's always a lament that comes from the Right—usually from the heterosexual Right, but occasionally one even hears it from right-wing homosexuals—that back in the good old days when we couldn't write about being gay, we wrote better plays. Well, that's just horseshit, and everybody knows it. I certainly know from my own personal experience. The reason that *Angels* is the best thing I have ever written is because I decided to write about being gay. That was tremendously liberating and it made me into a better writer than I was before.

ML: Now that a play that depicts a man getting fucked onstage can win a Pulitzer Prize, how does gay writing stay radical?

TK: That's a good question. We have to keep exploring that which genuinely makes us different, as opposed to that which makes us acceptable. I think sexual preference and desire is what our community is irreducibly defined by. For me, as a writer, it's the scariest and the most transgressive. That scene in the park was the thing that I got in the most trouble for when the play was first done.

But making strong statements for the spectacular variety of human desire, and for the ways in which desire creates human society, and the ways in which society is ultimately defeated by capitalism—this is where the radical potential in the movement has always been. Ever since Edward Carpenter and Oscar Wilde it's been clear that any radical defense of pleasure is going to seriously affront the nose of capitalism.

ML: Larry Kramer wrote in the *Advocate* last year that the gay novel is a dead form; the only interesting work happening in gay literature is in the theater. What is your reaction to that?

TK: Oh, Larry! I don't know what he's talking about, because he's gone off to write a novel as far as I know.

I just read Michael Cunningham's new novel *[Flesh and Blood]*, which is just astonishing. And Chris Bram has a new novel *[Father of Frankenstein]*, which is amazing. I think Sarah Schulman writes amazing novels. Certainly there's Dorothy Allison—I think *Bastard Out of Carolina* is one of the best things I've ever read. So I don't agree with that at all.

I think there's a certain *kind* of gay novel that's on the wane, in the same way that a certain kind of gay play is. Gay theater audiences are a little bored now with Gay Yuppie #1 and Gay Yuppie #2 meeting each other in the laundromat and having a cute little series of misadventures—sort of the *Mary Tyler Moore Show* for gay men. And I think people are not that interested in that version of the gay novel, either. We expect more now. Because we now *have* a Michael Cunningham, or we now *have* a Dorothy Allison. I think there's an elevation of standards.

ML: With the elevation of standards has also come an elevation in the level of recognition. Now that some out queers win Pulitzers and

National Book Awards, does this make it easier for the others to succeed, or harder?

TK: Both, probably. When you have a higher standard it becomes more daunting and the threat of silencing people who are intimidated is greater. High aesthetic standards in the absence of progressive democratic actions will eventually create an elite. On the other hand, I think high aesthetic standards *combined* with progressive democratic politics is something that one would aspire to. I don't think we want to try and keep the level artificially down so that everybody can just join in. But as long as people are being actively encouraged—as they are whenever there is a viable movement—people will come into their own voices.

Antecedent form is the name of the game in art. It's very important if you're a gay playwright to have Tennessee Williams, to have *Streetcar Named Desire*, or even something completely unattainable like Shakespeare. You need to define yourself against that, and you also need to know that it is possible for human beings to make something of that kind of beauty, even though you yourself will almost certainly fail in doing it.

ML: You've written that "In the modern era it isn't enough to write; you must also be a Writer, and play the part in a cautionary narrative in which you will fail or triumph, be in or out, hot or cold . . ." You are obviously very "in" right now. Have you thought about what it would be like if you became "out"?

TK: Only every fifteen minutes or so.

You never really know where the good stuff comes from, and there's always the possibility that it won't be there the next time you go looking for it. But apart from that there's also been [another] great fear. I'm an odd creature because I consider myself to be a mainstream writer. I have never really aspired to working in the cultural margins. I used to believe that that would probably be where I'd wind up, but I was never happy about it. I've always felt that my writing had the potential for appealing to bigger and bigger audiences. And *Angels* sort of made my wildest dreams come true in that regard. But I think we're at a point in American political history where it's much easier to say "I'm a homosexual" than it is to say "I'm a socialist." There's always the possibility that if I stay so unapologetically Left people will simply [dismiss me]. The more prominent you become, the more it's expected of you that you will eventually give up this "bullshit."

A very famous academic who's reasonably progressive wrote me a letter this year saying, "You write really good plays, but why do you preach to the converted? Why don't you shut up about the politics and concentrate on universal human truths?" And I was very shaken by that letter. But I'm just not interested in universal human truths. I'm interested in politics.

It's a test. Everything [in] life is a test. Eventually I'll be tested as to whether or not my political convictions or my income is more important.

ML: Gay writing in general also seems to be "in" right now. Do you think the "gay book boom" will go bust, and if so, what will be the consequences?

TK: I think there's a possibility of a kind of critical backlash. It's happened in London now—of course London critics are a pack of rabid dogs—but in London theater this year there has been a snarling backlash: "Why is it that every time I go to the theater I see a homosexual?" And I even feel that a little bit. I picked up a copy of *Granta* and I was reading a story in it last night. And the first paragraph is this guy in Cambridge talking about how much he loves being in Cambridge, and then the second paragraph is, "And then I met Paul, he was lean and wiry in black jeans and a leather motorcycle jacket," or something like that. And I sort of had this feeling: "Oh God, another homo . . ." And then I caught myself: "What the hell are you doing?"

I think that as a community we're great consumers of culture. We always have been. As long as we're given the option of consuming culture that is specifically about us, we're going to consume that, as well as other kinds of culture. So I think that the gay book boom is based entirely on the fact that in a country where the sales of novels are pitifully small, there's a very large and very reliable readership, and I can't imagine that that's going to go away. Because that's not straight people behind these books, it's homos.

Tony Kushner's *Angels*

Susan Jonas

Dramaturg and literary manager Susan Jonas, now with the New York State Council of the Arts, interviewed Kushner on February 9, 1995 at the Moonstruck Diner in the Chelsea section of New York City. Their conversation was published in a collection of interviews focused on American playwrights and their diversified relationships to dramaturgs.

SUSAN JONAS: I have before me the two lists of acknowledgment—official and unofficial dramaturgs you credit in the published versions of *Angels in America* and *Perestroika*. Did all of these people influence the development of these scripts?

TONY KUSHNER: Kim [Kimberly Flynn] had the biggest impact on the script of anyone. I've written in detail about her contribution in the afterword to *Perestroika,* both in the specific ideas and lines of dialogue she contributed, and the harder-to-define, profoundly shaping influence of our intellectual friendship, in which she's been mostly the leader and I the follower. None of it is conventional dramaturgy. With both plays, Ellen McLaughlin helped a lot in terms of cutting, which is a process that I find very difficult. With *Millennium,* Roberta Levitow was tremendously helpful in terms of reading through the script with me several times and making cuts. Because Ellen is a writer, I weighed her suggestions differently, and sometimes discarded them. When writers help you cut your material, they start unconsciously to make it sound like their material. When Philip Kan Gotanda was at the first

From *Dramaturgy in American Theater: A Source Book,* ed. Susan Jonas, Geoff Proehl, and Michael Lupu (New York: Harcourt Brace, 1997), 472–82. Copyright © 1997 by Harcourt Brace & Company, reprinted by permission of the publisher.

rehearsal of the workshop of *Millennium,* he was tremendously encouraging and, in several instances, urged me to keep things that I would have been persuaded to lose. Connie Congdon did an analogous thing with Eileen Nugent; she watched a couple of times and said things like, "I liked this. . . . This didn't work" very general suggestions.

sj: You've been recognized by dramaturgs as a great advocate of dramaturgy. You are one of the few playwrights who don't mind saying, "A lot of people influenced me and my work changed a lot."

tk: A lot of that has to do with Kim. I have been instructed through ten years and more of pitched battles over intellectual ownership and giving people credit. I really have to give credit to her for whatever generosity I seem to manifest. It's not something that comes naturally to me. It's basically the result of being called on the carpet by somebody who points out that, politically, it's deeply suspect that writers—especially male writers—feel that they have to produce everything completely on their own, and that the act of writing becomes in part an act of denying that one is in any way reliant on other people. I've thought that maybe other writers simply don't need other people's help as much I do, or maybe I'm just a bad writer. I suspect that some people are more solitary, and really dredge it all out of their own souls. But even there, there may be ways in which other people are feeding them about which they're not aware. Kim and I have really struggled with this for a very long time. I benefited a lot from that struggle. And I've survived; I haven't been diminished by admitting that other people have participated.

sj: What about when you're on the other side. **You** were the dramaturg on Anna Deavere Smith's play, *Twilight?*

tk: Well, Kim and I **both** were. She has not been given nearly enough credit. Kim did much, much more on the piece than I did. It's a weird feeling to have an idea absorbed into a piece. I've worked on plays as the director with writers and as a dramaturg with writers, and I've fed them lines that they've used. It requires a certain magnanimity of spirit that nobody is completely capable in this "fame-crazed" society. It's hard to feel totally great about that, and I don't think anybody does. Oskar Eustis has a great understanding of the pain of it, and the necessity of being able to not mind too much that we get absorbed.

sj: From everything you've said, Oskar was extraordinarily instrumental.

tk: Definitely. He's brilliant and spectacularly articulate. It was complicated with Oskar in *Angels.* He wasn't in any ordinary sense a dramaturg. I wrote the play specifically for Oskar to direct. Then, at the end of a very difficult and complicated process over five years, we decided to go our separate ways with it. We felt that in order to preserve a very, very important relationship, we needed to part company. It was insidiously difficult, especially for him, because he left the play at the moment at which it took off. And that's taken years of work afterwards to. . . .

The play was really begun in conversation with him. Certain features of my politics and his politics are similar, and we have always enjoyed talking about that. The title and the events and Roy Cohn and all that stuff was my idea. At the point when I started working on it, I was in New Hampshire directing *Mother Courage,* and I had just finished reading the [Nicholas Von Hoffman] biography of Roy Cohn, because I already knew I wanted to make him one of the characters in the play that Oskar had commissioned. I called Oskar, and we had a wonderful conversation about the American Right. It was a fifty-fifty conversation, but it was one of those moments of. . . . Well, for example, Prelapsarianov's monologue at the beginning of *Perestroika* is my writing, but it was Oskar's idea. Oskar and I were screaming and yelling at each other on the phone, about what Perestroika meant—in the early days of Perestroika. Oskar's feeling was, "It's not going to work because it doesn't have a theory." Because I don't completely agree with him, but also because I thought it was a very smart thing to say, the monologue is a kind of joking tribute to Oskar; it's Oskar's speech.

sj: You said in the notes from the British production that a lot of the play was written as an imaginary argument with Oskar.

tk: Exactly.

sj: You say that Oskar was not a dramaturg in any ordinary or traditional sense. What is a dramaturg in the ordinary or traditional sense, and does anyone on this list fit that bill?

tk: Well, I would say all of them in one form or another. The dramaturgy that every playwright fears is the play editor. Ellen's a very close friend as well as a writer I greatly admire. She helped me in terms of just talking through problem points and giving me insights. In the middle of *Perestroika,* which is the hardest thing that I ever had to write, she said, "One thing you should recognize about the character of Harper," which is a character Ellen always loved, "is that she's always at her best as a character and she's always most dramatically interesting when she's on stage with Joe." That was a small but incredibly important insight.

I had the best and the most dangerous thing that can happen with dramaturgy. The play was fed into by an astonishing number of in-credibly smart people. George Wolfe is completely brilliant. Without George, I would not have had the nerve to rewrite *Perestroika* as completely as I did for Broadway. With George in your corner, you feel you're protected against anything, because George is so tremendously powerful a person. We were closing *Angels,* a show that was completely selling out, that had won the Pulitzer and four Tony Awards. We were going to do four-performance weeks in the middle of a completely sold-out summer and then close for four weeks to put up *Perestroika,* a play that had not gotten good reviews when it went up in L.A. The play was not yet finished. It was long and difficult and complicated, and it could have easily sunk at once. It was literally back-breaking; I mean, I couldn't sit in a chair . . . and George made it okay. And the financial pressures were on him, in terms of the money that we were losing and so on. It was just staggering, and he was huge and indomita-ble. To me, that's a kind of dramaturgy. Also George is a writer, and he made incredibly smart suggestions. He could reconfigure things in his mind without even putting them on paper—come up with a whole new design for a scene. I hated one of the new scenes in *Perestroika,* but George loved it and said, "We're keeping it no matter what you say." It turned out to be an incredibly important scene in the play. The work on the Belize character, which was difficult for me, was greatly facili-tated by the fact that George, who is black, was directing the play. I felt that he was keeping me from making stupid mistakes.

sj: Did you feel that you were making any concessions to the venue?

tk: No. By the time it ended up on Broadway, the play was longer and more difficult than it was at the Taper. The big mistake—dramaturgically—was to listen to a number of people to whom I never should have listened. But then again, maybe it was right to have lis-tened, because we needed to try it. When I wrote *Perestroika,* it was a five-act play, but we all thought that it should be more like *Millennium,* so I turned it into a three-act play by the time it opened at the Taper. It was not and never should have been a three-act play. It had a totally different rhythm. It's not "bum, bum, bum." It's five acts; it has a more rolling structure. I let myself be talked into it in part because of the concern about intermission breaks, which is something that I shouldn't even have been thinking about. I learned a big lesson. Rewriting, which dramaturgy has a lot to do with, is tricky—to be smart enough to recognize what it is in the original impulse that makes the work yours and makes the work good—if it is good. It's difficult to be brave and daring in rewriting, while not being foolhardy, or betraying that original impulse. That's the impossible, terrifying thing. People kill things with rewrites all the time. They also kill things by not being able to rewrite.

sj: What did Leon Katz do?

tk: Leon wrote me wonderful long letters full of suggestions. It's hard to separate out the specific influences of so many people, and it's been a long time. Sometimes he was quite critical, but after he saw the first performance of *Millennium* at the Taper New Works Festival, he was rapturous. That meant the world to me, because I knew who he was, and I was somewhat in awe of him. After he saw *Perestroika*, he came backstage and said, "I have a lot of problems with what this is right now, but it doesn't really matter because no one's writing like this in this country." Whether that's true or not, hearing it was really lovely. It made me feel, "Well, even if I fuck up, I'm still doing something that moved somebody."

sj: This points to the other use of the word "dramaturgy." One of the critics said the play's dramaturgy, its actual structure, was "audacious."

tk: I think that some of the formal structures, which seem innovative **are** close to original, and some of them are not. I wrote in the introduction to Connie Congdon's book that I saw *Tales of the Lost Formicans* while I was working on *Angels* and it had a big impact. Caryl Churchill's work also had a huge impact on me.

The most unusual thing about *Angels* is that so much of the stage time is occupied. Well, first of all, the length of it . . . I had no idea if it would work, but it just had to happen. The size and ambition of it. . . . I think the subtitle *A Gay Fantasia on National Themes* may be one of the most important things about the play, because it announces immediately that it has immense ambition. Of course it's pretentious, and of course it's grandiose, but that's part of the fun of it. It's reclaiming something American. My favorite writer is Herman Melville, and part of what I adore about him is that he makes it *a trope* to be oversized and outrageous and much bigger than anyone could possibly be, and to say, "I will write this book and incorporate all of Thomas Browne and Shakespeare and opera and sailing and the entire globe and whales. . . . And of course it's going to fail. Of course it's going to collapse under its own weight. But isn't it great that we're doing this?" I think that's very American. O'Neill did it, and a lot better than I.

sj: There is a great deal of criticism directed against the way that new play development is done in this country. Many charge that in the process, dramaturgs and others do a lot of damage trying to normalize the play, using their own preconceived notions of play structure. Yet with all this input, plays survived, and they are absolutely and gloriously **not** normalized.

TK: The person I always quote when I talk to playwrights is Maria Irene Fornes, who thinks that you should do your own dramaturgy yourself. As with so many other things, she's right in a certain sense. Of course, there are a lot of very smart people around and the theater is a collective enterprise. Because it has a tradition of collective creation, playwrights should—and if they're smart they will—take advantage of the community sense of it. It's not like writing a novel; you're not stuck in a room alone with your brain. You're out in the world and a lot of voices can contribute to what you're doing. But I also think that you should be "Fornesian" about saying it's yours. You have absolute final responsibility for it. It is your work, and if you don't know how to fix it, don't touch it.

SJ: It is a common and fundamental mistake on the part of dramaturgs to assume artistic responsibility in the making of plays, and a common and fundamental mistake on the part of writers to abnegate or deflect responsibility by being influenced in that way.

TK: There are a lot of people in this country who are dramaturgs because they weren't able to write plays or direct well enough to have careers. They wind up being damaged by the jobs that they're given— by becoming literary managers and having to sift through hundreds and hundreds and hundreds of bad plays every year. And being a person without power or respect within an organization also diminishes you. As a writer, you have to be careful of these people. The nightmare age of dramaturgy is finally over, but when it was this new thing, artistic directors would literally say, "We are paying this person on our staff to be a dramaturg. You take their suggestions or get out of our theater."

SJ: It seems that because you have a strong sense of self, you can afford to hear these suggestions and negotiate with them, without losing your impulse, your vision or yourself.

TK: Well, I've been doing it for ten years now. It's a process that develops slowly. It's hard because of painful episodes, like taking a five-act play, doing all the work necessary to turn it into a three-act play, and then realizing in the middle of one of the scariest try-out situations in American theatrical history, that you've made a terrible mistake and you have to turn it into a five-act play again. I've learned something from that. I'll never make that mistake again. And you become more familiar with yourself. You learn whether you're the sort of a writer like Whitman, who should never have rewritten anything because his first drafts were always best (every time he rewrote *Leaves of Grass* he fucked it up even more), or whether you're the sort of writer who writes very, very slowly and needs to sort of grope his way. Most of us are in between. It's just a matter of becoming familiar with yourself. And of being wary and recognizing that people with the best hopes in the world for your work can fuck it up very, very badly.

sj: You trained as a director. Did you have the intention of writing plays as you were training?

tk: I think I always wanted to. I'm a very fearful person and I was very afraid of writing—and writing badly.

sj: And directing seemed less scary?

tk: Much less. You're not alone. You're not starting from nothing. I do think it's harder to be a playwright than anything else. But then it's much easier for me to be a playwright than to not be one. Maybe other writers don't find it so hard.

sj: I don't know any of them.

tk: I don't either. Everybody struggles terribly. Creating something from nothing is hideous. Theater, as tough as it can be, always has the world of the rehearsal room, which is a chance to be an artistically creative person, but not do it in isolation—to be part of this wonderful crazy family, and you really want to do that. Playwrights live halfway between what writers usually are, which is isolated and lonely, and are also denizens of a garrulous, promiscuous and wonderful place—the theater. There are many things that destroy playwrights. One of them is to become sucked into that whole world, which, on the one hand, you rely on entirely and have to know incredibly well, but then on the other hand, you have to avoid like the plague. If you want to do really serious work, you have to be alone with your books and your pens and your thinking, or in the real world, trying to understand it better.

One of my biggest grouses about dramaturgy, especially when it starts to bleed into what playwrights do, is the kind of research that dramaturgs do in this country, which is absent of ideology and partisan politics. It's too sociological and too ethnographic. I don't think that art comes from that. I think it comes from places in the spirit that are inimical to that; it's completely subjective and completely unfair and completely judgmental and closeminded and prejudicial and prejudiced in advance. I see dramaturgs from the La Jolla model say, "Here's a table of all of our research," then do the *Cherry Orchard* and not talk about Bolshevism and what's in this play. I think playwrights sometimes pick up that model of research.

SJ: What I'm hearing is that there should be more discussion of ideology and an ideological basis for all the participants, and that art is not merely a function of history, sociology, or other things that can be researched.

TK: Right. Art comes from interrogating yourself as to what you want to say with this work of art, not from pretending that you're going to recapitulate some kind of objective truth about existence. As an actor, as a dramaturg, as a set designer, as an associate assistant wigmaker, you are doing this because you want to say something to an audience. What the hell is it that you want to say? We so rarely ask that. Instead you find out what a Russian middle-class intellectual would eat for breakfast in a highway hotel room halfway between Moscow and St. Petersberg—that kind of boring, detailed, unimportant homework. I don't think you need that shit to do Chekhov. What you need to find out is: What is this play saying? What is this passionately partisan, political, harsh play saying about life that I want to say. Some research is necessary, but when actors do *Angels in America,* they spend too much time studying valium addiction, studying Mormonism so that they can cite all one hundred and eighty-five articles of faith, when it is utterly unnecessary.

SJ: If you were counseling someone who's dramaturging an extant script, what would you say?

TK: I would say, "Look at what Kim does when she works dramaturgically with a director." She's done it for me when I've directed. When I did *Fen,* she laid the bedrock for that whole production. She did not go out and say, "Here's how Fen women pick potatoes: they stick their hand here, and they do this with their elbow. And here's the history of the potato and the history of all of that stuff," that Caryl Churchill obviously already did—to the extent that playwrights do it. Brecht says in his journals that playwrights don't know anything about what they're writing about, and the great thing about being a playwright is that you can know so little and sound like you're an expert, and it's all fake. And it is; it's theater; it's completely fake. We forget that, so we expect this person on salary to go to the library and clean out eight shelves, put it all in the back of the car, and bring it to the rehearsal room. And there it is—this great unappetizing lump.

What Kim does is she reads the play, then analyzes it as a work of literature and, because she's an immensely political person, as a work that comes with ideological baggage and with an ideological design.

She presents research and reading materials and thinking about the deepest core of the play in terms of what it means as a work of art. That creates in the rehearsal room a sense of the immediate importance of what one is doing, rather than creating a museum era sort of thing. Actors, because they are badly trained in this, think their job is to do all this research. They hate doing it; they read about halfway through any book you give them. But they don't know **why** they're up on stage, and they don't **want** to know, because soon they're going to go and play Joe and Jane Doe, and do commercials trashing national health insurance, so it's best **not** to ask. Dramaturgs **should** be the intellectuals. That's what they **should** do.

sj: What if someone is doing this kind of dramaturgical "take" on *your* work? It's not Chekhov; it's *your* play? Is it weird to hear it?

tk: No, because it means somebody's performing an act that we should all be performing. Even if it's wrong, it starts the process. Kim is enormously smart, so when she came in and talked to these women about *Fen,* she brought in a vast amount of digested information about British socialist feminism, which you need to know if you're going to approach Caryl Churchill's world. And all of those issues are electrifying. Every single woman in this room responded, "This is my life." They read this stuff and they were turned on by it. Then ideas start to get fun, and people start to own the play in a way that's deep and important and real. That's what directors don't understand. They think that they should come in with this pre-first-reading chat about what the play means: "Why *I'm* doing this play and you people are all lucky to be in *my* vision of this play." But dramaturgs should not have an official place in the rehearsal room process. Dramaturgs should be as welcome in the rehearsal place as anyone, which is on the sufferance of the director. The relationship between the playwright and the director should not be intruded upon by anyone. Dramaturgs who feel they are getting in the way should know that if they **do** get in the way, they are probably going to do vast damage to the rehearsal, and consequently to the production. There are very famous dramaturgs who are nightmares, because they believe their job is to forcibly insert themselves in between. Their job is to absolutely never, ever get in between. The director and playwright have to talk to one another, or the playwright has to go away. I've done that.

sj: Who goes out for a drink with the dramaturg after rehearsal?

tk: The dramaturg should have the right to be an absolutely loathsome person, because what you want in a dramaturg is an absolutely brilliant mind. They don't need to know anything about the theater at all. They need to be able to come in and take the play and say, "This is what this is, and this is what this person is trying to do." Theoretically, it would be best if they didn't hate the play and could say, "This is why this is exciting."

sj: But with no conversation with the playwright?

tk: That's what my idea of what a dramaturg is. I'm incredibly prolix as a playwright and need help from somebody to say, "Cut this, cut this, cut this," but I would never go into a theater with a new script and sit down with someone I just met and let that person do that with me. It's much too scary because I'm suggestible enough. I would go and find Roberta Levitow or Ellen McLaughlin or K. C. Davis, or Oskar, although I know that Oskar isn't great about cutting. He's a sissy about it; he doesn't like losing words. He loves words, which is why he's great as another kind of dramaturg. He has very articulate suggestions about what he thinks you're trying to do, but Oskar isn't a great editor because he doesn't mind having an audience sit for eight hours. So if I need cutting, I go to people I think can cut. I have to know them and trust them, otherwise I don't want them around.

Scary dramaturgy asks, "What's **wrong** with this play?" Every writer has a list of people whom he or she can trust. They shouldn't trust them too much. I don't entirely trust Kim, who is my closest friend in the whole world, when she makes a suggestion. I think about the suggestion. I think about it very seriously. But she didn't write the play, and nobody but I will know if it's the right thing. You should be open to everybody and listen, but you should be armed to say, "Okay, that's interesting, but it's not this play." How do you train for that kind of thing? I don't know.

sj: It sounds like, whether or not you take their suggestions, you enjoy the conversations.

tk: It's great. Great things come out of it. After working for three and a half years on the angel's antimigratory epistle in *Perestroika*, I finally figured out what I was trying to say with it, at Joe Allen's at three o'clock in the morning in a conversation with Ellen McLaughlin, Jeffrey Wright, Stephen Spinella, George Wolfe, and Kimberly. We sat around and said, "What does this mean? What is this trying to say?" We came up with a couple of lines as a result of that conversation. We cracked the spine of the problem it presented, and I did a rewrite, but **they** made it work dramatically. Another time I was doing *The Illusion,* and there was something missing. Mark Lamos came over during previews and said, "Jerry, Mark's lover, watched the play last night and said, 'What am I watching? Why am I watching this play?' "

My first reaction was, "Well, I'm a very postmodern playwright. I don't give the audience that kind of moment. You have to figure it out for yourself." Then I thought, "What a bullshit defensive stance to take." I said, "I don't know how to write that." And Mark said, "I think you absolutely do. And I think you just have to ask yourself what is this play about for you? There has to be this moment towards the end where the penny drops, and the audience goes, 'Oh, I get it.' "

Connie Congdon loved the line where the father finds out that the kid is still alive, which was passed over rather quickly. She said, "I wish there was more of that moment, because it's very moving when you suddenly realize that his son is alive." So I repeated several times, "He's alive." I expanded it until it became the emotional center of the play.

One of the actors said to me early on in rehearsals, "Well, of course, what the play is saying is that there are many kinds of illusion. One is love, because what is love after all? You can say it exists; it's an illusion." It's an obvious point, but I never thought of it in that way. So I took that idea and I wrote it down. Then I had this great dream with Mark Lamos in a chef's suit, cooking something in a big white bowl. I woke up the next morning and I thought, "What a peculiar dream. What is that?" I was agonizing over how to write this moment. We didn't have any previews left and I had to get it written and I suddenly realized, "Oh! It's the Emperor of Ice Cream in the Wallace Stevens poem. . . ." You know . . . "Out with the maker of big cigars, the row of big cigars, the person who's whipping concupiscent curds in a bowl. . . ." Then I thought of the last line of that moment—the finale of the scene. I went for a run at the Hartford gym and literally wrote that speech while I was running around—the speech that the wizard had in the end about love being an illusion. It's about the nicest thing I ever wrote. All of those people fed into that. And that's why in the play's introductory material, I refer to Mark as "The Emperor of Ice Cream." That kind of process comes from a community of people focusing on one thing over and over and over again.

SJ: I noticed in one of the interviews you gave, you said that you liked to be referred to as "a gay playwright."

TK: I said that partly because I always hate it when I read a gay playwright saying in an interview, "Well, I'm not a **gay** playwright. I'm a person and I'm a playwright and my plays aren't gay." It always feels like denial. "You're a **gay playwright.** You're gay, and you're a play-wright." It feels like, "Don't reduce my market share by making me. . . ." I believe that there's a gay sensibility, and that my work participates in and partakes of it fully, and it's **my** sensibility. In the same way, I would never in any way balk at being called a Jewish playwright, because my sensibility is very Jewish.

sj: But you don't write for a Jewish audience, or a gay audience?

tk: Oh, I do in a way. I write for people like myself. You preach to the converted. That's what you're there to do. You envision an audience that's every bit as smart as you are, every bit as culturally knowing as you are, as far advanced evolutionarily as you are. Gener-ally speaking, audiences are smarter than theater people, so we have to assume that and run to keep up with them, rather than go slow so they can "learn"; that's the worst kind of teaching. Your challenge comes from trying to keep **those** people entertained. It would not be a challenge to keep Jesse Helms entertained, because the man doesn't know anything!

sj: I look in *American Theatre* and every year see the same ten plays being done at all the regional theaters around the country. I'd love you to suggest to the dramaturgs, directors, teachers and playwrights who read this conversation some plays and playwrights that you really love, that aren't being read and done, so that they'll continue to be circulated.

tk: Suzi-Lori Parks is the most exciting playwright in America today. I think that her work will be done very widely. It better be, or there's no point in doing theater. Phyllis Nagy is a remarkable play-wright who has not yet had a fair hearing in this country, but probably will very soon. A young woman, Naomi Wallace, whom I taught at University of Iowa and whose play I just directed, just won the Susan Blackburn Prize. She's extraordinary. Ellen McLaughlin is phenome-nal. Her huge play, *Infinity's House,* is a masterpiece, and nobody's touched it. I think David Greenspan is remarkable and ought to be done a lot more. Fornes is an immensely important writer. I would love to see a great deal more attention paid to her, because she's neglected. There's a lot of interesting Adrienne Kennedy that should be reexamined. I would love to see someone give Amiri Baraka's work a reexamination. Even though politically he's sometimes very difficult, and sometimes he says things that are really sexist and homophobic, within those plays there are things that are hair-raisingly great. I'd love to see people dig into Richard Foreman's body of work, because I think he's a genius, and that isn't a term that I use lightly. I'd love to see more Gertrude Stein done. There's a lot of early John Guare that I think needs to be reexamined, like *Landscape of the Body*. It's become neglected, and it's so prescient. What's going to happen is the British are going to do it first. Why do they always get to that stuff first?

sj: How would you feel if in ten, twenty, thirty years, you looked at *Angels* and said, "You know what? Its time has come and gone?"

tk: You always run that risk. I would love it if *Angels in America* were still of value twenty years from now. But I think the worst thing, besides trying to write for everybody, is to write for immortality. It's impossible and a mistake.

On Art and Politics

Susan Sontag

San Francisco's City Arts & Lectures series *On Art and Politics*
presented Susan Sontag and Tony Kushner in conversation
on April 5, 1995. Steven Barclay, associate director of City
Arts & Lectures, remarked to the packed house that Sontag
and Kushner had been invited "to participate in a dialogue
during which they will interview each other on a broad range
of topics; there is no third party, no interlocutor. They have
many things in common, including the fact they are both
intelligent, articulate voices, committed to political and social
justices and human rights."

The evening's discussion was a benefit for The Women's
Foundation, an organization that raises money to distribute
to fifty of northern California's fifty-eight counties whose
own grassroots organizations "benefit poor income women's
and girls' projects."

TONY KUSHNER: We're going to talk about a few subjects largely
grouped under the heading "Art and Politics." We're here representing high culture and low culture, Susan . . . *[Laughter.]*

SUSAN SONTAG: Tony, don't do that to us.

TK: There are a number of questions that I've always wanted to
ask you, and I'm going to use this evening to do that.

We live in an incredibly difficult and dangerous time, which is not
news to anybody. It's become increasingly difficult to get out of bed in

From City Arts & Lectures, Inc., Herbst Theater, San Francisco, April 5, 1995. This
previously unpublished interview took place before a crowd of nine hundred people,
each of whom paid $16 a ticket, with the proceeds going toward grant allocations to The
Women's Foundation's constituents.

the morning, increasingly difficult to open a newspaper and see what new horrors have been cooked up overnight. I wanted to come here and talk to you about what your work has meant to me over the years. It occurred to me that there is a contradiction at the heart of your work, between an extraordinarily beautiful, great, and very deep isolation that comes from a refusal to participate in the formula which shared experiences, political experiences generate. A modernist loneliness, a search for the self. Melancholia that is like Walter Benjamin's, a critic that I know you admire. This loneliness is to a great degree in contradiction with both a powerful force in your writing and in your life toward political engagement, social commitment, and political activism, and a very courageous one at that.

I wanted to start by asking about the challenge that your work seems to present to partisan thinking, and also to people who refuse to participate in a partisan struggle.

ss: That's the most comprehensive question of all. My whole life is organized around this question, or disorganized by this question. For starters, I'm in tremendous conflict all the time about almost everything. As soon as I have an idea, I recall the truth of some very different way of thinking about the same subject. I have a natural suspicion of my own certitudes, of the positions I most want to maintain and to promote.

Also, there are some fundamental collisions. For instance, to take a flying leap into a pair of big abstractions, there is, there can be, a very real conflict between truth and justice. Sometimes going all the way with truth will not get you to be very active on the side of justice, and vice versa. I'm not saying truth and justice are in opposition. But I am saying there are situations where they can't simply be mapped one on the other. My way of dealing with this is to live in a certain way, learning from my experiences, which are informed by my principles, rather than first having an idea and then applying it. I'm not just an artist or writer. I'm also someone who has commitments, and when pursuing or implementing these, while I might bring to these actions certain talents, and the privilege of being heard at all, basically I'm functioning as a human being, a citizen. I believe in righteous action, I believe that one should do good. I'm sure you'll agree that it's hard to pronounce these words without feeling embarrassed.

However—and there is a however—I'm not sure that I want the work I do as a writer to be measured against the standard of doing good, of righteous action. For there are other imperatives, such as one's own spiritual development, or one's own greater individuation—more words that are hard to use without blushing. Some issues that are addressed in art, and embodied in many great works of art, seem to be beyond morality. While I don't want to be beyond morality in my life, I do want to confront certain issues that are beyond morality as an artist.

So, there is a conflict. But I think part of it is resolved by saying, "Well, I do certain things—I write and I also direct in the theater and I've made some films, whatever—the art activity. And then I act, as a citizen, and as a soul." The sphere of public action suggests options I might not choose to take up as an artist.

To throw all this back to you, Tony, I have the impression that you've not been as concerned as I have to carve out a part of your life where you're precisely not functioning as a writer. I know that you are admirably public spirited. As you remember, we actually met for the first time doing a very nuts-and-bolts kind of civic action, testifying at a low-profile meeting of the Board of Education of the City of New York against some monstrous cuts in the education budget that would drastically affect working-class students and students of color. So we both do these things—it's one of the many bonds between us. But I think you feel more unified as a writer and a citizen than I do.

TK: Are there truths that lie? This is the question that I'm asking myself a lot these days. I'm finding it harder to maintain hope in the face of this century resolutely heading toward self destruction. Are there truths that lie beyond justice, or is it simply that there are deeper and more complex forms of justice? I've always assumed that the kinkier and darker parts of myself that don't fit well, or don't map, as you say, nicely with a political agenda, could be understood if one tried hard enough to fit into some larger system of truth that would still be consonant with what we understand as moral, just, and righteous. Is that just an American illusion; is that just a false hope?

SS: Well, Americans are very devoted to the idea of hope, aren't we? This is a society built on the notion of the new life, the second chance, the frontier, start all over again, be reborn, you can always change yourself, if you want it to be so you can make it so—all those ideas of improvement and self-remaking, which usually involve breaking away from one's own individual history or past, or some collective history or identity such as the country or culture you came from.

And there is—well, there was—a very strong idea of justice in this country. But I think most of our ideas about justice and righteous action involved shunting to the side a sense of how large the capacity for wickedness in human beings is. I'm not talking about anything as trivial as kinkiness, whatever that may be. I mean the capacity to kill, to injure. To be utterly unmoved by the suffering of others, to enjoy inflicting suffering. To be cynical, to be without compassion. Most decent people don't want to take in the bad news that human beings have an enormous aptitude for this. Americans don't like to think that human beings are not basically good, or that problems can't have a good solution, that they can't be resolved. It's not that we insist on happy endings, but we do want our glimmer of hope. We do want to feel that if we have the right attitude and put our shoulders to the wheel, things could get seriously better. I've been saying this is particularly true of Americans. But of course in some sense the basis of all action is a degree of optimism—if only, as the old phrase goes, "pessimism of the intellect, optimism of the will."

However, truth-telling in art leads you to more pessimistic conclusions. You can call people's attention to injustice—that's a very important thing to do. But even more important now, I think, is the job of keeping alive people's capacity for feeling, feeling in a responsible rather than a facile way. By feeling, I don't mean sentimentality. Sentimentality is thoroughly compatible with brutality and heartlessness. Aren't we all haunted by the image of the Auschwitz commandant who, after a day's work of bayonetting babies and ordering people into gas chambers, comes home, hugs his wife and kids, and sits down at the piano and plays Schubert? It's perfectly possible for people to be lovingly attached to their families and appreciate beauty in art and also be capable of unimaginable cruelty and bestiality.

So we have to be very suspicious of sentimentality, and of "niceness." There is a deeper education of the heart which, I believe, the art of our time that means to be serious ought to promote—although, for the obvious reasons, it mostly promotes the opposite: heartlessness. The job serious art has to do now is, I think, unprecedented. Maybe one always thinks one's own time is the worst. But, don't you agree, some times *are* worse than others. A lot worse. We live in a culture, high and low, which is committed to desensitizing us. Evoking sentimental responses, maybe. But still, making us heartless. So art is partly thrown back to doing something which we would never have imagined in the past. We would have thought that keeping alive the capacity to be serious, or the capacity really to feel, was taken care of or guaranteed by other things in the culture. But it isn't. Not any more.

Yet, having said all this, I agree that you do have to have some kind of hopefulness. And, Tony, your epic play does hold out hope. Surely one of the reasons that *Angels in America* has touched so many people, has meant so much to so many people, is the way you've kept this horizon of hopefulness which even you, at moments, must have felt was more an evangelical position, a position you felt was important to express and make coherent, than one you could confidently defend as a prediction.

TK: A lot of people have responded to *Angels in America* by saying that they're excited by the fact that it offers hope at the end. I find myself very dissatisfied by theater that opts for what seems to be a very easy but enormously dispiriting nihilism that hasn't been earned in any way. On the other hand, expressing hope, as you say, can become an evangelical position; it can become an automatic task that you feel that you have to have by the end of the play, or the book, or the essay that you're writing, some door that you leave open. So, I'm wondering more and more about the political uses of despair. Yet on mornings when I can't find a particularly good reason to hope—and there are mornings like that these days—I question whether or not it's politically irresponsible to create work that expresses that despair.

SS: I agree that so much of the despair is unearned. My own experience is that the more I live and make work of different kinds, the more I have to acknowledge how much of what I do is reactive. I am hinged to the time in which I live. For instance, in the first fifteen years or so I was writing, I was fascinated by certain extreme positions that seemed to be more profound, more usefully critical, than positions that were more reconciling or moderate in their purpose and in their ambitions. I didn't underestimate the cost of taking these extreme positions—think of Artaud, someone who fascinated me for a long time. It's almost unbearable to think how much Artaud, Artaud the human being, suffered. I never forgot that. I certainly didn't think that madness was the true sanity, or any of those clichés one did hear in those years. But I felt strengthened by what Artaud had produced out of his martyrdom, out of his unconfined visionary seriousness.

If I think back on it now, my attraction to Artaud and some other martyrs of poetry and thought was an expression of my sense of how inert and spiritless most people were. What I felt most oppressed by was that people didn't seem to care enough, that they didn't get excited about things. So my attraction to some of these extreme figures and the imaginative work that I did based on the idea of extreme acts was an affirmation of passion. I thought: This may be crazy, but it's alive, it's ambitious, it's passionate. . . .

Then, after about fifteen years or so, what began to flood my consciousness, what began to oppress me, wasn't anymore how inert and unenthusiastic and mindlessly conformist people were. The signal I was getting from the culture was of something even more horrifying—cruelty, unearned nihilism, easy, all too easy, acceptance of the violation of every taboo without any consideration of the consequences. So I started to back-pedal, I had to. It was clear to me that the whole range of human experience was being condescended to.

This revelation didn't correspond to something that was happening to me in my life, which actually had great continuity. But I suddenly realized that one now had to defend the things I thought could be taken for granted. For instance, romantic love. Certainly I had taken that for granted, as did the Hollywood movies I adored when I was a child in the 1940s. I never thought you had to defend romantic love. Or tenderness. I thought, you don't have to defend wholesome passions; those take care of themselves. But then I saw not only a general decrease of passionateness of all kinds but a facile cynicism, an acceptance of craziness, an abandonment of any belief in rationality or objectivity. Enlightenment values were not only criticized, people didn't even understand the values of rationality, and the humility which comes with authentic belief in reason, anymore. So it was a very reactive thing. I had to think on behalf of values which I'd up to then taken for granted.

When I think back now that I spent about a third of seven years of my life working on a critical edition of Artaud, I realize how far I, and the culture, have come since that time. Little did I think that the hatred of rationality and the promotion of mindless violence and taboo-breaking would become mainstream values of the mass culture. So I think we have to go in another direction. You, Tony, as a younger artist, seem to have understood right from the start that you had to address a much larger and more central body of experience—as you do in your plays.

TK: The phases that you're talking about correspond with the late 1950s and early 1960s in terms of . . .

SS: That's when I was in college.

TK: . . . a sense of nihilism that turned the 1960s into the 1970s.

SS: Yes, it was in the mid-70s.

TK: Did your work on Roland Barthes follow the work on Artaud?

ss: You know, I didn't work on Barthes, in the sense I've been talking about working on Artaud—which was a scholarly edition with a new translation and research and a big essay, and sixty pages of scholarly notes, and so on. I read Barthes. And I loved his work. There's no deep problem with Barthes's writing. It's just wonderful— as writing. Reading Barthes makes you smarter. And it's pure pleasure, at least for me. I did put together an anthology of his work, which I'm proud of, because it's designed to make you see what a good writer he is, like Valéry. I wanted to challenge the view of Barthes that subsumes him under various academic labels.

But since you asked that question, it occurs to me that the figures we're mentioning are all French. So I guess what my interest in Artaud and Barthes has in common is that I did think I wasn't going to find the mental nourishment I craved in America.

Of course there were certain American writers who mattered a lot to me from the beginning. When I was a small child, Poe was my favorite writer. And Poe, particularly his stories, is certainly one of the formative influences on my imagination. And then there was Whitman, whom I've always loved, and then Dickinson, and finally Emerson. But still I always thought the good stuff was mostly not in the United States. And I was sure it was mainly in the past. You have to understand that I grew up in the American provinces. The only books for sale in the small town in which I spent the first thirteen years of my life were in the back of a stationery store. So literature wasn't handed to me. I didn't come from a book-reading family. When I discovered books, it had the force of a revelation. And the books, after Shakespeare, were mostly the nineteenth and early twentieth century European classics. I loved these books because they were *not* about what I knew and where I lived. They were about something better, deeper.

Books were like space capsules. They were going to get me out of this world in which people were talking about Frank Sinatra and Gene Autry and what they were going to have for dinner. Books taught me about feelings and standards. In fact, I never heard an elevated thought or a real discussion of anything serious in my vicinity until I got to university, which was—by that time my family had moved to California—Berkeley. There I met, for the first time, people who had read the books I had read, and learned that Proust was pronounced "Proost" and Yeats was pronounced "Yates." All this time in my head I'd been saying "Prowst" and "Yeets"!

So I guess I'm a cosmopolitan from way back. But so are you,

Tony, and you probably have a very different background from mine. You feel very comfortable in the past, and in European subjects. Sometimes I think that Americans make particularly good cosmopolitans— maybe because we're an anthology country to begin with. We're made up of everything, so we export ourselves very well. But still, we have to come to terms with this country and what this country has made of itself, and not only because we're both natives of this country but because America exerts such enormous influence elsewhere.

So you have written a play, a marvelous play, which has made more of an impression on everybody than any play written by an American in many, many years, called *Angels in America,* and the novel I'm writing now is called *In America,* and . . .

TK: And Larry Kramer is finishing a book called *The American People.* So something is in the air, I guess.

SS: But we aren't doing this as the most normal thing to do. We are both, you and I, people who have made a certain journey to get to this point. I mean, although your journey is not as long as mine chronologically, I sense that it's similar. You worked on a play of Corneille, *The Illusion.* You have done an adaptation of Ansky's *The Dybbuk.* A classic French play. A Polish play. So you too, I would guess, have been as a writer influenced by European models at least as much as, if not more than, by anything coming from American culture.

TK: Although I come from a family that did read a lot. Probably because of that, I feel like I'm still actively engaged in trying to overcome my parents' politics and go beyond them. I'm still working on refining certain aspects of it that I find fatally attractive, and I am terrified at the thought that I'll wind up living out my days as a New Deal liberal *[laughter].*

SS: Well, Tony, I think that's pretty . . .

TK: More and more exotic as the years go on.

SS: Exotic isn't the word for it. Now we have a leading political figure, Newt Gingrich, who has announced that his aim, even before he becomes president, is to get the New Deal repealed.

TK: At the same time saying that his personal model as a politician is FDR, which is . . .

SS: Who hasn't said that?

TK: I know. It's very strange *[laughter].*

SS: Ronald Reagan said that too.

TK: It's eerie. He's the most opposite person you could have mentioned.

SS: I don't know anything about your parents, but I think it'll be very hard to end up in the present circumstances as a New Deal liberal. It really isn't an option. One has to go for something more radical, or one is going to be just swept away. The forces that are being marshaled now against the things that you and I care about, justice and truth, whatever we might perceive as the complex interface of those things—these forces are very powerful. They are triumphant. We're talking here in a part of the country where the liberal or progressive agenda is more acceptable than anywhere else in the United States, including the city where you and I live most of the time—New York. But those values are just as imperiled here, too. The country has been changing in a very large way. Maybe we are actually living in a new period. Eric Hobsbawm says the twentieth century was a short century—1914 to 1989. That means we're already some six years into the twenty-first century. Certainly, anybody over forty—and I'm sure that quite a lot of people in this auditorium besides myself are over forty—is living in a society that's fundamentally different from the society in which she or he was born. If you're in your forties, and certainly if you're in your fifties or sixties, the ground rules are really different from the ones that you accepted, or at least were inculcated with, when you were a child. Though you're not over forty, Tony, does this make any sense to you?

TK: Yes. But still you read things that make you wonder how different it was. If this is a period of transition, then it's both true and not true. It seems to me that one doesn't want to look to the past for solutions; and yet, because of the reactionary nature of our times and because of the ground that we've lost recently, pushing ahead into a new form of social organization is difficult because we need to rebuild what's been stripped away. One has to go all the way back to Federalism to effectively argue against the kind of politics of the 104th Congress. And, I find myself asking questions about the extent of the change that we're witnessing. It is still the case that only one-fifth to one-sixth of the voting public elected these guys. Are we simply looking at a country that has been demoralized and demobilized by Clinton's wishy-washy nonadministration, or are we looking at a fundamental ground shift—that's the sad part.

SS: What has changed is reflected in all this talk about the budget and the deficit. It is now acceptable to treat ethical issues, issues of justice and the mental and physical well-being of citizens, purely as fiscal issues—to talk about them in terms of whether we can afford to do something or whether it's economically rational to do this or that. It wasn't so in the past. And it's not as if materialism or bottom-line thinking were something new in American society—read Tocqueville, who came here in the 1830s. There has always been a very powerful, fanatical materialism in this country, which is linked to our form of egalitarianism. Measuring people by how much money they had, or what they could buy, was a way of denying or transcending the traditional class structure which has to do with birth, and manners, and attitudes, and markers of taste. But materialism—or, if you will, the capitalist ideology—has gone into a new gear since the 1980s. No restraints. No protected zones of concern. All sorts of issues are talked about now in terms of money, of profit, that were never talked about that way before. People acknowledge doing things for money they wouldn't have done before.

You might say it's just a failure of hypocrisy now, that they're just more honest than they used to be. I don't think so. I think there is a real change of attitude. Maybe it's the single most surprising thing I've witnessed in my life. The death of high-mindedness. It's my impression that most people now find quite alien, almost incomprehensible, the idea that you might do something out of principle, something altruistic, whatever the financial incentives to do otherwise, or the degree of inconvenience or discomfort or personal danger. "My principles dictate . . ." or "My principles forbid . . ." or "I believe this is the right thing; therefore I'm going to do it," or "I have to do it even though it's dangerous . . ."—that kind of language, of thinking, is dying. It actually makes no sense to most people.

Not even the virtue of courage, which used to be considered something admirable in itself, covers the gap. Why should you be brave if you don't have to be, most people think, or if there isn't anything in it for you?

TK: But don't you think the extent to which people are willing to sacrifice is completely tied in to the extent to which they believe that the sacrifice will result in a benefit for the greater good?

SS: No, I don't. Here's our first disagreement. I don't think the reason for my commitment to Sarajevo, which has involved spending a good part of the last two years there, came about because I thought it would do any good. I mean, for me, it's like volunteering for paramedical duties in an AIDS hospice. I mean, people like to be visited. I'm this crazy foreigner who keeps coming back. I don't have to come back again and again; I'm not a journalist on assignment, and I'm not "me," the writer, there either. It's just that by now I know lots of people.

They're happy to see me. I'm happy to see them. It means something even to people in Sarajevo I don't know personally that I keep coming back. But in real terms, it doesn't mean a thing. It doesn't change anything. I'm not doing it because I think it's a contribution to the greater good, or that it is particularly effective. I'm doing it because I think one should do things like this even if they don't achieve any good. Let me put it this way: the good that is achieved is affirming the possibility of that kind of action. It's not that I have to think of the results I'll achieve on my elementary school project in Sarajevo . . .

TK: No.

SS: . . . which is one of the things I'm doing there, trying to organize some primary schooling in the large apartment house projects, which have relatively secure basements where children can be brought; almost all the schools are closed, since so many children have been killed in classrooms and schoolyards by shells and sniper bullets. But, I have to tell you, the last time I was there, this past November and December [1994], the whole project collapsed. After more than two years of siege, and you have to imagine daily life without electricity, running water, heat, mail, telephone, hardly any food, constant bombardment, so many deaths and injuries, constant terror, it seems completely understandable that people are in a state of catatonic despair. You can start something up. And then . . . nobody comes. They agree to do it. And then they can't. So in fact it was a huge failure, the work I was doing last time. It didn't produce anything.

TK: There is a big difference between saying that you honestly believe that it will never mean anything in the universe anywhere, and saying that. . . . For instance, one could say that one actually was doing a great deal of good visiting people in an AIDS hospice. And even if you're not aware of an immediate return on your investment of time or courage, or personal risk, you believe that your action will, in some way. . . . Derrick Bell writes about it very beautifully: You engage in action even if you have absolutely no way of knowing that you're ultimately going to . . .

SS: No, you're right, you're right. I'm overstating it. I'm really speaking out of heartbreak here, which is I suppose why I reached for the AIDS analogy. Because, of course, what one wants to do is save them. It's that crazy. One wants to save them. When you go to a hospice, you can't actually say, "I'm not doing any good at all." Of course that's not true. You are, you are doing something worthwhile. The important point is to continue to reach out.

Saying that makes me want to go back to the earlier question of why we write and why we make things and why we talk in public. Because all that is a form of reaching out.

But there is another part of it. I want to tell the audience about what we were doing before we came on stage. From about 7:30 on, Tony and I were sitting in a little dressing room. We weren't going on with our longstanding conversation about diets. We were talking about whether one can write at home or whether one really needs to go to an office every morning. It turned out that we both have discovered, reluctantly I think, that it works better if you leave your apartment—where you are alone to begin with—in order to sit, alone, in some cubicle of an office. That's what Tony told me he has started to do, and I was saying, "Oh, where is your office? Do you think there's another one for rent in the building?" *[Laughter.]* And this too is part of what we're talking about. We're talking about reaching out and at the same time doing a kind of work of which it is true, as Kafka said, "You can never be alone enough to write."

But why is that true? There are many voices, many people, in one's head. I think writing comes, first of all, out of the desire to emulate. It's because one loves literature, one loves theater, one loves whatever the art is one practices. And then one is doing it for others. You write for an ideal audience. You write to move people. You write to make people cry. I take it as the greatest compliment when people have told me that they cried at the end of *The Volcano Lover*. At that moment it seems to me the thing I want most for my writing to do. By that I mean the fellowship of feeling, of seriousness, of compassion which is transmitted by the receptivity to art and to literature. This seems to me so much more alluring than the concerns people have been taught to value in this society, such as making money and being suspicious of your neighbor and being armed in various ways, literally and metaphorically.

So making things is an opening out of yourself. And at the same time it involves this going inside yourself because, how are you going to find where the good stuff is. Or if you don't go far inside yourself, which may mean leaving your perfectly nice apartment to sit in some broom closet office you've rented to do it—if you don't go to that place, then you'll be just repeating the communal drone. You want to go to some other place which is more original. There are of course plenty of original things which are quite irresponsible, of the "Well, I'll do that because nobody's done it before" kind. That's not the originality I'm talking about. You want to speak to others, to connect with and support what is deeper and better in them.

TK: It's very hard to go back and forth between the deep inner places and the outer world. It's very hard to stay, I find, politically engaged *and* to be working hard on a project because you get reclusive and cut off, and frequently the energies, the pace, and the rhythm of writing are really at odds with the energy of organizing or the energy of . . .

SS: Let me ask you, because your principal medium is the theater, and I say "principal" because I have a hunch that plays are not going to be your only fictional form. But for now you are writing plays and then the plays have to be put on. So, for instance, there have already been countless productions of *Angels in America,* quite a few of which I'm sure you've seen. Is the fact that a play can be done in so many different ways part of why you've chosen to write for the theater? Because you're not the one doing the staging, I mean you're choosing mainly not to direct your own work, although I know you have done that. You prefer to be the writer and let others do the directing. Or would you like to control your own work as much as possible if you could clone yourself and be in a lot of different places?

TK: Practically speaking, there's no way to really . . . well, I don't know. There have been some people who have directed their work well. But I think that there are real problems with directing your own work, including a time problem. I'm very, very slow as a writer, and so it takes me too much time to write a play to be able to think about then spending the time shepherding it through the world. I write plays because I'm not very bright, and there aren't very many words involved in writing a script *[laughter]* well, I mean except *Angels in America.*

SS: There's a better reason you might want to use instead of this preposterous one about not being very bright: You don't like to write descriptions. That's what Heiner Müller once said to me. "The reason I write plays," he said—of course he does write other things—"is because I'm very bored by descriptions. I like to cut to the chase, go right to the dialogue."

TK: He's very, very brave not to write any descriptions. The more you work in the theater and the more you see what people do with your plays, if you don't describe a lot, the more *[laughter]*. . . . I'm starting to get like Eugene O'Neill—every word is accompanied by little stage directions. *"Then you say this word this way, and then that word . . ."*

SS: *"Softly."*

TK: *". . . softly, quietly"* [laughter] *"with seeming indifference to her, Don pointed his* [laughter] *thing."* But, you know, it's true. When you write for the theater, you create for a certain scatterbrained, lazy kind of intellectual. Yet it's a very good form because you write something, and then you can hand it over to a whole other group of people who provide a level of meaning that isn't necessarily in the text *[laughter]*. Sometimes it's not a meaning that you would ever choose to want to have your name associated with. . . .

I'm terrified at the thought of writing a novel. I'm actually thinking of writing a novel but I . . .

ss: I knew it. *[Laughter.]*

TK: . . . but I'm really afraid of writing.

ss: Well, write it in the first person.

TK: Oh that's . . . the scariest thing of all. That seems like an endless self confession, to give all of my worst and most dearly held secrets away. I'm much more likely to do a bad *Moby Dick* kind of exercise with lots of pieces and clumps of things thrown in.

ss: And a lot of information.

TK: A lot of information, right.

AUDIENCE MEMBER: [inaudible]

ss: The question is, If things are so different, what happened, and aren't these people we think have led us to ruin, aren't they, after all, us?

My answer would be that there is such a thing as politics, that there is such a thing as the economy, and that there is such a thing as the concentration of power in the hands of a few. I worry a lot that many decent people have fallen for a naive populism in which they end up thinking that, well, all that evil, it's done by, you know, people. And there are people like us, and then there are some other people who aren't so much like us, and so on. As if the world doesn't have any structures!

The fact is that we live in a culture whose values support nihilism—it's very good for consumerism—which is also very ingeniously organized. This culture, and this organization of power, is called capitalism. New-style capitalism, for capitalism has evolved. There is a new world out there that's really a different world structurally. The rise of global capitalism, which has essentially transformed the nation-state and drastically reduced national sovereignty, is the big reality of our time. It's not about personality, that's just the biggest hoax and diversion to get everyone thinking that personality and personal life history is all that's interesting, all that counts. It's not about kinds of people. About whether you or I like Clinton or don't like

Clinton. And it isn't about feeling indignant, and calling up our friends, and going on a demonstration. It's about power, who has it and in whose interests it's being exercised.

A lot of people say to me, "It's really terrible that we haven't done anything about Bosnia. We know what's going on, there's so much information about Bosnia, so many appalling images of Sarajevo under siege, and everybody just sits in front of their television sets and watches what's going on there. We didn't do anything." At that point, I have to say, "Please. You don't know how the world works." *We* didn't do anything? Well, it wasn't for *us* to do something. The people who made the decision to let free Bosnia die were a very small number of people. Let's start by understanding that, that a very small number of people on the planet—a couple of thousand, maximum—make all the big decisions, those that determine the life and death of whole peoples, of cultures. They aren't made on the basis of lobbying or the mobilization of public opinion.

I don't mean that no local initiatives and no demonstrations ever have any consequences. But we'd be kidding ourselves to think that once upon a time there was public spiritedness and people went out and marched and demonstrated and made better things happen, but now this spirit is lacking and everybody is staying home and playing video games. As I said, in the last fifteen years there have been radical structural changes in the world of a very, very important kind—in the economy, above all—which explain a great deal of what is happening and what is decided in the world. What looks like politics. And like culture. Until we have a concrete political and economic understanding of what's going on, we're being merely sentimental about what our options and possibilities are.

TK: Right. Although the global economic changes are undeniable and we don't know yet exactly where we're heading or what that's going to add up to, I think it's incredibly important that at this particular moment we not decide that we've failed. Action is demanded, in this country at least, about domestic issues which we can directly affect urgently. There is a movement of resistance that's building against what's going on in Washington now. The Clinton administration has been a disaster in many ways but I still believe that there are a good 40 percent of the people in this country that don't want this kind of antigovernment. A resistance to it is not only possible but absolutely necessary.

SS: Unfortunately, I don't think that resistance is going to kick in until a lot more people are a lot more uncomfortable. But that may come quite soon. I've been told by journalists in Washington that the Gingrich people believe there will be major riots in the cities, if not this summer then the following summer. And they think those will only play into their own hands, so people will say, "Oh look at those animals, those barbarians. They're setting fire to their own stores and looting" and so on. It's interesting that *they* think there will be a reaction to this stepping up of the pauperization of large numbers of people in this country.

AUDIENCE MEMBER: Do you experience this as a time when things have changed, or did you experience this all your life?

TK: Experience this, meaning where we are now? . . . Well, I never imagined that an hour and a half was going to go so quickly because there were points of disagreement that we didn't have time to settle. But I still tend to feel optimistic, maybe even more so after the hour and a half, than I think Susan does. I actually began not from Europe to America, but in America, and I'm now thinking about leaving. There is clearly some sort of immense transition in effect, as I said. I'm clinging to the things that give me hope. I do believe that there is a strong basis for resistance to the new world order and that it will be slow in mobilizing. And I agree with Susan that unfortunately people tend to mobilize after the bodies started to pile up in the streets [of Sarajevo], and that that's probably going to be the case this time. There is an early resistance forming, and everybody who can do it should join in wholeheartedly. I look back to the 1960s, which I didn't really participate in because I was a kid in Louisiana, with a kind of nostalgia for that level of social mobilization. But I believe that nostalgia isn't necessary; it's also an antecedent to draw from.

SS: Because we're talking about the way things were, and how much they've changed, I'd like to mention once more the radically enlarged acceptance of violence. It's not just that people take outrageous violence for granted. They appreciate it; they consume it. What's the figure . . . that the average American child will have watched 20,000 murders on television by the time she or he reaches high school? So it must seem quite normal, perfectly human, almost comical, that a guy who has five thousand dollars worth of debt, a former postal worker, goes into a post office, shoots five people, killing four of them; and with the five thousand dollars he gets from this robbery the next day meticulously pays off his bills. This happened in Montclair, New Jersey about two weeks ago. And when he was caught, which happened immediately, because one of the five people he shot, though horribly wounded, didn't die and could identify him, he said,

"But I had to get some money right away! I had this mountain of debt!" You have the feeling that for a lot of people now violence is a . . . solution, a normal kind of solution. It's not a big deal to kill somebody. There's always been murder, sure. What's different now is the notion that it's not a big deal. Take *Pulp Fiction*. . . .

TK: Yeah, exactly.

SS: I'm stunned by the fact that *Pulp Fiction* is regarded by practically everybody as simply a charming, witty, intelligent, well-made movie, which it is . . . *[Applause.]* Maybe it's being so afraid of not being hip that makes everybody slide over what the movie is being charming, witty, intelligent, and well-made about. Let me appeal to those of you who are over fifty. Do you think you could have imagined thirty years ago when you were going to the movies, or forty years ago, when you were a child, that one day the movie about which everyone would say, "At last, an intelligent Hollywood filmmaker," "this is going to revive American movies," "this gives hope for the future of the industry," stuff like that, would be about people casually slaughtering each other? I'm not saying that slaughter isn't a legitimate subject. What's astonishing, at least to me, is the silence around the presumed normality of the subject.

I have an idea about why this horrendously brutal movie seems so charming to people. Two things. One is that it's the most color-blind movie to come down the pike in a long time, and that seems positive. The other is that in the midst of all this mayhem something about the couple is being affirmed. Remember when Bruce Willis comes back from the voyage to hell, he doesn't even think of bothering his bimbo girlfriend with the story of what he's been through. Instead he asks her with genuine concern if she got the pancakes she was craving; he's concerned that she got frustrated while he was away. Hey, he loves her. And that's appealing, very.

I was talking earlier about the connection between sentimentality and brutality. There's a sentimental core at the heart of *Pulp Fiction*, in the depiction of the couple-like relation of the two hired killers and of the other, conjugal couples, which sets you up for the acceptance of nihilism as the central dramatic story of our time. Didn't you feel that?

TK: Well, in addition to *Pulp Fiction* being very frightening and violent, I found it to be racist in a dreary, obvious way and incredibly homophobic. Getting fucked by another man is the only thing that can bring these two completely . . .

SS: Exactly.

TK: . . . opposed people together. I thought it was a terrifying movie, and I was very *[applause]* disgusted by it.

SS: But let's not forget *Forrest Gump.* Somebody has said that *Forrest Gump* and *Pulp Fiction* are just the two sides of America. What a thought! What a culture! *Forrest Gump* says it's good to be dumb because being smart never really gets you anywhere, and it's threatening to others and may make you uncomfortable too. So one movie praises the charm of stupidity, the other the charm of heartlessness.

TK: Mayhem.

SS: . . . and mayhem. Of course, it's not as if people don't go on leading their lives, whose main concerns aren't reflected in these movies. But I don't think you can say, "Oh, it's just entertainment." After all, if advertising works, and it does, then so does art, and in the same way. These images and stories influence us; they create legitimacy and credibility. They make things which used to be central marginal, difficult to defend. I'd go back to an earlier point I was making: That although many people I know actually are capable of acting on principle, most of them could not defend what they're doing as acting on principle. They no longer have a language for ethical action. It's collapsed, it's dropped away. Whereas new forms of cynicism and cruelty, of indifference to violence, have become central in the culture. And that's a change. I think that's a big change.

The Theater and the Barricades

Craig Kinzer, Sandra Richards, Frank Galati, and Lawrence Bommer

On April 12, 1995, Northwestern University honored Tony Kushner as Hope Abelson Artist in Residence. Through her generous endowment, Abelson established a program at the School of Speech whose purpose was, according to Dean David Zarefsky, "to make it possible each year to bring to campus, for a short period of residency, a distinguished artist whose work was on the cutting edge, who would challenge and stimulate our students and faculty with perspectives that went beyond and were different from those that they might encounter in the normal curriculum." The dean concluded his introductory remarks at the free, public occasion by announcing a discovery that Kushner and he made earlier that day: Kushner's last visit to Northwestern's campus was twenty-three years ago when he was a student of debate at the National High School Institute—a program that was, at the time, under Zarefsky's direction. Accordingly, Zarefsky took great pride in calling Kushner "a former student of mine."

Associate Professor Craig Kinzer of the Department of Theater, serving as the panel's moderator, introduced Sandra Richards, Professor of Theater and African American Studies at Northwestern and distinguished theater studies scholar; Frank Galati, Professor of Performance Studies at Northwestern, a member of the Steppenwolf Theatre Ensemble,

From the previously unpublished transcript of the presentation of the University Medallion Hope Abelson Artist in Residence Award to Tony Kushner, Barber Theater, Northwestern University (Evanston, Illinois), April 12, 1995. This presentation filled the 450-seat Barber Theater to capacity.

Sir Thomas Browne (Jason Butler) in bed as (left to right) Maccabee (Christian Lincoln), Dr. Dogwater (Sam Catlin), and Dr. Schadenfreude (Matthew Miller) anxiously await his response, in *Hydriotaphia or The Death of Doctor Browne*. Produced by the Graduate Acting Program's third-year class, Tisch School of the Arts, New York University, directed by Michael Wilson (April 1997). (*Photo courtesy of Sasha Stollman.*)

Associate Artistic Director of the Goodman Theatre, and Tony Award–winning director; and Lawrence Bommer, playwright and distinguished theater critic for the *Chicago Tribune*.

CRAIG KINZER: In an interview in *Vogue* magazine, on the occasion of the opening of *Angels* in Los Angeles, you said, and I quote, "Politically, basically, I'm a foot soldier. Art is never enough, but maybe I'm more effective writing plays." If you're a foot soldier, who are the generals? *[Laughter.]* And more importantly, what do you regard is the battle that you're engaged in as an artist and a man of the theater?

TONY KUSHNER: Well, I suppose my sense of myself has changed since that was an interview about two or three years ago, before this happened. I feel to a degree that I've become, although I'm uncomfortable with it, an on-again, off-again spokesperson for one particular political movement, for the lesbian and gay movement. Or at least for the gay male liberation movement. It's something that I don't think that I'm very good at. I would prefer to go back to being a foot soldier again, if I can figure out how to do that. I miss the obscurity *[laughter]* that felt sheltering and protective. I've been wrestling with this a lot ever since I started writing. But it's become more and more acute since the success of *Angels*.

The demands of political activism are especially in a time of emergency and crisis, as we've been in since November. Well, that's putting it mildly. *[Laughter.]* Also known as the shit has hit the fan. *[Laughter.]* It becomes very difficult to be both an artist and an activist. It's an unsolvable dilemma, which many artists solve simply by retreating from the world, and that retreat may in some ways be necessary. I don't know if I'm answering your question, but that's the thing that's weighing on me a lot these days. I basically don't know many artists who succeed in both staying completely committed and active politically and also continuing to write—I think especially that's true of writers—and continuing to write as well as they can. That's a concern and a fear of mine. So it might be that you have to do it for a while, and then back away for a while and keep going back and forth. I don't think that there's any real solution to it.

I don't know where the generals are. There are two possible answers to that. One is that somehow capitalism has finally produced simply a generic sort of character disorder *[laughter]* that makes it impossible for people to lead. I'd like to believe that that's not true, and I don't, in fact, believe that it's true. There are structural problems that [the] progressive [sector], the 40 percent of this country that is reliably progressive and that rejected Reaganism in 1992 and that sat back and was dispirited and didn't vote in the last election, is lacking—maybe not personalities and leaders so much as a party. The Democratic party . . . I'm really beginning to believe that they are the problem, because there's going to be reaction, and of course there's going to be a Right initiative. Then, there's going to be a counterrevolution. But in this country we have a great deal of trouble organizing progress. I'm wondering if the Democrat party isn't occupying that position and dropping the ball so decisively that we're being disempowered. I'm not sure that the problem is in a lack of generals as in a lack of a structure for the generals to appear in, because there are a lot of very talented people that one encounters. Some of them are problematic figures in one way or another, but they're very galvanizing and exciting and inspiring. There's simply no supporting structure for them.

CK: You spoke about the dilemma of being an artist and an activist at the same time. Where does that sort of press down on you? Is the dilemma that we in this culture have an impatience with both politics and arts, so to be both is to be doubly damned? Or does the perception of you as an artist diminish your political voice and vice versa?

TK: No, I certainly haven't experienced anything like that. I find that people are very, very hungry for political discourse in the theater, and for political discourse in art. People are tired of plays where you can't tell who the characters might have voted for in the last election. *[Laughter.]* At least in traditional psychological realist drama, actually since the fifties, there's been a conscious attempt to erase the kind of talk that occupies most people's lives, which has a lot to do with politics. People are immediately obsessed with what they've read in the paper, and they never talk about it onstage. People are hungry and excited to see that.

A problem with a lot of political theater is that the politics are maybe better than the theater. *[Laughter.]* Because we're all told that political art is bad. When you see a bad psychological drama that doesn't work you say, "I didn't like the play." When you see a bad political play that doesn't work you say, "I don't like political theater." You have to be aware of that prejudice. I need a lot of time to be alone. I'm very, very slow. I think very slowly. I read appallingly slowly. It was the iodine in milk, or something, when I was a kid. *[Laughter.]* It takes me about a year and a half or two years to produce a play. And it's just very hard when every day some new piece of outrageous legislation bursts like a bomb on the front pages of the *New York Times,* and you have to run to the fax machine and start freaking out about what we're going to do. Because by the summer we're really going to start to feel what these people are up to on the streets. And it's going to be, I think, unimaginably ugly. That, for me, is the biggest terror.

SANDRA RICHARDS: Are you still involved with ACT UP? Would that be one avenue where you would make the day-to-day responses while you're perhaps hibernating on part of the longer script?

TK: ACT UP was really great. I was involved in ACT UP at the point that I was actually working on the first part of *Angels,* and it was a really great time to be involved in it. Like a lot of people I've fallen out of the group rather than out with the group. I still admire it a lot, and I still think it has a very important job to do. I'm thinking more and more that I should probably get reinvolved with it. It crested in an odd sort of way, in New York at least, around the cathedral action. I don't know if people remember that. It was December 1989 when we disrupted High Mass at St. Patrick's Cathedral. It's an action that I'm still very proud of, but the political effectiveness of it was very much injured. ACT UP was basically an anarcho-parliamentarian group. There was no controlling its members. It was really kind of astonishing when it was going full guns. And one of the people that participated in the action brought a Communion wafer and crumbled it and threw it on the floor of the church, which is something that the rest of us deplored, but was, of course, seized on by the media. A great deal was made of it. It caused a lot of splits in the group, and a lot of unhappiness. I sort of stopped working with them at that point.

The group is going through a very painful transition now for two reasons. One is that the demographics of AIDS are shifting and the group was primarily originally a response of gay white men. The disease is now hitting with equal savagery communities of color and women—and that has to change. The struggle over that has been hair-raising. Also, the first impulse with AIDS activist militancy was to get drugs into bodies, and to overcome the barriers that the FDA, the Center for Disease Control, and pharmaceutical corporations were presenting to people who needed the drugs. There was a feeling that if we pushed hard enough we could get people up off their butts and a cure would be found, and we would be free of this nightmare. It's an unbelievably difficult thing to fight, the virus. And the pace of biological research, in a way, like the pace of art, is much slower than the kind of political urgency that ACT UP mobilizes. I fell back from ACT UP a little bit because I wasn't clear about what exactly we were trying to do.

A lot of work now is being done about housing and community support for people who have AIDS. That's very important. I now support them more through fund-raising. I also feel like I'm a little old. ACT UP was very young. *[Laughter.]* You know, you have to look good in those T-shirts. *[Laughter.]*

For some bizarre reason I seem to always be drawn back to the Catholic Church, which is an odd thing for a Jewish boy to be. *[Laughter.]* Four years ago a group called the Irish Lesbian and Gay Organization tried to be allowed to march in the St. Patrick's Day Parade and they were denied through a really nefarious conspiracy between the Catholic Church in New York and the homophobic city government. This has been going on for four years now. I was very moved by these people because there are only about thirteen of them. Most of them are very recent immigrants to New York, and they're very, very brave. They put up a huge struggle. So I've been involved with them a lot. It's a very tiny little cause, but I've become a little more Foucauldian in my old age, and thinking—especially when everything is falling apart—that you just need to pick a battle that you can really address with your complete energy, and address that. And the connections between that struggle and other struggles will be made for you.

SR: This may be a reversion of the sixties when you used to hear a lot about protest playwrights being co-opted by the media. Do you think that's a constant problem? That you have to run twice as hard to stay in the same place and still be cutting edge and activist and in their faces? And yet they constantly want to market it and defang it and domesticate it?

TK: I'm uneasy calling myself a protest playwright. I'm not as far Left as it gets. I sometimes chastise myself for that, and I sometimes think, "Well, it's OK." My politics are genuinely right in between radical and liberal. I'm a real believer in democracy and pluralist democracy and in citizenship. My work consequently is of less interest to people whose politics are more to the Left than mine are, who I respect, but I think find my stuff to be kind of stuffy bourgeois. It's made it easier for me to be successful without having to change my politics. I'm the son of New Deal Democrats and Old New York, you know, CP USA [Communist Party of the United States of America] sort of fellow travelers. They never actually belonged. It's that tradition of aggressive, old-fashioned liberalism that I'm critical of, and that is not definitive in any way. It was always sexist and racist and homophobic. It needs to be improved upon. The notion of citizenship needs to be an ever-expanding thing.

I sometimes worry if I don't have a kind of comfort level that pushes me into a politics that promises a kind of an evolution toward a new social order rather than a revolution. My suspicion has grown deeper and deeper as the years go by with a revolutionary ethos and a revolutionary model of social change. Everybody should worry about this. Is it because you just don't want to have to leave your home, and you don't want the subways to stop working and you don't want to live through a general strike in Manhattan, and so on and so forth. Are you just too wedded to luxury and comfort. It's possible that I am. I feel like that's part of the struggle and part of what I like to explore in the play.

SR: How do you measure the success of your politics in the theater, because that's a question that plagues political theater? How do we know we're being successful?

TK: My job as a playwright is not to necessarily change people from a conservative politics to a more progressive politics, because I don't actually believe that people do change that way in the theater. I've gotten letters from people who have said that the play made them rethink some fundamental position. But I feel that those people are actually being very generous and kind toward me because they like the play, and that in point of fact a whole host of social forces are working on them, and the play happened to be the thing where they had their little epiphany. *[Laughter.]* They're giving me more credit than I deserve. No playwright exists, not even Shakespeare, who could make Bob Dole into a smart or an honest *[laughter]* or a decent man. And we won't even talk about Newt Gingrich *[laughter]*, who as far as I know doesn't go to the theater. *[Laughter.]* As Brecht said, "Conservatives may have to be the way they are, but they do not have to be." *[Laughter; applause.]* When I read in the paper today that Alfonse D'Amato [New York senator] was in the hospital with chest pains, and I thought, "God forgive me, but . . . *[laughter]* . . . wouldn't it be nice, and wouldn't there be some kind of justice served if . . ." *[Laughter.]* He really must be a very unhappy man or why else would he behave that way? So it would be a mercy if he . . . *[Laughter.]*

There's this great image from Melville, in a letter that he wrote to one of his friends, that the people he admires are people he calls "deep-sea divers," who go down to the bottom and come up with bloodshot eyes, but they're holding the truth in their hands. It's really finally more about the truth than it is about politics. You have to ask the questions finally yourself. Have you been as truthful as you could possibly be? Have you been unafraid to ask difficult questions? And if you're committed to being useful to a politically progressive movement, sometimes those questions are hard to ask in big public forums,

194

because they're tricky and perhaps not necessarily useful in a political struggle.

We're going through that right now in the gay movement with the whole question of the second wave of AIDS infection. And how much is it the ancient question, "Is it good for the Jews?" Do you "air your dirty laundry in front of the goyim?" *[Laughter.]* Do you want to tell the *New York Times* that gay men are not having safe sex, or is the Right going to use that and say, "See, these are just a bunch of sex maniacs who can't even stay safe and clean in an epidemic." Those questions are very difficult, and finally you're going to make mistakes. You have to be willing to be a victim of history along with everybody else, because nobody is spared that. The people who think that they're spared that are the people who believe that Newt Gingrich can cut taxes and the deficit at the same time. You're not going to be happy, and you're not going to be spared the indignities that history forces on everyone in this age. You have to be willing to take risks and make mistakes. Hopefully your successes will outweigh your mistakes. But you shouldn't think about that while you're alive.

SR: And the success is putting your vision in front of a public?

TK: Yes. For me the question is exploring the problems that people have in being political and being active in a social order that provokes complacency and disconnection. And I'm very concerned about questions of collectivity and whether or not people can reconfigure themselves in ways that allow for collective action. There are lots of large questions like that. If I feel when I've written a play that I've done the best that I can do at considering those things, then I consider that to be a success. Also entertaining people, because that's what theater is irreducibly, or at least it is for me.

FRANK GALATI: You're so modest when you say that your work is only a catalyst for an audience member who may have some discovery or change of heart during the experience of the play. And you also say that there are social forces that are at work on that individual. But how do you feel personally about having tapped or touched a vein that we feel so profoundly in such great multitudes. When I was in college the whole idea of zeitgeist was something that we were sort of mesmerized by. I remember trying to figure out what that was. How did it happen that certain individuals could feel what was in the air and in the atmosphere. You seem to have emerged as someone to whom we all, I think, look as a visionary who has explained to us in the terms of the poet what it means at this point in history to be where we are. You're very modest when you say that you're only a part of larger social forces. How do you feel about this? What was it like to come to the threshold of writing this masterpiece and from whence did it come? Social forces work on us, and they worked on you. You have made a political play, perhaps, or a political epic or narrative. But you've also made a great work of theater art. Many of us are fascinated by the sheer force of the creative process that must have been a part of your personal experience.

TK: Wow! *[Laughter; applause.]* I'm going to go home now and die happy! *[Laughter; applause.]* That was really lovely! Thank you. I don't think that I'm being falsely modest, though. I'm very stingy with the use of the word "genius." There are writers of genius who come along very, very rarely. I'm reading Maynard Solomon's biography of Mozart. You really realize that there's this gulf between *[laughter]* anything that you thought you were good at and what . . . Mozart was probably dropped from a spaceship or something. *[Laughter.]* No, I mean, it really is. The book is genuinely terrifying. You're reading and thinking, "This is just not . . . this is impossible." But then all you have to do is look at a stack of Phillip's CDs, who collected the complete Mozart, and it's like this tall . . . and he died when he was thirty-five. *[Laughter.]* And he felt he wasn't that tall at that point! *[Laughter.]*

I feel like . . . I mean . . . I'm a talented writer. It's taken me a long time to be willing to say that and to feel that I can say that without embarrassment. I think that I'm good at writing jokes. I think that I have a good ear for dialogue. I think that I have a good ear for a certain kind of stage poetry, which is not real poetry, but it sounds like poetry. If it goes by really quickly and you don't think about it too long *[laughter]*, you can think, "Oh, that's really poetic!" And I'm a real magpie; I'm a very good imitator. So I learn very quickly from people that I'm really impressed with—also known as, I steal a lot. I see it as a bunch of accidents that all happened, and that I got incredibly lucky. That it really could have been the case that things could have worked out differently.

. . .

I really think that [Pat Buchanan's speech at the 1992 Republican National Convention] was a watershed moment in the fortunes of the lesbian and gay movement. You can read Derrick Bell and become profoundly and reasonably depressed about what he calls the permanence of racism. It may be a very strange thing that racism became socially unacceptable in the sense that you weren't allowed to make overtly racist jokes on national television but you could make covertly racist jokes. What you could do in the thirties and forties you couldn't do anymore because people would get mad at you. Yet the real underlying deep structures of racism seem to be unchanged and to be the sort of thing the Republicans can cash in on every election time. Whereas there's an odd flip that happens with homophobia. It seemed to be the very last socially acceptable prejudice. It was allowed; making open, unapologetic fag jokes was the last thing in a way to go. I think that we turned that corner in 1992. It may now turn out to be the case—it's too soon to tell—that the deep structures of homophobia may yield up a lot easier than we had expected, while race remains as it has always been, the issue in this country that's just the stark dividing line between people committed to social justice and people who are essentially the enemies of social justice. And gender may also be that. I don't know.

FG: I was curious about those initial moments when it began to come in your imagination, when it presented itself to you as a narrative, as a series of images. The angel itself as a metaphor.

TK: The first thing that I had was a dream. Right after the first person that I had known closely died of AIDS, I had a dream of an angel crashing through somebody's bedroom ceiling. I finally figured out about three or four years ago that it comes from Flaubert's short story "A Simple Heart," that it's the parrot at the end. It's a great short story about a maid who dies and at the end of her life, end of this life of kind of unimaginable drudgery, is vouchsafed this vision which is this kind of slightly ludicrous, but also completely spectacular, celestial vision. I came up with that after my friend Bill died because the play was actually knocking at my door. I did it because I needed comfort. And then everything followed from that . . . the title *Angels in America*.

I was also involved in this six-month-long sort of flirtation with a Mormon missionary in the subway in Brooklyn near my house where I lived, and became very fond of these two guys who were standing there in New York City talking to crazy people all day long about the *Book of Mormon*, and became interested all over again in Mormonism. I read Fawn Brodie's astonishing biography of Joseph Smith, *No Man Knows My History*, which is like one of the great all-time reads. It's a perfect beach book. Everybody should get it this summer. And Wallace Stegner's amazing book, *The Gathering of Zion*, which sort of picks up from there. The whole epic of Mormonism, which I think also gave me a sense . . .

And then completely silly accidental things like the fact that the

Eureka Theater, which commissioned the play, was in San Francisco, which I think gave me the permission to decide to write a play about being gay, but when we were approached I had said, "Well, I'm going to write a play for you if you want me to write a play for you, and it'll be about five gay men. There will probably be an angel in it. And one of them is Roy Cohn and one of them is a Mormon, and I don't know who the others are yet." Oskar Eustis, who ran the Eureka Theater at that point, said, "Well, why don't we apply for an NEA special projects grant, which gives you a lot of money, like $57,000 to write a play for a theater with a standing company." So we applied. Reagan was still president, and we thought, "Well, this is a joke! We're never going to get this money, so it doesn't really matter that I'm proposing a play for five gay men." And the Eureka Theater Company was three straight women and one straight man, who had nothing to do with, you know . . . So, then we got the grant, because this was before Bush, who actually tried to make good on the promises that Reagan had made the religious Right. The NEA controversy hadn't started yet. We got this grant and suddenly were faced with this immense amount of money for us. It was enough money to produce the play, but it didn't make any sense with the company, so I had to add three female parts and they had to be really good parts, because those actresses were mad about the whole thing. *[Laughter.]*

SR: Understandably!

TK: Yeah! Understandably! They knew. And they were also wonderful actors, and I wanted to write for them. So the play became suddenly eight lead characters, which, of course, is going to make for a long play. We all tried to pretend otherwise, but it *[laughter]* just kept getting bigger and bigger. The whole time I was writing *Millennium* I hated it. I almost stopped after the first sixty pages, because I thought I was writing a soap opera. I sent it to several friends. At least half of them wrote back and said, "Yeah, it's not really good." I was going to write a play instead about Sir Thomas Browne, the prose stylist, the seventeenth-century English prose stylist. And I just said, "Why don't you go back to that. It's a more interesting subject." *[Laughter.]* Only a couple of people said, "No, I really think you're on to something. Keep going." But I hated it the whole time. I thought it was really badly written, and didn't make any sense, because it was two hundred twelve pages long up to the angel crashing through the ceiling, which was supposed to be intermission in a two-and-a-half-hour-long play. *[Laughter.]* And again, accidentally this person who I don't actually have an immense amount of respect for, but somebody who works at the [Mark] Taper [Forum], called up and said, "Maybe this is a play by itself, and you don't need to do a second half, or the second half could be another play." I thought, "Well, this guy's a jerk and this is silly." But then I started thinking about it and said, "Well, you know, maybe that's right." And we did a reading of it and it worked, and so it feels like the whole thing was just luck. It really, certainly wasn't, you know, like Joyce sitting down to write *Ulysses* and saying, "Well, I'm going to write . . ." I still think that the jury is very much out on the play. I'll be very curious to see what happens to it in ten years. If it's still held in high regard. I would be very, very happy if it is, and I'd like to actually continue working on it and continue adding more and more installments of it. But we just don't know those things, and history is very harsh, exacting, and unrelenting, and especially with works of art. This thing could become the *Miss Lulu Bett* of its time. So we'll see!

SR: Or *Leaves of Grass,* as you keep writing . . .

TK: Oh, I love it. I'd rather it be *Leaves of Grass* than *Miss Lulu Bett,* but we'll see.

SR: I think of people like Nzotake Shange or Marsha Norman, with the tremendous success of their first plays, then they kind of . . . it's almost as though they're set up for failure with what comes next. Where do you go after a successful run so that you can take those kinds of risks? Where do you go next?

TK: I'm lucky because I tend to write about a lot of different kinds of things, and I tend to switch styles a lot. So I think that I'm going to escape, to a certain extent, the sort of follow-up. In a way, I escaped it already, because *Perestroika* was the follow-up to *Millennium,* and I had no choice about it. It had to be written. Going into rehearsal in August, with *Perestroika* . . . certainly the people in the biz and even people beyond the biz . . . I think definitely the lesbian and gay community were sort of caught up in the drama of whether or not I would solve the problems, because we had already shown the play to the world at the Taper, and everybody came and reviewed it there and said, "Well, it's interesting but it's got a lot of problems." So it became this sort of, "Is he going to screw up?" "What's gonna happen?" And I liked that.

There's this great quote in Hugh Kenner's book on Pound where he's talking about Goethe—and anybody who writes a long play has to think a lot about *Faust*—and Goethe spending sixty years writing *Faust,* which at times I thought was going to happen to me with *Perestroika.* He says that the job of the epic poet is to become, while writing the poem in public, the poet worthy of finishing it. That's a great thing. I could puff myself up to thinking, "Well, I mean, this is all, you know, it's a diminished age, so it's not good and it's not *Faust* and it's not Kenner or Pound, or any of those people. But people have gotten caught up in the drama of this thing, and it would be exciting again I think in five years, if I do a part 3 or a part 4, to see how long you can keep the ball in the air and if you're going to flub it, and when you do whether you'll be forgiven." It becomes sort of part of the drama itself.

Since I wrote *Angels* I've written an adaptation of *The Good Person of Sezuan* for Lisa Peterson and the rock group "Los Lobos" in La Jolla, California. I did *A Dybbuk* for Mark Lamos, and I did this tiny little pocket epic play, *Slavs!* And they're all very different. So, it makes it easier for people to see differences between plays and less likely that they can say, "Oh, well, he's repeating himself now." I just think I should never look for this level of success to happen again, because I don't think it will, and I think it would break my heart and stop me from writing if I . . .

SR: I'm thinking about structures. To what extent do we have in the theater structures for a playwright to go and perhaps fail and then have the production after that and the production after that?

TK: Yeah. That's a really important question. I think that that has a lot to do with the NEA. What playwrights of my generation have that Tennessee Williams didn't have is the regional theater movement, which was created by a few foundations and the National Endowment. The destruction of that is going to threaten a very good system that exists now. Theaters are becoming more conservative and more cagey the more they're being asked to rely on their own ticket revenues, which no successful theater in the history of the world, anywhere, ever, ever has done! And it's just not what theater is. Theater is an event of the tribe, and the tribe has to support it or you'll have *Cats,* which is the *[laughter],* you know, *[applause]* the event of some tribe, but I . . . *[laughter]* silly people in fur suits.

SR: So would you venture to sort of crystal ball gaze as to what kinds of infrastructures we might have in the future to support a kind of progressive politics?

TK: Pessimistically I would say that what we're going to wind up with is a redisenfranchisement of all the people who the regional theater movement has enfranchised in the theater. You'll see less plays by women, less plays by African Americans, less plays by Latinos, less plays by Chicanos, less plays by Asian Americans, probably less plays by, certainly less plays by lesbians, and I think probably less plays by gay men, white gay men, although we've done better in that regard than most other groups of disenfranchised people have, because we're white and we're men, even though we're gay. *[Laughter.]* But a theater that needs to make up a certain percentage of its operating budget off of ticket sales is simply not going to take chances. I've seen theaters that said, "Well, I can't book Anna Deavere Smith, because I don't know that people will come." It's astonishing to hear that. It takes your breath away. But people get very freaked out about the bottom line, and there's no safety net for theaters, any more than there soon will be for people who need public assistance.

What I would like to see happen is the federal government quintuple the size of the NEA. And the federal government ought to buy ten of the Broadway theaters and turn that into the National Theater of the United States. *[Applause.]* . . . Andrew Lloyd Webber just bought the theater in Vienna where *The Magic Flute* was premiered, and he owns it now, and he's permanently installed *Phantom of the Opera* and he's going to run it there, he says, forever! And because Vienna gets truckloads of tourists every minute, it probably will run there forever. They probably think it's a Viennese opera. *[Laughter.]* It makes you want to kill yourself. It's really distressing. But until we rediscover the value of having a federal government and federal intervention . . . States rights versus the federal government has been a struggle since the dawn of the Constitution. We're all in trouble when the states get to be too powerful. The structures that we need are not going to be in place until we manage to beat back this counterrevolution.

SR: I'm trying to find some light at the end of the dark ages that you're predicting, and I don't think you're off the mark. Shelley said that poets are the unacknowledged legislators of the world. Do you think in this benighted period that playwrights will regain their souls in the way of Clifford Odets and Arthur Miller and become conscience keepers in the absence of any true moral authorities, certainly not the ideologically bankrupt hypocrites that you are quite properly castigating. Do you see that as something that might fill the ethical vacuum that . . .

TK: Yeah, it's tricky, because you don't want to anticipate profit from a national disaster. There's always been a difficulty with the rhetoric of AIDS. You're trying to find positive things in a holocaust like this, so you say, "Well, it has taught people certain things and it's made us a different kind of community," and it has actually forged alliances between the lesbian community and the gay community that didn't exist. Those are good things, but still, wouldn't we all much rather never have had it. I think that Reagan politicized the arts community. People don't remember, but in 1981 he announced, "Arts shouldn't be political and I don't like political art." Of course, he did nothing about it, but announced it and immediately got people going. One of the few positive things that he did was to make people so angry that they realized that they're fighting for their lives and then art becomes more political. I'm happy to see that, but it also becomes really disheartening that the world only seems to learn by the example of holocaust. And you say, "Well, why couldn't Clinton, uncertain an object of attachment and affection as he ever was, have inspired us to levels of activism and political engagement." For the first time in thirteen years somebody was there who could give us at least some possibilities. And there were some good people with him, and why didn't we mobilize around him so that the 104th Congress never happened. Why is it only once that happens . . . and it's still not happening! There's still not massive unrest, and there won't be until you literally can't walk down the street without seeing whole families starving to death on your corner. Then maybe you'll start to think, "This is . . ." But you're gonna see that. That's the terrifying thing—that we can't imagine that, because we feel like we've been through hell already, and how much worse can it get? It's going to get so much worse. We're going to see that. Then people will respond, but by that point hundreds of thousands of people will have died.

SR: Do you think theater should hit the barricades then? Not in the false way of *Les Misérables* but in street theater, agitprop . . .

TK: Well, I think that that is going to happen. The people that are successful at it should do it, and people who are good at it should do it. It's the kind of theater that I'm not very good at. It's a very legitimate form of theater, and you have to be somebody like Peter Schumann of Bread and Puppet Theater, and really have a great gift for creating that kind of buildingless event. He's actually the signal success of that. There are very few . . . well, there were more in the sixties, I guess.

SR: San Francisco Mime.

TK: The Mime Troupe, yeah. Although the Mime Troupe always was more a sedentary, stationary event. It had its connection to the movement, but it wasn't . . . the Bread and Puppet created an aesthetic that would work at any demonstration. In the seventies when I arrived in New York, you couldn't go to a demonstration without these big, weird birds flying over everybody's head. But it was an aesthetic that really worked, that really spoke to something, and it was in this amazing way genuinely multicultural. It's not condescending. The images are timeless and have a kind of classic authority. And they're very moving.

I think everybody's going to have to hit the barricades and theater artists as well. None of us can say, we can't say anymore than lawyers can say or school teachers can say or doctors can say, "Our work is our political commitment," because your work is one thing and then your engagement has to be something else.

SR: But one would hope that theater could at least confront people with the same moral choices they face in their daily lives on the stage. I think of the recent scandal at Steinmetz High School [Chicago] that just exploded yesterday [Steinmetz's Academic Decathlon team cheated and lied to win the title]. It would be very good if some play could come out of [that] that would make sense of this moral malaise, this mess where students are apologizing for liars and cheaters. We seem to have a shifting sands morality where expediency rules the roost. And it's scary stuff.

TK: For me the new thing that I'm going to try and do in the next three plays that I write—which I see as being connected, although they're not, it's three very different stories—is to start to talk about money again. I'm inspired by working on *Good Person of Sezuan,* which is a play completely about haggling and transactions, and is amazing in that way. What makes me nuts is not a collapse of morality, because then I start to feel like Gertrude Himmelfarb, and I don't want to ever feel like Gertrude Himmelfarb *[laughter]* saying, you know, "Let's get shame back into the . . ." You know, what are these people, what are they talking about?

What makes me crazy is that nobody can talk about economics anymore. Nobody can talk about capitalism. Nobody can talk about the notion that workers have rights, or that maybe the rich aren't entitled to maximize profit to the moon and have no regard for human life or the environment or jobs. Maybe downsizing is immoral. Maybe these things need to be looked at again. That's where I feel more than anything else that the Right has stolen *[applause]*. . . they've eliminated the possibility of talking about that. It's much easier now to write a play saying, "I'm gay and I'm proud," than to say, "I'm a socialist and I'm proud." And I want to know why . . . *[laughter]* why that is, because we're never gonna get out of this. It's just very, very clear. The answers to all of these problems are more money. Why isn't there more money? Where did the money go? Who has the money? Why suddenly do we now have no money and we have to cut everything because there's no money? It doesn't make any sense. It only is because we can't ask certain questions, that we can't envision certain answers. And so I've become very interested in writing plays, at least the next three plays, that deal with questions of the international character of capital. That's *[laughter]* what I think would be fun to do.

SR: You heard it here first.

TK: It is actually the first time I've said it. There we go.

LAWRENCE BOMMER: You mentioned earlier today that this freshmen class was the least politicized in many years.

TK: It's a study that was released in the *New York Times.* They've been doing it since 1965, asking a questionnaire with about two hundred questions on it to college freshmen. This year's entering class scored the lowest of any class since the survey began in terms of a sense of being, of believing in political agency, and of being politically concerned. Scary.

LB: It is indeed, yes.

TK: It has [nothing] to do with these people being less moral. They're being told there are no jobs.

LB: Yes.

TK: No one will support you. Your parents have no money. You will inherit nothing *[laughter],* and sink or swim, baby. And you're about to be a citizen of a country that really is prepared to let you sink, straight down to the bottom. The lack of a social net creates fascism. You have to cling to a job in order not to plummet into the most abysmal poverty. They'll do anything to hold onto that job—including electing Adolf Hitler or Newt Gingrich. Had Gingrich been alive in the Third Reich, we know which side of the fence he'd have been on, without question.

The students at City University of New York, who are among the poorest in the nation, who are primarily from communities of color and who already know that their lives are now being threatened by what's happening, are beginning to mobilize. It's scary because the New York City government is reacting to it with an unbelievable level of harshness and severity, because they've sort of learned the lesson of the sixties, which is student movements can grow and you have to watch them very carefully. But it's also exciting, because you feel everybody else in New York sort of saying, "Well, these kids are doing it, what are we doing?" I still believe, even in America, we're not completely a nation of infanticides. We still feel a certain need to protect people under the age of twenty-one from mace and riot gear and being beaten up and put in jail for long periods of time. These kids may help lead the way.

The nurses marching on Washington, that was a great thing. Those labor guys going to Marietta, Georgia, and crashing into [Gingrich's] office, that was a great thing. It's starting. I hope it doesn't take too long. I was very active politically when I was a college student, because I hated classes and I hated writing papers, and it was so much more fun *[laughter],* and I think you can always count on that *[laughter]*—that seems to me to be entirely appropriate. The spirit of the revolution should always be allied to the spirit of carnival. *[Laughter.]* You put a bunch of kids together in one place and carnival is pretty reliably what you're gonna get, unless you've got a Princeton. And then, but that's a whole other . . . *[Laughter.]*

CK: I wanted to bring up the name Arlene Croce for a moment *[laughter],* who about two or three months ago, I believe, in the *New Yorker* magazine [December 1994] refused to review Bill T. Jones's piece *Still/Here,* largely on the basis of the fact that it represented what she called "victim art." Her contention, and I'm paraphrasing here and perhaps inaccurately, but it doesn't really matter *[laughter],* was that there is a strain in American entertainment and in American art that privileges victimization to the degree that it is impossible to critique it, and has eliminated any discussions of beauty or aesthetics from the dialogue. How do you respond to that? I know you responded to it directly to the *New Yorker* in a letter [January 1995], but I wonder if you'd speak to that for a moment, as an issue, particularly in terms of a shifting aesthetic paradigm in your work, and in looking again in the crystal ball down to the future.

TK: It's scary to think that Croce's paradigm, which is hardly new, would become a standard. The woman is deeply reactionary. I don't follow dance, and so I don't read her dance criticism. I'm told she's a very good dance critic. I'm very happy for her. *[Laughter.]* I called around to ask about her when I was contacted by the *New Yorker* to write a response. I found out very quickly that she used to work for the *National Review,* and that she's an absolute, committed conservative ideologue. She has a slightly odd relationship to it, because apparently she's also promoted the work of gay artists and lesbian artists, and artists of color. She's not stupid, although that thing that she wrote certainly gave a lot of evidence that she's becoming stupid. *[Laughter.]* It's the Forrest Gump disease *[laughter],* much more dangerous than the flesh-eating strep A bacteria. We have to *[laughter]* hold on to our brains.

The thing about reviewing a piece without going to see it was a big smokescreen. I was angry that everybody in the *New Yorker* was sort of saying, "Oh, but that's ridiculous!" or "You shouldn't do it" or "You should do that," because that's, of course, obviously insane. You can't review something if you don't see it. Bill T. Jones is a great choreographer and his work is admired by people because he's a great choreographer. He's also a very political artist. What she was basically saying is that she doesn't like political art and she's invoking the canon and she's invoking some sort of empyrean of the nineteenth century. The artist, of course (as I said in my letter), who she's admiring so fervently, people like Keats, was beaten over the head relentlessly by the kind of tired, cobwebby old journalists like Arlene Croce in the nineteenth century. There are always those people around to hold the gates against the barbarians who are coming in to take our privileges away. The term "victim art" is like political correctness. It's an invention of the Right to shame people literally into becoming victims, into ceasing from the activity of identifying oppression for what it is, and for being willing to be angry about it, which is a hard thing to do.

As I said in the letter, there's no victimization in Bill T. Jones's work. Go say that to his face. It's not at all about being self-pitying or whining, or sort of blaming other people. What the political art of the Left is all about is finding power and taking power from people who are really determined not to give it to you, and really determined that you not get it. It's a canard and I think it's cheap and fraudulent. And I was angry at the *New Yorker* for pandering to it to make a sensation, which they absolutely did. Sontag then responded to Joyce Carol Oates's article responding to Arlene Croce by saying that we have to remember that there are standards. That's the sort of Sontag thing where I think she somehow winds up sounding like she's allied with somebody of the Right when she's actually not. Standards are important. But it's a little hard to feel sorry for Arlene Croce. Bill T. Jones's *Still/Here* uses videotapes of people who are talking about having terminal illnesses. And she's saying, "Well, what if I don't like this dance? How can I say I didn't like this dance? There are people who are dying in this dance." And it's like, "Well, no, you can still say, 'You know, I'm sorry. I didn't like the dance. I was moved. I'm sorry that you're dying,' " which she's, of course, terrified of doing. She says in her article that she doesn't want to say that. And it's that telltale lack of compassion that you always find in the Right, that really *[laughter]* lets you know, don't turn your back because these are not very nice people. What's the worst that's going to happen to her? Somebody who's angry saying, "You asshole, that guy was dying and you trashed his whatever."

I don't understand what her problem really is, I guess finally. I think canon defense is . . . all of this academic stuff is really just about preserving white-boy culture. And it's gone! It's over! These people are just screaming after something that they lost. They're veterans of a battle that was lost a long time ago, and they've not gotten it yet. But they don't get anything, so it's not surprising.

. . .

AUDIENCE MEMBER: With your plays do you intend to simply move your audiences or move them to action? Also, I'm interested in how you and Robert Altman are going to divide the artistic control. *[Laughter.]*

TK: The second question is easy. We're *not* dividing the artistic control. He has it and I don't! *[Laughter.]*

The first question is an interesting one. The kind of theater that I do, which is very much in the tradition of psychological narrative realism, may not actually be about moving people to action, or at least it would be an odd ambition for an artist in that tradition to have. I really believe that this kind of theater works in the way that dreams work, that the deal you make with the audience is you can sit in the dark and nobody's gonna come up and put their hand on you, and nobody's gonna come up and scream in your face that you're not doing enough to save the whales, or something. You're going to be left alone, and you can be in this kind of semitrance state with a bunch of other people who will be sharing a vision that you're watching. That's the deal. What we get to do, since you've agreed to come and pay your money and sit in the dark, is enact scenes of pity and terror that you really wouldn't want to be in the middle of in daily life. Because you're safe, you're willing to watch them. You'll control your anxieties. We're presenting them to you in metaphors, in aesthetic forms, in vessels that make them watchable. And then it's up to you to decide whether you forget the dream when you wake up or when the lights come up, or whether you remember it.

One of the moments when I decided on my little road to become a playwright was in a Shakespeare class that I took at Columbia. The big speeches at the top of act 5 [of *A Midsummer Night's Dream*], the Theseus and Hippolyta speeches, where the dialectic of theater is laid out and Theseus says that he doesn't believe the fantastic stories these lovers are telling, that they took place in the night. They're just dreams. And then Hippolyta answers:

But all the story the night told over,
And all their minds transfigured so together,
More witnesseth than fancy's images
And grows to something of great constancy;
But howsoever, strange and admirable.

I believe that everybody in a room together having the same experience creates something. It creates an energy. It creates a community. It creates a phenomenon that didn't exist before, and that in almost a mystical way creates good in the world, and it also empowers people and makes it more likely that they will act.

. . .

I always like to believe that my audience is smarter than I am and more politically sophisticated than I am, and knows pretty much everything I know, and I really have to work very hard to keep them from being bored, and to keep them from being ahead of me. I've never found that to be a false assumption. Sometimes, of course, you get the audience from hell who sit there and they just hate the play and you hate them and the actors. And they start hating each other in a contest to see who's going to hate each other most by curtain call. *[Laughter.]* That's part of the fun of being in the theater, to see something that you've worked on for nine years . . . Usually it happens when John Simon is in the audience. *[Laughter.]* And it happens because John Simon is in the audience, too. It's always been my experience that audiences are just immense. When you get three hundred people in a room together the IQ level of everyone goes up about twenty-five points, and everybody becomes, you know, "Eeuh-eeuh-eeuh . . . I don't get that," but they got that. And this thing starts to happen and that's why live performance is so exciting.

I would never want to write a play that was about convincing people that it was OK to be gay, because if you don't know that already, go rent *Philadelphia* and figure it out. *[Laughter.]* That's not what serious theater should be about. It should be preaching to the converted in the sense of Martin Luther King, Jr. and John Donne and the great preachers of the ages who have done impressive things when they preach to the converted. That's what one should aspire to.

AUDIENCE MEMBER: Joseph Smith once said that he was trying to look for an alternative to a society that was becoming a society of bankers, lawyers, and businessmen. If you read some of the writings of

208

Smith, and I'm not speaking as a Mormon myself but as a scholar of this, you do see elements of something like a radical social critique. I wondered if you received any interesting criticisms from that part of the Mormon perspective, and two, do you see your *Angels* in the future perhaps going more in that direction, and mining that tradition further?

TK: You're certainly right. There is a whole history of utopian social experimentation in the years of the early Mormon Church. And Brigham Young was like Lenin. He was willing to try anything and damn the consequences, which is a problem. They certainly had tried collective ownership of property, and various forms of economic organization that would have solved the deficit, if we had gone further with them. But those were all abandoned because, as is always the fate of revolutions, they were surrounded by a country that wasn't about to let that. Along with polygamy, one of the things that the Mormons had to abandon was that form of experimentation with property ownership when it became clear that they weren't going to become a kingdom unto themselves, and needed to become part of the United States. I'm very intrigued by it.

I'm also very intrigued by the whole utopian movement in this country, in the nineteenth century, and I would like to continue exploring it. You're very perceptive. *[Angels]* comes out of that tradition. That's my Americana. Jews in the twentieth century in this country have been immediately drawn to that. It's why the culture industry of rediscovering American studies happens to a certain degree because of Jews in the New York Public Library reading room discovering these social visionaries of the nineteenth century, and getting very excited about them. I feel connected to those Jews and through them to Emerson and beyond.

When you ask if *Angels* in the future, if you mean the play *Angels* or the angels that will be in the play, because I'm thinking a lot about those angels recently . . . One of the places where I felt that a better writer than I am would have done better in *Perestroika* was when the angel finally opens her mouth and speaks. I'm sort of happy with what it is. I feel that it's somewhat inadequately realized, and I think it's also an accurate reflection of where I am. I never intended to write a play with any theology in it at all. I'm an agnostic with no evangelical ambitions at all. So it was surprising to me that the play became as religious as it did, and I'm curious about where I seem to be tending in that. And, again, that's sort of the zeitgeist. Its most banal manifestation being New Ageism, and its more exciting manifestations being things like liberation theology. I like the mix-upedness of the angel. I like that she is so Luddite and so terrified by progress. I'd like to explore her.

My great antecedent in that is James Merrill's *The Changing Light at Sandover*. It's a much better work of art, but it's a work of art that—it's this seven-hundred-page theology, cosmology rather—that's really astonishing. With each book that he wrote, he refines, perfects, elaborates, and expands, and each successive wave of spirits, angels, and dead people that appear to him and his lover as they work on the Ouija board and discover all these things tells him that the generation before were liars, or were confused, or weren't high enough to really know what they were talking about. So it's a constantly opening series of doors into ever deeper and deeper chambers of the sublime. That's a fun, sort of Blakean thing. And it would be fun to play around with that and see where it goes. Madness, probably. *[Laughter.]*

AUDIENCE MEMBER: You spoke a lot today about advocating support for the arts. Do you think that the American theater is producing a telling art form these days? What do you think is the state of the American theater today? And secondly, do you think the American theater is becoming more and more of a director's art?

TK: God forbid! I think that this is the most fertile, without question, the most fertile period of American playwriting ever. I don't know that we have playwrights who are quite as great as O'Neill and Williams. But I think other than O'Neill and Williams, we have certainly many, many more really good playwrights right now than we've ever had in our country's history. Don't you think that's true? I mean, I think that that's true. I think it really is a kind of a weird little sort of tarnished golden age. *[Laughter.]*

. . .

Society needs us. Do doctors earn the right to be doctors? Well, no, of course. Most doctors are awful. *[Laughter.]* But we need them, and we'd all die without them. So we have to make them better doctors and society has to make us better theater people. This medium will never be more a director's medium than a writer's medium. Of course, I would say this; if I were somebody else, a director maybe, I might not be saying this. But I really feel that it is not an art of narrative and it's not an art of image. It's an art of dialectic. And it's an art of argument. To that extent it's always going to be about the words. It's becoming more and more increasingly the case that it's the only semipopular form that is completely and totally and irreducibly literate. Poetry still exists and is immensely important, and everything flows from poetry. But nobody, except for maybe like twenty-five people, most of them poets, reads poetry anymore. *[Laughter.]* I believe in trickle-down only to that extent. The rest of us can leech off of what those people are doing, because they're the best writers. But they don't have a popular audience. They never really have and they never really will. Theater people do. I find the theater of images sometimes very compelling and frequently really slippery and maddening. Certainly for any kind of usefulness as a partisan political aesthetic, the theater of images doesn't work. You need the certainty to the extent that words are certain of language.

AUDIENCE MEMBER: Whenever I am part of a conversation like this and we're talking about a political theater, we kind of agree that there's political theater and then there's theater that ignores politics. I wonder if doing so we give ammunition to the Right. Isn't there a Right, conservative political theater as well? And where do you locate the politics in theater? Is there a theater practice that's not political?

TK: Well, I don't think there's anything that's not political. As they say, the absence of an ideology is an ideology. It's a conservative ideology. And a politics that seeks to efface its presence is part of the great mythmaking project of bourgeois, capital society. That's what it's about. It's pretending that it's nature instead of culture. It's fate instead of political struggle. It's essentialism versus social construction, and I'm all for social construction and culture and political struggle.

I feel uncomfortable talking about theater artists. I will say that, for instance, Steven Spielberg is apparently a Democrat. He just gave a big party for Bill Clinton. I guess that means he's probably idiotic. I feel I can trash people in the film industry and, of course, they read about these terrible things that I say about them and then I'm having a smaller and smaller market in Hollywood as a result. *[Laughter.]* *Forrest Gump* is bad reactionary art and *Jurassic Park* is sublimely good, hideously reactionary art. *E.T.* and *Close Encounters of the Third Kind* are the flagship aesthetic statements of Reaganism. They're fascinating for that reason, because Spielberg is somebody who has just an astonishing ear for the rumblings of reaction, and he just goes right for it and he knows exactly what to do with it.

He makes very entertaining and very competent and skilled work. It's very rare that you find somebody who is really reactionary and a really great artist. You find people like Céline. But there you're dealing with a level of depth and complexity that Newt Gingrich would be very hard pressed to recognize. *[Laughter.]* Only the French could think of somebody like that as actually being on the Right.

What it really boils down to is those people are fundamentally either nihilists or anarchists of some form or another. And that is really, honestly a position when you meet a real libertarian like Barry Goldwater now, in his most recent benevolent incarnation. *[Laughter.]* Now that he's decided to have the courage of his convictions and to really speak like a libertarian, he's become unbelievably a person of the Left. Newt Gingrich, who pretends to be a libertarian, is, of course, a fascist and is in no sense to be confused with that. People like Dostoyevsky are finally not . . . I think you'd really be hard pressed to say. They are people that don't believe in the transformability of human society. But I prefer to think of that as nihilism, rather than anything that the Right could really take up as a political statement. Who can use Dostoyevsky? He's sort of so great and so frightening that he's beyond any kind of partisan political use.

AUDIENCE MEMBER: What would you say about, or to, the politically apathetic young people of today. If we're faced with such daunting prospects, what is there in it for us to get involved? What is our reason, what will rally us?

TK: I don't consider you the apathetic young people of today, because I feel like that's unfair. I'm completely sympathetic. Sooner or later everyone will come to a realization that their lives are at stake and will start to do something to save themselves, because people will finally act in their own best interests. Finally, I hope even with virtual reality and all of that stuff, that that's still going to be recognizable, and that people will—if the rich get a lot richer and everybody else gets poor again, and even worse than was the case five or six years ago—that people will start to fight.

People of your generation are being told now, if you behave yourself you'll survive. That's a lie. You won't survive. Not even rich people will survive, because when every state is its own little separate sovereignty and there is no federal government to control environmental despoilation, for instance, what does it matter whether you're rich if they're burning nuclear waste across the state line. It's going to drift into your . . . nobody can stop that. You won't be able to sue anybody. There'll be no laws to protect you, so you'll die. And when enough of that happens *[laughter]* people will get freaked and they'll rise up in revolt and throw the bastards out.

If you want to do something now, first of all, every single person who cares about art in the United States needs to call the Republican leadership in the Senate, as distasteful as that prospect is, in the next few weeks. They really are hearing from people that the NEA is for everybody and everybody listens to NPR and everybody loves PBS and everybody wants the NEH to continue and everybody likes the new history standards. It doesn't do any good to call Carol Moseley Braun [Illinois senator] about it, or for me to call some liberal congressperson from New York, because they're already going to vote for it. You need to call Gingrich. You need to tie up his phone lines. All they care about is votes. They have no real scruples or morals. They'll vote if they feel that they're going to get in trouble. They'll keep the NEA in some kind of shadow existence until we can get more energy mobilized behind it. And that's just an absolute imperative. If you don't do it, art in this country is going to suffer horrendously. If you want to work in the arts in this country, you're depriving yourself of employment, because there will be no place for you to work. So you have to educate, organize, agitate, educate, organ—— . . . whatever that . . . [Laughter.] A long time ago we had this slogan and I don't remember what it was. [Laughter.] I just think it's the same old same old.

AUDIENCE MEMBER: In the beginning of *Perestroika* there is the line that if a snake sheds its skin without growing another one, it breeds chaos. In a large way that's what the youth of today is being affected by, that we don't really have a true theory. Being a theater artist and being from New York, I had the opportunity of seeing the snowball effect that *Angels in America* was beginning to have and is still continuing to have. As a result of that, a lot of people are looking at the play as a theory, and as the next theory. I was wondering how you feel about that and the responsibility that brings. You said that you didn't intend the play in the beginning to be religious, and now it's starting in a way to be its own religion. [Laughter.]

TK: Very odd religion, I would imagine. Not a church I would go to. [Laughter.] As the joke goes, "That synagogue I don't go to!" [Laughter.] You know that joke, this Jewish guy who washes up on a desert island? He washes up on a desert island and he's there for twenty years by himself, and finally some sailors see him and they come to pick him up and take him back to civilization. They find on the island that in the twenty years that he's been there he's built two synagogues side by side. One of the sailors, as he's getting into the lifeboat, says, "Excuse me, sir, I just have to ask you. I can understand building one synagogue, but why did you build two?" And he points to one of them, and he goes, "That synagogue I don't go to!" *[Laughter.]*

Part of what I'm trying to get at with *Perestroika,* and what all the characters in it are wrestling with, is that we've earned the right now, after what happened to communism in Russia and the transmogrification of the ideal of socialism into Stalinism, that big theories are very dangerous things. I think that we absolutely need them. We have a responsibility to create them. But at the same time we also have to find perhaps theories that are less totalizing. We can't really trust a total theory anymore. I could certainly never believe in any theory that said, "This theory explains everything." I don't believe it in Marx, Freud, or Stephen J. Gould. Hence, the glories of postmodernism—that all theories now have to also reveal their own lies and their own slippages. That's very important. At the same time, we have to recognize that human beings are as much creatures of idea as they are of materiality, and that we need ideas. Wallace Stevens is very important. We live in—we are made of—words. God is the imagination. I think that we are both created by and create history, and that we have to have an idea of what we're creating in order to have the thing that we create create us into something that we want to be. That kind of Möbius strip is important to me.

Angels obviously isn't a theory. It's a big, messy play. I'm very happy when I see people that seem to have been influenced by it. Sometimes I feel ripped off and annoyed, and sometimes I feel really good. I would prefer it if people copied the political side of the play than the theological, only because I don't want to be part of unleashing . . . What does Gabriel García Márquez feel like in the morning when he gets up and thinks, "I am to blame for the words 'magic realism,' and I am to blame" *[laughter]* "for all these horrible, horrible," you know, "for *Chewing Gum and Chocolate,*" or whatever that terrible, terrible movie *[Like Water for Chocolate]* . . . *[Laughter.]* I don't want to be responsible for every play being spooky things with wings and tails crashing through ceilings. But I'm happy if the play is useful in that way. I think that's exciting.

One of the things I'm proud of with the play is that it's reminded people that there are a lot of nifty things that the theater can do, and that we need to push it more in terms of that whole sort of illusion-reality paradigm. The best thing about the theater is that when the angel comes through at the end of *Millennium* you see the wires, and that's the magic of the theater, and that's the magic of the theater that I think speaks most powerfully to our current political conundrum, in that capitalism always seeks to erase the work behind the commodity form, the work that produced, the human labor that produced the effect. What's great about theater is that it never can do that successfully. And it should try very, very hard to, because that makes its failure ultimately to do it all the more thrilling. For five seconds, you are actually watching this thing swing down and saying, "It's an angel! I'm seeing an angel!" Then you're saying, "It's a woman in a silly wig and fly wires," and that doubleness is the kind of consciousness that citizens of capitalism need to survive, and are constantly being winnowed away from. Making stage magic is an important thing, and I think a lot of people of my generation have sort of reembraced that, and are doing that. As part of that movement, I'm happy about that.

AUDIENCE MEMBER: When I saw your play the audience was predominantly young, and I listened to a discussion this morning on WBEC about closing [a local theater], and their comments were that the audiences are middle-aged. I know I and my contemporaries are great supporters of the theater all the time. And I wondered if you have concerns about the younger people getting more interested in coming to the theater? We're not the ladies that come from the sewing club in the suburbs. We come to the theater because we love the theater, maybe because many of us are also politically inclined. Do you have concerns at all about more young people getting involved as supporters of the theater, not necessarily as writers and authors?

TK: There really has been a shift of the profoundest significance, and we can't begin to know yet what it's going to be, but I think that electronics and cyberspace are a new frontier. I don't understand it. It doesn't do a lot for me. I don't have E-mail. *[Laughter.]* I find it sort of alarming to think that in twenty years I'll be able to take a pill, put a helmet on my head, and actually believe that I'm having sex with Brad Pitt. *[Laughter; applause.]* Which is not to say that if I could go back to my hotel room tonight and take the pill and the helmet that I wouldn't seriously think about doing it.

It's part of the terror of progress. I think that your generation, and to an extent my generation, but I think certainly my parents' generation is . . . I adore them. In a weird way I find myself feeling that I have an audience of people who are in their fifties and sixties who really get what I'm doing, who really like what I'm doing, who speak about it with a kind of excitement. A lot of young people think that I'm this stodgy old, square, geeky guy, and I feel partly that's because I am all those things; I'm thirty-eight and they're twenty-one, and there should be that split. And partly it's because they're already citizens of cyberspace. There's been a change. It isn't a change like anything in human history that precedes it. We're kidding ourselves if we think it is. What it means and what its political . . . I don't know.

I hope that people continue to go to the theater. It's like the great thing that Ford discovered when he first was being a Taylorite and trying to find new and efficient ways of using a workforce. He shoved all of his workers together into big barracks. Of course, what happened was they organized *[laughter]* and they became a big pain in the ass for him. So he said, "Oh, no, no, no! Barracks are bad things. You should all be with your families. I believe in family values. Now go live in your separate houses." Absentee ballots are always more conservative. The results of absentee balloting are always more conservative than people just going into a polling place and being together. So computer voting—of which a really big fan is Mr. Gingrich—is a very scary thing to me.

It's just the most important truth for me—that two people, not one person, is the indivisible human unit and that the theater brings people together in artificial communities, that exciting things happen. I really believe that young people will be coming. They may be coming to theater that you wouldn't like or that I wouldn't like, but they're going to be coming to theater. Like poetry, it simply can't ever go away, because it's too essential—and universal to the extent that anything is universal—a part of the human condition. It's always sick and it's always in trouble, and you always hate 99 percent of it, because it's so hard to do. But it's always around and there's always that 1 percent that is part of what makes life possible.

sr: Reality doesn't get anymore virtual.

tk: Yes, exactly. Or virtuous, at least.

Wrestling with Angels

Rabbi Norman J. Cohen

On the evening of the Day of Remembrance (erev Yom Hashoah) in 1995, Kushner was invited to speak with Rabbi Norman J. Cohen, then Dean, and now Provost of Hebrew Union College–Jewish Institute of Religion, New York. The interview was a significant program in the college–institute's Holocaust commemoration. The audience consisted of both members of the student body and the general public.

NORMAN J. COHEN: This evening is erev Yom Hashoah. It's the eve of our Holocaust commemoration. We struggled long and hard here at the College to talk about an appropriate program for this evening, and we really thought about the fact that if we had a program that would deal with shaping Jewish identity, in a post-Holocaust era, we really would hit the point of exactly what an evening like this should be all about. And as Tony and I were talking before, I mentioned to him that in an interview in the *Forward* approximately two months ago, he said the following: "The model I used in the process of coming out was everything I knew about the Jewish experience in the twentieth century." And so we thought we'd start by simply posing the question of what the impact, Tony, of the Jewish experience in the twentieth century has been on you, on your life, and particularly on your writing.

TONY KUSHNER: It's been a bad century, so it's hard to know. What I meant in the interview was, and I think this has been true of most gay Jewish men, that in being Jewish one is born into a history of oppression and persecution, and a history that offered, at various points, a

From erev Yom Hashoah program, Minnie Petrie Synagogue, Hebrew Union College–Jewish Institute of Religion, Brookdale Center, New York, April 26, 1995. This previously unpublished interview took place before an audience of sixty people.

sort of false possibility of a kind of an assimilation that demanded as one of its prerequisites that you abandon your identity as a Jew. The possibility of passing which is not, let's say, available to people whose oppression stems from racial difference or gender difference. For me, as I think is true for most Jewish homosexuals, the business of claiming an identity, the business of coming out of the closet, the business of learning one of the central lessons of the Holocaust, which is that, as Hannah Arendt says, it's better to be a pariah than a parvenu. If you're hated by a social order, don't try and make friends with it. Identify yourself as other, and identify your determining characteristics as those characteristics which make you other and unliked and despised. So, it was central to me.

It was also a way within my family to explain to my parents, especially my father, why I felt it was necessary to not only be gay in the privacy of my own life and bedroom, but to actually announce it publicly. My father and I had a very complicated, difficult relationship for most of my childhood. His sense of my sexual difference, my preferential difference, was all channeled into a lot of political hostility. So we screamed and fought about everything. But one thing that we both agreed [on] was that Jews do badly when they try to pretend to not be Jews. And so it was a way of making inroads into something that was emotionally very, very difficult for him.

There are also big differences. I just saw the opera *Harvey Milk* at New York City Opera, which I didn't like at all, and they made a very simple equation. There's a moment in the opera where a giant pink triangle descends, and then an upside-down triangle, which is the symbol for gay oppression and liberation. On top of that a sort of a big, right-side-up yellow triangle comes down, huge—thousands of feet in diameter—and makes this gigantic Mogen David. I found that peculiar. You don't want to collapse the specifics of your own, of a very particular kind of oppression into another history. There are always complicated feelings that come up when that happens. You can see that in the way that African Americans are frequently angry at lesbians and gay men for using too intimately the civil rights struggle model as a model for lesbian and gay oppression. Because, of course, each form of oppression is very particular and specific. I have found that among homosexual Jews there's a certain ease of politicization of the process of coming out that I think people who come from cultures that are not thought of as being oppressed don't have.

NJC: In the same *Forward* interview you acknowledged how Jewish you thought *Angels* was as a play. In rereading it several times, I couldn't help but focus from the very outset on the Rabbi's eulogy of Sarah Ironson and the Jewish journey that's depicted. If you would allow me at least to read just a little part of it. I'm not auditioning for the next Rabbi part.

TK: The first time it's ever been done by a rabbi!

NJC: All of my professional development training, right? He's talking about the grandmother, right, of Louis, at her funeral with the coffin present:

> She was . . . a whole kind of person, the ones who crossed the ocean, who brought with us to America the villages of Russia and Lithuania—and how we struggled, and how we fought, for the family, for the Jewish home, so that you would not grow up *here,* in this strange place, in the melting pot where nothing melted. Descendants of this immigrant woman, you do not grow up in America, you and your children and their children with the goyiche names. You do not live in America. No such place exists. Your clay is the clay of some Litvak shtetl, your air the air of the steppes—because she carried the old world on her back across the ocean, in a boat, and she put it down on Grand Concourse Avenue, or in Flatbush, and she worked that earth into your bones, and you pass it to your children, this ancient, ancient culture and home. You never make that crossing that she made, for such Great Voyages in this world do not any more exist. But every day of your lives the miles that voyage between that place and this one you cross. Every day. You understand me? In you that journey is.

And so as I read those lines I said to myself, "In what way is that journey in you?" How do you see yourself, and how does it manifest itself in your life, that journey of the past and Jewish experience of the past? And your ancestors. How does it manifest itself in you?

TK: The play is the clearest evidence of it, because I had absolutely no intention when I sat down and made a laundry list of the things that *Angels in America* was going to be about. Judaism and being Jewish were not on the list consciously. It was going to be a play about AIDS, gay men, Reagan, and Roy Cohn, and Mormons, and angels, I guess, and . . .

NJC: You can keep on adding things.

TK: Yeah, I can keep adding things. But those are the things that I wrote down on pieces of paper at the beginning of the process, and thought, you know, these are the kind of disparate elements that I wanted to pull together. I think by bringing Roy in the first place I guaranteed that a certain amount of energy was going to be going into the Jewish question, because Roy was Jewish in a very interesting way. Then I immediately began to create this character Louis Ironson, who is the closest character to myself that I've ever written. And between, in the sort of thematic struggle in a way that's going on between Louis and Roy in the two plays, I think I guaranteed that the thing was going to be to a certain extent about being Jewish. And I'm sort of mystified by that, because I didn't come from a religious family, and I grew up in a Jewish community in the South, but most of my friends were not Jewish. In fact, until I came to New York I had not had any Jewish friends. I didn't like the kids too much that were in my congregation, so I didn't have very much to do with them. Somehow osmotically this culture has seeped into my bones.

At the point that I started working on *Angels in America,* my grandmother on my mother's side, Sarah Deutscher, died after ten years in a nursing home. That had a huge impact on what the play was. In fact, the Rabbi is based on the rabbi who came from the Bronx Home for Aged Hebrews to talk at her service. We didn't know him. We'd never even seen him the times we went up to visit her in the nursing home. He was just the guy they sent down, and he was this terrifying old rabbi who basically said all of these things to us. We were all very moved because it was Grandma. It was that whole sensibility of belonging and not belonging, and being very proud of being here and a very aggressive assimilator, which she was in some ways. But she hung onto that outrageous accent until the day she died. She didn't vote, she "woted." *[Laughter.]* She was an American and very much not an American all the days of her life. My mother and aunts and uncles and my father absorbed that, and then so did we. We didn't know Yiddish, we didn't know Hebrew, we didn't know prayers. We went to a very, very Reform—I mean sort of reformed out of existence—Jewish congregation. Still it's all in there somehow, so that when I read translated Talmud . . . you can sort of smell it out. The Jewish essence or some essence of the culture is still in there, and waiting to flower. And I find that . . .

NJC: And you begin to resonate with that.

TK: Yes. It makes sense, in a way that nothing else quite makes sense.

NJC: You talk about your grandmother's death, clearly your mother's death had a tremendous impact upon you. We're talking a little bit about the similarity of our experiences, both our mothers dying of cancer at a relatively young age before we flowered and matured, and the impact that that had on both of our professional lives and our personal lives. You've been quoted as expressing interest, for example, in a dybbuk, which is a world so foreign to everything you've been immersed in, a world of the shtetl and East European folklore. To an extent it was an outgrowth of *Angels,* but very much the result of your mother's death because you became interested in Jewish things, even Yiddish. I wonder if you could just elaborate about who your mother was for you, and what in a real way her death meant to you and the impact of her death upon you.

TK: God, I'm in analysis, so this is a very difficult *[laughter]* and dangerous thing to do at this . . . Is there a couch? Can I lie down? It's sort of "Who is she this week?" is the question. *[Laughter.]* She died the summer after the very first performance of *Millennium Approaches,* the first production of it, which is the first part of *Angels in America* at the Mark Taper Forum in 1990. She had had breast cancer and a total mastectomy when I was twelve, and very nearly died. Although she was a very small person, she was a tremendously strong person, with kind of an awesome will in a rather frail body. She fought herself back from . . . really from death's doorstep when we were very young. Then, for twenty years, [she was] without cancer, which was kind of a miracle. And then it reappeared very, very suddenly, and very quickly she died; from diagnosis of cancer to her death was only three months.

Her death had more of an impact directly on *Perestroika,* the second part of *Angels in America,* which is the hardest thing I ever had to write. I wrote the entire first draft of it, which is twice as long as the finished version. It's three hundred pages long. It's the longest play, just by itself. It's seven hours; it takes seven hours to perform it. We actually did one performance of the seven-hour play for people from a Jewish old folks' home, oddly enough, in San Francisco, who were brought in because it was free tickets. They were the King Solomon Old Folks' Home, I think, in San Francisco. They showed up at seven o'clock in the evening, and they were there until two o'clock or three o'clock in the morning. *[Laughter.]* But, if you've got a big mess of a play to perform, Jews of that generation are the people that you want to perform for *[laughter]* because they're not leaving until it's done, even if they're miserable and they hate it. *[Laughter.]* And it really is one of the great evenings of my theatrical career. They moaned and they groaned every time a new scene started. *[Laughter.]* When we got to act 5, which was about one o'clock in the morning, I made the director get up and apologize to them. He said, "I'm really sorry, but there's one act more to go." And this man calls out, "There oughta be a law!" *[Laughter.]* And this other woman sitting near him goes, "Well, if you don't like it, get back on the bus!" And they started screaming and yelling at each other. They were wonderful! Apparently they went back to the old folks' home and they slept the entire rest of the day, and then wrote and said, "Thank you very much. It was very interesting. We think you should cut it a little bit." *[Laughter.]*

I wrote the entire thing in ten days, and finished it on my parents' anniversary the year after she died. This rather extraordinary [event] happened. I got in the car . . . and I finished it. I was in Russian River, and I wrote the thing. It was like being in a trance. I wrote literally about sixteen, seventeen hours a day, and I couldn't stop. And this immense pile of paper built up. It was really thrilling. Everything that's essentially in *Perestroika* just sort of came flying onto the page. I really began to feel that she was . . . I had wanted to see a ghost or something after she died. The night that my grandmother died, I actually saw a rosebush wrapped in a white sheet in New Hampshire, which is where I was when she died. I was directing a play there. I thought it was a ghost, and thought it was her, and then found out a couple of hours later that she had died that night. I didn't know it at the time. So I sort of believe that that might be something. Who knows. Some sort of dybbuk. I got in the car after I finished writing *Perestroika* and drove back to San Francisco and I turned on the car radio and in succession, without my having to turn the dial, I passed through four different radio zones. "American Pie" was the first song that came on, and then "We've All Gone to Look for America," the Simon and Garfunkel song. And then another song with the word "America" in the title. Then a song by the rock group the Black Crows, "She Talks to Angels." Then the last thing was the Mozart bassoon concerto, which was one of my mother's practice pieces. And it appeared just at this one moment of this incredibly recognizable bassoon piece, and then went away. So, what was the question? *[Laughter.]*

NJC: How we get to *A Dybbuk* from that.

TK: Well, you can see. I was haunted in a way. I've always been attracted to pictures and photographs of the Yiddish theater of the teens and the twenties and the thirties. I've heard lots of stories and heard phonograph recordings. Vanessa Redgrave did a benefit for a group called Memorial for the Victims of Stalin's Oppression in New York about four or five years ago, and one of the people that performed

In *A Dybbuk: Between Two Worlds,* Khonen (Michael Hayden), a Ye-
shiva student in momentary reflection, is observed and his behavior
scrutinized by others. Kushner's adaptation from Sy Ansky's *The
Dybbuk* was produced by the Hartford Stage Company (Hartford,
CT, February–March, 1995) under the direction of Mark Lamos.
(*Photo by T. Charles Erickson.*)

was an eighty-five-year-old actress from the original Jewish theater in Moscow, who was this beanpole of a woman in this fabulous black velvet dress, and white face paint. She did a Yiddish poem about the Holocaust. It consisted primarily of the names of Jewish towns that don't exist anymore in Russia. I'd never heard Yiddish spoken that way. I always think of, you know, that Leo Rosten Yiddish. But this was incredibly elegant, and fluid and melodious. And I thought, "God, this is an astonishingly beautiful language." So I became very fond of hearing it, and decided that I'd be interested in working on a play, and *The Dybbuk* seemed like the obvious place to start, and it's this great play.

It was an interesting challenge, because it's not a very good play. Many of the things that make it not a very good play are the things that make it work so well, because Ansky wasn't a playwright, he was an ethnographer. The more I read about him, the more I felt that we had very similar backgrounds. He was somebody born into a nonreligious home, who went toward Judaism, but who was always inhibited in his thinking about Judaism by his political convictions, which flew very much in the face. He was a social democrat and a "menshavik." His sense of himself as a political revolutionary was very much at odds with this sort of emotional tie that he has with Judaism. He struggled with that all of his life. *The Dybbuk* is definitely a product of that struggle. So the play drew me, because it's not this little fairy tale. It's actually more complicated than that. I think very much about a very insular, premodern shtetl world, but one that's already being impacted upon by modernity and the arrival of the nineteenth century, and everything that would come after that. So, I was very drawn to it for that reason.

NJC: You lived in Lake Charles between the ages of two and seventeen, and you returned to Manhattan and Columbia University. You were quoted as saying, "Growing up in Lake Charles for a gay Jewish man was the best of all worlds." Could you elaborate for us? *[Laughter.]*

TK: God, when did I say that? Bizarre! What a stupid thing to say! *[Laughter.]* I feel that there are a lot of different influences on my work, and one of the things that can help make up for deficits in talent is an interesting background. I've benefited from growing up in the Deep South. I don't know if being a gay Jew in the Deep South was necessarily the easiest thing. I've certainly arrived with a lot of baggage. You can ask my analyst about that. But I think it was an exciting place to grow up. I grew up in a more integrated society, paradoxically, because so much effort was put into integrating the South. All of my cousins in the North grew up in virtually apartheid social conditions. They knew no African Americans. They had no contact, except people that you would see on the subway, whereas I went to a completely integrated, public elementary-secondary school system. I was in the South at a very exciting, transformative time, which has left me with a certain conviction about the efficacy of political action, and a very deep conviction that the federal government is a good thing and that we shouldn't dismantle it. Contemporary wisdom to the contrary.

The South is a very good place for writers to grow up. I'm not entirely sure yet why that's so, except that I think that the South has a very lively mix of linguistic traditions, that it has a very ornate, sort of purple relationship to language that the more industrial North has ground out a little bit. Louisiana, especially, is a place of endless birth and decay. I grew up in the middle of a woods with a swamp in the backyard. I got to watch a lot of birth and decay. It's a very humid, sort of tragic, beautiful landscape. A good place, I think, to grow up for that reason.

In terms of understanding things about oppression through Judaism, there were experiences of anti-Semitism. They were fairly mild, but they existed in Louisiana. Had I grown up in New York, being a Jew might not have been necessarily as immediate an instructive experience, in terms of feeling marginal. But there were a hundred Jewish families in the town that I grew up in, so we definitely felt . . . I mean, even as recently as two years ago my sister and I were asked by a hospital worker in Lake Charles where our horns were. It was unbelievable. Our jaws fell. A very nice person, but a person—a white Southern Baptist—who believed that we have little horns.

NJC: Do you think that some of those experiences, the sense of oppression of the Jewish, the otherness that the Jew feels, is one of the reasons why you might be drawn to the golem as a possible focus of your work?

TK: Well, I wouldn't call the golem a focus of my work. I like doing adaptations when I've finished a new play. I'm working on a completely original play now. And then after that I'm going to do *The Golem*. Really, I think it just started from having enjoyed working on *The Dybbuk*. I came up with an idea for a play that I'd like to do after I do *The Golem*. It's a true cornerstone of the Jewish theater. They intrigue me. As I begin to read more and more about the golem, I'm not sure that this is completely true. But it seemed to me at the time when I was working on *The Dybbuk* that it is very much a play about interiority and about the Jew's relationship to him- or herself, and Jews' relationship to one another within the confines of the shtetl, that anti-Semitism and Cossacks exist, but never onstage, and they're sort of bad memories, and always [a] threatening possibility. But they're not the big problem. The big problem is a Jewish problem. It's a problem about somebody making an oath and breaking it. And a rabbinical cord. The outside world is threatening, but only as a kind of a scent that drifts through the play. One of the traditions of the golem, of course, is that the golem is created as a protector of the Jews. It's an urban play as opposed to *The Dybbuk* which is a rural play, and it's a play about the Jews in a very big city, in Prague, and the need for a protectorate. And about how do you confront anti-Semitism? How do you confront the genocidal intent of the world without yourself becoming a murderer, and without usurping certain things which are proscribed by God. I'm intrigued in wrestling with that, with *The Golem.*

NJC: Change gears a little bit. You write and talk about your relationship with Kimberly Flynn quite a bit. You wrote in the piece in *Perestroika* that you share equally complicated powerful religious traditions, and a deep ambivalence toward those traditions. I wonder if you could articulate a little bit what some of your ambivalences are to the Jewish tradition, Jewish religious tradition?

TK: Being gay, I can't help but have a deep ambivalence, because there is a fantastically powerful homophobic tradition within Judaism. When I was at the Wailing Wall with a gay journalist from Tel Aviv (when they were doing *Angels in America* in Tel Aviv), I was looking at these varieties of orthodox and Hasidic Jews who were praying at the Wall. And I said, "You know, it hurts me that these people who, even though they don't dress the way I dress, or are very, very Jewish, it hurts me that they don't think of me as a Jew." And he said, "Oh, well, they think of you as a Jew. They think of you as a Jew who should be killed." *[Laughter.]*

When I was first coming out, the first political activity that I engaged myself with was trying to get the Gay and Lesbian Rights Bill passed in the New York City Council, which went on and on and on. Every year one would find oneself surrounded by—in the City Council chambers when people were testifying—surrounded by on one hand Catholics from Queens who had been shipped in by the Archdiocese, and then in a very unlikely alliance, the Lubavitchers—including Menachem Schneerson—who would show up. It was sort of first come, first served theoretically, so we usually got there first. I remember once this busload of Lubavitchers pulling up, and these guys with yarmulkes and gabardine suits really shoving and pushing and knocking us out of the way to get to the door. I thought, "This is horrible!" And this is a part of what being a Jew is that I don't want to think about and don't want to deal with. But this is real, and this is there. Of course, the Lubavitchers are not a particularly good example of that. There are orthodox Jews who think that it's a sin to be gay but who are tolerant and respectful, and I even know a gay American Jewish man who's in Israel now studying to be an orthodox rabbi in Safed. So he's in the middle of the whole mystical tradition. They know that he's gay and that he actually has sex with other men; in one way or another they deal with it.

NJC: The irony for me is interesting here, because I know you've received letters, and since you're in a Reform Jewish institution, about your Reform Jewish upbringing in Lake Charles, which you've characterized as a kind of an assimilationist experience. That element of Reform removed everything that was beautiful out of Judaism. But on the other hand, being here in an institution like this which underscores human autonomy, and the importance of the individual, and inclusivity as primary kinds of expressions, it's an interesting tension here, you know?

TK: Yeah.

NJC: Between what Reform is in terms of its principles, and how you perceive it from the point of view of its practice. Reform has changed a lot since your days in Lake Charles twenty-five years ago. But what intrigued me most of all was that implicit in your critique of Reform was your appreciation for the aesthetic part of Judaism, which is ritual, and I'm wondering how you balance the issue of your self-perception as an agnostic or a secular Jew, on one hand, but your real appreciation for ritual, on the other, which is implicit in the critique of what Reform was back then. How do they jive?

TK: Secular and agnostic are very different.

NJC: That's for sure. I only use it because both words have been used in relationship to interviews that you've had.

TK: I'm a very serious agnostic.

NJC: The question is, What does a serious agnostic believe in?

TK: A serious agnostic accepts something that seems to me to be a very Jewish thing, which is that you're engaged in probably an interminable struggle with the unknowability of God. It's not an atheist. It's not the same thing as atheism. It's not a certainty that there is no God, or an indifference to that. It's a willingness to be tormented by the fact that as of age thirty-eight, God has not revealed him- or herself to me in a way that I can sufficiently abandon my agnosticism and move on.

Ritual is actually a part of what I think of as the road toward at least a more developed agnosticism, or possibly into faith. I'm very interested in prayer. I can't pray. I've been thinking about it and looking at it from various perspectives. And I've always been very moved by Jewish prayer. I think the most moving scene in both parts of *Angels in America* is when Ethel Rosenberg says the Kaddish for Roy Cohn. And the Kaddish has always been a prayer that . . . I mean, I think it's a sort of a genetic thing. It's almost worked into the gene structure at this point. It has tremendous resonance for me. So does the Sh'ma. And I do believe—I wouldn't be in theater if I didn't believe this—that certain forms of ritual practice can transform one's consciousness through gesture and through design and through ritual. It's about a discipline, also, which, God knows, is a big part of Judaism.

NJC: On some level we might be talking semantics here, and that is that there's such a positivistic tone to *Perestroika,* especially by the time it ends. In your afterword ["With a Little Help from My Friends"], which I thought was beautiful, you wrote, "The world howls without; it is at this moment a very terrible world." Yet we recognize "amidst the gathering dark, paths of resistance, pockets of peace, and places from whence hope may be plausibly expected." And then you go on to talk in several interviews about the fact that it isn't politics that lets you down anymore than Judaism . . . [it's] God that lets you down. "It is we who have failed to make ourselves worthy." And then the interesting line "We who have not prepared the way for the Messianic." If we're talking about definition of a divine presence in the world, you intuitively respond to the world around you and people around you and say that people not only have the ability to change, but people have the ability to change the fabric of their very existence. And that, on some level from a Jewish perspective, resonates with at least one way of looking at God's presence in the world. When we talk about resonances of the divine presence, we talk about looking into people's faces and seeing their potential.

. . .

Your work is almost a kind of postmodern critique of modernity. For two hundred years, we have talked about the power of reason, right? And the triumph of enlightenment. We thought that technology could solve all of the world's problems. We were convinced that reason could pierce anything. And then all of a sudden we wake up in the twentieth century and post-Holocaust era especially, and we realize that reason is only partial, and that the radical individualism of rationalism and modernity has led us to a point where we are individuals simply adrift and not connected. And that reason in and of itself can lead to the use of power that can oppress and hurt people. Ultimately what postmodernism tells us is that we have to be relational selves, that we define ourselves in relationship to the other. We have to take responsibility for ourselves.

I was thinking of Louis in *Angels,* his struggle to relate to other people, the struggle to walk . . . the impulse to walk away, and yet the ability slowly and with great difficulty of coming back as he does at the end of *Perestroika.* And again, the tremendous Jewish sense of that struggle, you know? That ultimately it's through our relation with other people and in community that we come to some higher sense of existence. Louis is really a very powerful Jewish figure struggling with that sense of his Jewishness. Since you said that Louis is the closest character, it's really you, on some level, who's struggling with the other. And the other is other human beings. But the Otherness—that is, with the big "O"—[is] that sense of something divine in other people that can make you even more whole.

TK: Yeah. *[Laughter.]* Postmodern and modernism are very complicated things, because I think of myself as being a modernist and not quite ready for postmodernism in the sense that I'm too terrified by the notion of the decentered subject, and too frightened of the idea of some of the things that postmodernists seem to be rather eager to embrace. It's a radicalism that's more radical than I'm prepared to go. I'm sort of a premodern modernist. I just read an essay describing Susan Sontag as an elegaic modernist, [in] Sohnya Sayres's book on her. And I like that. I identify with the tradition within modernism that is a socialist tradition, and is consequently very concerned with interrelationships. I fully recognize the political usefulness of a lot of postmodernism, and we are clearly past the modernist era, although I think that certainly the literature of modernism predicted the Holocaust. It certainly wouldn't have been a surprise to any of the great writers of modernism, that something like that could happen.

I think that the massacres in Rwanda, or the fact that the war in Sarajevo continues, or the Oklahoma City bombing indicate a movement into a new era. We're starting to deal with a character in this sense that is profoundly disaffected from itself and alienated. I wouldn't know how to write a character like Timothy McVeigh. Except to make him your garden-variety psychotic. But there's probably something more interesting going on there that I'm missing. Or there was a very scary *Nightline* last night with Ted Koppel, talking to these people from Michigan, this town that seems to grow these meshugene people.

NJC: We won't mention his name now.

TK: They were all standing up and talking; they were pretty scary. There's something out there . . . people were putting too much alcohol in their test tubes, or something. I felt afraid that these are not the kind of people that I would be able to write, and so possibly there's a kind of irrelevance on the horizon for me. So in terms of the question of modernism, I don't know.

On the other hand, on a more optimistic note, the kids that were arrested yesterday blocking the four main traffic arteries into Manhattan are instantly recognizable as people who are not only willing to sacrifice, but really sacrifice. Most of them are still in jail. As of five o'clock they were all still in jail, and had been kept there without food and water, some of them by the Giuliani [mayor of New York] administration, which is unprecedented and obscene. These are people who, when you talk to them, not only say, "We're doing this because we can't go to school if we don't stop this budget," but who are also saying, "There are kids coming after us who will never get near CUNY [City University of New York] if we don't stop this." So there's a spirit of sacrifice there and a spirit of commitment and connectiveness that's thrilling and flies in the face of all the wisdom about upcoming generations, the generation X, and that they're not interested in anything but, you know, dancing in clubs. It's not true.

Not on Broadway

Kim Myers

Independent producer Kim Myers interviewed Kushner as a special segment in her ongoing project of filming American playwrights discussing their opinions of and relationship to noncommercial theater. Kushner's experience as a veteran of off-off-, off-, and on-Broadway productions bridged the gaps among the various theater worlds that were Myers's subjects. The interview took place at the Joseph Papp Public Theater in New York, with only Kushner, Myers, and the film crew present.

The first broadcast of segments from the Kushner-Myers hour-long conversation aired on *City Arts*, WNET-TV (Channel 13), in New York, on December 9, 1995. The following is the interview in its entirety.

KIM MYERS: This special, *Not on Broadway,* looks at what is happening in the contemporary theater scene that is not on Broadway. Do you feel in some way a part of a community of writers, of other artists, of people working in the theater—do you feel a sense of community in today's theater world in New York?

TONY KUSHNER: Absolutely. I don't know that the sense of community that I have is limited to New York City, but I feel very much a part of a variety of groups who are attempting various things in the theater. The writing that I am doing is part of a movement of playwrights who are doing similar things or making similar experiments

From *City Arts*, WNET-TV (Channel 13), New York, December 9, 1995. This previously unpublished interview took place on November 11, 1995. The estimated viewing audience was one million people.

with dramatic literary form. I feel very closely connected to a generation of directors and actors that I entered the profession with about six
or seven years ago who are now working pretty much full-time. It's a
very close and important community structure, as opposed to the
sense that one gets when one works in film, where you really feel that
you're in an industry. The theater community is small and belea-
guered but to a certain extent a collective and to a certain extent
communal—the people are supportive of each other and working to
make good theater and genuinely excited as well as jealous and other
things when good theater happens.

KM: What was your first play that was produced in New York?

TK: When I was a graduate student in directing at New York
University's Tisch School of the Arts Graduate Theatre Program—
this was in the early 1980s—I founded, with a group of about twelve
other people, most of them actors, a few designers, a couple of other
writers, a company that was originally called 3P Productions—three
"Ps" were politics, poetry, and popcorn—and then it became Heat and
Light Company. We did a variety of plays, about three or four of
mine—I wrote and directed them—and the very first one was a play
called *The Age of Assassins* about anarchist assassinations at the turn of
the century. It was staged at a wonderful space that's no longer a
theater on Eighteenth Street called the Newfoundland Theater. It
used to be the home of a company called the Medicine Show, which
was a very interesting theater company. We raised the money by send-
ing letters to every person we had ever met asking them to send us five
dollars, and I think we raised about five thousand—no probably much
less than that—two thousand dollars, and we did the whole show with
a cast of eighteen. It was three hours long. It was a fully staged,
nineteenth-century costumed event. It was wild. It was a lot of fun.
Most of our productions were done that way, with money sort of
grubbed up from people who didn't have a lot of money. But you
could do theater for very, very little back then, and there were many,
many wonderful spaces to be rented for very little money. It was
always possible to get a play up on its feet.

KM: Where did your audience come from for that particular play?

TK: We pasted posters all over Soho. It was an exciting time.
People were looking for things happening on the street. There was a
sense that art was happening in New York City and that you really had
to look to find it and that it wouldn't be delivered to your doorstep
every morning by the *New York Times*. I mean, if you really wanted to be
hip to what was happening in the city, you had to pay attention to

what was being put up on the sides of buildings. So we actually got a huge number of our audience, I think, from people who had seen the poster—it was a good poster. And we begged and prayed for a review from the *Village Voice*. We didn't get one. We tried very hard to get one. But that was impossible. In those days, the *New York Times* never reviewed anything; it very, very rarely reviewed anything below Fourteenth Street or in Chelsea. So, we didn't even think about the *New York Times*. That was also a time when a good review in the *Village Voice* could sell out a show for months. We had no ambition like that. We just wanted to sell out a couple of weeks' performances. We did pretty well. We raised enough money to do our next production.

KM: When you wanted to mount a play, originally, did it occur to you to go to an existing venue? Or did it seem the right thing to do—or the only thing to do—to start on your own?

TK: We felt very, very far removed from any existing theater. It would never have occurred to any of us to go to the Public Theater. And we also wanted to be a theater collective. We were very impressed by the legends that were reaching us from England: 784, Monstrous Regiment, and the feminist and socialist theater collectives in Britain that had generated a lot of extraordinary productions and some really great writers, like Caryl Churchill. And there were still a lot of collectives in New York functioning that were inspiring. Mabou Mines was still going. The Wooster Group was beginning. The Performance Group had sort of stopped. Little companies like Medicine Show. Bread and Puppet Theater used to be around a lot. There were a number of companies formed, and that seemed to us to be the ideal. We really wanted to create theater that way. And, of course, we thought eventually we'd get good enough to be asked to come to the Public and perform. But the goal at that point was to build a working community of theater artists in microcosm that could generate material.

It wasn't until four years of doing this that I started to think about taking the work I was writing and showing it to . . . and actually I never did show it. Somebody had come to see one of my productions. Oskar Eustis was visiting from the Eureka Theater in California and he saw the last of our productions, *A Bright Room Called Day*. He saw the play and asked if he could bring [the script] to the Eureka. His company gave it a reading, and then a production, and it had several other productions, including one here at the New York Shakespeare Festival. It just didn't occur to me to go out and hustle scripts. I didn't even really think of myself as a playwright. I wanted to be, you know, JoAnne Akalaitis. I thought myself as a director who created events, and it wasn't until some time had passed that I started thinking of myself as a writer.

KM: How do you collaborate with a director, now that you are thinking of yourself as a writer?

TK: Well, it's all become very institutional. The director-playwright relationship is immensely complicated and difficult. I collaborate very differently with different directors. I have one kind of relationship with George Wolfe, and another kind of relationship with Lisa Peterson. These are people I've worked with. At this point I consider that I have an active relationship with about five or six directors. George is directing my next play *[Henry Box Brown]*. It's a complicated relationship that's made more complicated by the fact that I used to direct and still sometimes think that I should be directing. I've had a lot of struggles with directors, because I tend to give notes like a director and I think like a director, and sometimes I can be a real pain in the butt. Some people have more tolerance for it, others . . . George is particularly great because he isn't terribly ruffled by it. He just ignores me when I start to be too much of a nuisance, and he pays attention when he should. Some directors have seriously thought about not working with me anymore because it gets to be too exasperating.

KM: Is there a desire for you to keep working with the same people again, again, and again—that sense of wanting a continuing creative . . .

TK: Yes. I'm very lucky because I've met a number of directors that I love working with, a number of actors that I love working with. I always envy a little bit people who, like Mamet, find a director [Gregory Mosher] that they work with constantly. Craig Lucas and Norman Renee. These teams of playwright-director. It would be very easy to simply know that the next thing you write will be directed by this person, because this person directs everything you write. And similarly, I envy writers who have had that kind of relationship with a group of actors. In a funny way I sort of developed a company of actors who will simply always be in my plays because I write the parts for them. Stephen Spinella, who played Prior Walter in *Angels,* I've been working with since 1982. He was in this company that I was part of in the early 1980s and I'm sure I will always write lead roles for Stephen. Stephen, Kathy Chalfant, Ellen McLaughlin are some of the actors that I just know I'll work with repeatedly. The idea of companies and of collaboratives and collectives in theater is incredibly good, useful, and important. Lack of material support for that kind of work happening is very much to the detriment of the development and maturation of theater in the United States. It's a great thing to see a group of actors who have worked together for ten years. It's great to see a director who has worked with those actors for ten years. Most companies seem to have a life span. They don't go on forever. But all of the theater that is historically significant and generative of other kinds of theater comes out of some sort of collective movement. Maybe Williams, Miller, and Albee are exceptions. But O'Neill certainly came out of a collective. The Group Theater, all the stuff that was happening off-Broadway and off-off-Broadway. And then nearly everything in Europe. There are places to incubate theater there that we simply don't have.

KM: What writers have influenced your own work? They could be contemporaries as well, who you really consider to be influences or have fed you in some way.

TK: There are so many of them. American, European, classic, anything? It's just this huge list. I'm tremendously influenced by Shakespeare—everybody is, in the sense that that's the Parnassus. You spend your life wishing that you could write two seconds of material that compare to the least graceful two seconds that Shakespeare wrote. It's very depressing actually because it doesn't seem to be human. It's from Mars or something. I tell my playwriting students not to read him when they are getting ready to write, because you just sort of say, "Why bother, it's all been done before." But Shakespeare, Chekhov, Beckett, and Brecht, to some extent Ibsen, are hugely important to me in terms of classic drama. Ben Jonson. I've become a very big O'Neill fan. I didn't used to be, but I'm now very much under the influence, very excited and impressed by the plays and also by the life. I'm really spending a lot of time reading and thinking about it these days. Tennessee Williams is probably all-in-all my favorite playwright and probably all-in-all our greatest playwright. He was a much better writer than O'Neill, maybe even much less powerful ultimately as a dramatist, but a sublime poet.

And then more contemporary people. I'm very influenced by a lot of British writers. Caryl Churchill is a huge influence. Edward Bond, Howard Brenton, David Hare to some extent, David Edgar. The whole British socialist tradition has had a big impact on me. In America—John Guare, Maria Irene Fornes, David Mamet are playwrights that I admire immensely and have drawn a lot from and probably wouldn't be a playwright without them. Among my contemporaries, Mac Wellman, Suzan-Lori Parks, who I think is a phenomenon. Connie Congdon, Ellen McLaughlin—I'm going to leave out people and they're going to be angry with me—Holly Hughes, a lesbian performance artist/playwright, who is astonishing. David Greenspan. It's a pretty big list.

I feel that I'm very lucky that this is a very, very exciting time—I think almost entirely because of the money that has been spent in public support for playwriting through the NEA and through the Ford Foundation or Lila Wallace grants. There are more interesting writers writing now for the theater than at any point in American history. That's completely inarguable. We may not have anybody who is as absolutely great as Tennessee Williams, although there are a couple of people who I think will be up there. Suzan-Lori Parks will be for sure. The rest of us may occasionally do something that will last. But there are a lot of very remarkable people writing now. Donald Margulies is an amazing writer. And I feel embedded in that—you had asked about community—I feel very much a part of that hubbub. I always envy Jacobean writers. It would have been so exciting, dangerous and scary at the same time, but exciting to have been a writer in England at the beginning of the seventeenth century with all those writers and so much at stake politically and culturally. This is a similarly dangerous and provocative time and there are a lot of people doing it. The Elizabethans and Jacobeans had patronage from the aristocracy and the crown, and we used to have the NEA and foundation grants. We're in a lot of trouble now. It will be another dark age of playwriting when that money dries up, which it seems to be in the process of doing.

KM: That leads me to the themes for your work. Is the impulse for your writing, one might say, of a political nature or at least partially of a political nature?

TK: Yes. I'm just completely a political animal. It's something I can't help. I don't think of things without thinking of them politically. It's not a good thing or a bad thing. It's just my particular take on the world. I feel that politics is life. Politics and everyday life are inseparable. The political is simply the striving for better life, striving for a decent life. It's the side of struggle in life, and so what else can you do as a playwright, but write about politics. It's always dialectical. The theater is always about dialogue. It's about debate. It's about "he said," "she said." You know, back-and-forth controversy and contention. And that, I think, automatically makes it political, even when it's trying desperately not to be. Simply the presence of the dialectic makes it political. I want very much to write political theater because I think it's exciting. Those stages always seem to me to be debating platforms for society. It's the old sort of Athenian ideal—you go to see the biggest issues of your society's life debated in some hopefully exciting way.

Right now I'm writing a big three-play trilogy about money, because I feel that the most appalling thing about what's going on in Washington now is that we—in this country and in the world (this is in France as well after the strikes)—the people have lost the ability to talk and think critically and politically about the economy. It's great to see people in France saying, "Well, we don't care that you say you must have a balanced budget. We expect certain things out of life and you better go and figure out another way to get them for us, because that is what your job is. We're not accepting this economic nonsense. You're not screwing up our lives." We don't do that in America anymore. We've sort of come to accept these things as givens, as though somebody was going to say, "It's going to snow tomorrow." It's time to start to talk politically about money again. So these plays are all plays about money.

I don't know if you saw in the coverage of the French uprising—this worker, this middle-aged guy, who as reported in the *New York Times*, turned to the television camera when asked, "Why are you demonstrating, why are you protesting?" And he said, "Well, because money has gotten so tight that now one simply can't afford to go to the theater anymore." It was so amazing to see that interview in the *Times*—it was apparently repeated a number of times on French television. Here you would be laughed at for saying that, but they made an incredibly important point: because of the level of government participation and the high standard of living that's maintained in France, this man, who is a worker, believes that going to the theater is part of what a guarantee of happiness and a decent life should be about, not just subsistence living, but actually also having a way into culture. I thought that was unbelievably great.

KM: Would you say that the theater does have a vital place still in this culture?

TK: Absolutely. In part because it's more political than the narrative mimetic art forms like film. Film can be political, but I don't think it has to be. There is a dreamlike quality to film, and film is a finished process. There are ways in which film has a less immediate political taste and presence. It's less dangerous in a certain sense, because it's finished—it's a finished product. Theater is political for that reason. Also it's labor intensive and not capital intensive, so you don't have the banks getting involved as much. It's why there might be more political

237

potential possibly in cable television than in network, and maybe more than in film, because the more big money is necessary—and big money is necessary to make even a small film—the less freedom you have. When you start getting into major motion pictures—the closest thing we have to a political filmmaker is Oliver Stone. I mean, what are his politics? What is *Nixon*? What was *JFK*? It's like we say in Yiddish, "a gedulah mein babe," like, you know, "Thanks Grandma." He's hopeless, confused.

KM: I agree with you. I think he's a nut—

TK: He is.

KM: Conspiracy theory is not politics.

TK: No. And *Nixon* is unbelievable. Have you seen it?

KM: I haven't seen it.

TK: It's unbelievable. He basically . . .

KM: . . . supports him?

TK: Yeah. Three hours and he never talks about Watergate as this incredible challenge to due process and constitutional democracy.

KM: [Oliver Stone] is definitely out there.

That segues into your Broadway experience. Unlike many younger playwrights, you have had the Broadway experience. Could you speak about that and what some of the realities were that you may have faced in that transition.

TK: I had a great time on Broadway. My time on Broadway was not typical. So, I don't think that everyone who goes to Broadway is going to have a great time. And there are a lot of problems with it. I had very, very good producers. They were very respectful of the play and the play was successful. They were generous. They have by this point almost made all their money back, and the national tour is in the black. But it was a rough road. And they never got silly, or they never got spooked and tried to do anything sleazy and commercial to make it sell. All went very nicely. It ran for eighty-five weeks, which is a very respectable run.

It's scary to have a bottom line of profit that you have to watch each week. It cost close to $170,000 a week to run *Angels* on Broadway. You had to sell that many tickets or more and that got to be frightening. There are repertory theaters in Europe where *Angels* has been running now for two or three years, and it draws half audiences. But it doesn't matter. That's a much nicer way of doing it.

By being on Broadway the play had a chance to be sort of a cultural event that it just wouldn't have had off-off-Broadway. Probably if you talked to Anna Deavere Smith, she would say something similar. It's stupid. It really shouldn't be the case. Seriously, it doesn't happen on Broadway anymore at all. It's entirely the product of off-Broadway and the regional theater. And it has always been that. Every single important playwright that this country has ever produced and every single important piece of theater that this country has ever produced—except for the big great musicals—were all developed regionally. And even all the big musicals were developed on the road and then brought into New York. Nothing really gets born in the theater district. It's a showcase. But it still is the heart of the American theatrical history in a funny way. You get a kind of attention there that you don't get anywhere else. You get money there that you don't get anywhere else. You get opening-night presents like you get nowhere else. Very nice things. It's a very snazzy event. And I loved all of that. It was great.

I don't know that I will ever be back on Broadway again. It's not my goal. It wasn't my goal when I wrote *Angels in America* to get on Broadway. I think if it happens it happens. But you have to be willing to let it happen if it happens and not care if it doesn't. To write plays to go to Broadway, you would have to write *Moon over Buffalo* or something and good luck to you; I hope you make a lot of money and die happy.

I had a play in the New York Theater Workshop—*Slavs!*—that ran for two months. It was completely sold out. It was too big to move. A lot of people read the book [*Thinking about the Longstanding Problems of Virtue and Happiness*] now and say, "When is the play going to be done in New York?" New York Theater Workshop is an astonishing place, a great, great, great theater. So it's a mixed bag. On the other hand, working off-off-Broadway again was a great joy, because it's smaller and more intimate. The money is not hemorrhaging in the kind of horrifying way that it did . . . you know I was six days late turning in the rewrite for *Perestroika*. If it hadn't been for George I would have just committed suicide. I was being screamed at daily by everyone, because I was really costing people tens of thousands of dollars. And George is completely and totally impassable if he wants to be. He just says, "Leave him alone and go away," and people do, because he's an immensely strong person. But still, because I was six days late, he was six days late in tech, so we had to cancel six performances of *Millennium Approaches*, which was already running. It cost like $360,000 because I had a block about getting *Perestroika* finished. It's the most expensive writer's block in history, maybe. It's really horrifying when I think about that. If I'm a little late off-off-Broadway, people will adjust and finagle and things will be fine. It's a much healthier way. I could never have written any kind of serious play, I think, for that arena in that arena. It just wouldn't work.

KM: That means when you wrote *Slavs!* you must have known that you weren't writing for Broadway. That you absolutely knew. So this was not in your consciousness—you were just like moving on to the next thing. You wanted to write. Is that how you think of yourself in the future?

TK: Yes. I think it's nice to know specifically what you're writing for. The next play *[Henry Box Brown]* will be at the National Theatre in London. That's a coproduction with the New York Shakespeare Festival. And then George will bring it here. It seems like something that might conceivably be Broadway material, but it isn't important to me that it gets there. The important thing is that I write something that I really like. It's a very big play. I tend to write really big plays. But some big plays, like *Angels,* only have casts of eight people. So it's a big little play. You can actually do it with very little money, and theater companies are now doing that. This new play has a cast of billions of people, so it's going to be huge and expensive, and only a theater the size of the National or of the Public could produce it. Oddly enough, the bigger the play now the more impossible to get it to Broadway. It's not that Broadway's more accommodating to theatrical ambition. It's considerably less accommodating, unless you're Andrew Lloyd Webber—God help you. And if you don't have a chandelier going up and down, a serious play on Broadway is going to have to be pretty small to be a moneymaking proposition.

KM: So, it's virtually impossible to develop, to create serious work for Broadway. Do you think that there was a reason why *Angels* was able to make the move to Broadway when it did—I know you had good producers and all of that, but was there something about the nature of that play at that moment in time?

TK: Yes, I think it was really lucky. I think it came along at a good historical moment for it. The January when Clinton was being inaugurated, the play started rehearsals in New York for the Broadway opening. It opened in Los Angeles for its sort of out-of-town tryout—the big performance at the [Mark] Taper [Forum] was the weekend of the election and I think that there was a very strong sense in the country that it was time to overturn the Reagan Revolution. The play that was very critical of the Reagan Revolution was sort of well timed. It was also right after Pat Buchanan had made his hideous speech about a cultural war here in the United States and he tried to use homophobia as sort of the most salable and palpable form of bigotry available. People were ready to look at AIDS and look at their own homophobia in a new way to prove him wrong. And the gays in the military thing was happening. It was a good time for the play to show up, and then, quite frankly, the most influential drama critic [Frank Rich] the country has ever had had written three rave reviews for the play—twice in London and then once in L.A. It had already been a hit at the National. It was sort of primed. It was a pretty safe bet in that regard. So when it opened, its first box-office day was the biggest single ticket sale for a serious play ever on Broadway. It was something people wanted to see. A lot of that is just good luck. Some of it is good timing, but a lot of it is just luck.

KM: What do you think it takes to maintain a life in the theater? What do you think about that for yourself as you look forward?

TK: Well, I'm thinking of Rosemary Tischler, the associate producer at the Public, who said to me when I was working on *Perestroika*, "It always feels like it's the next play—it's all about the next play—and it has to be great and it has to be everything you want it to be." But then she said, "You really have to think of yourself as an artist with a lifetime of work ahead and it's finally the shape of the entire life and it's the shape of the entire body of work that matters." I'd like very much to have written, let's say, twenty full-length plays, and I'd like very much for three or four or five of them to be really good, and I'd like to see that I keep getting better, that everything that I write is a little bit better than the last thing that I wrote, and that I don't feel that I started to get stale or slide. If I feel that way, I hope that I'll have the strength of character to say, "Try something else, you're not doing this as well as you use to." And I think I probably would, because I am not addicted to theater in the way that some people are. I'm reasonably suspicious of theater. There are other noble things that one can do with one's life.

[Theater] is not a profession in which people, generally speaking, grow old gracefully, and in part because it's so marginal. It's all sort of by the seat of your pants and the economics of it are so shaky. There is no tenure and there are no pensions. You can be sixty and still facing a life of insecurity after having done a life of good work and that's very hard. But there are people who have been around for a long time and have really contributed mightily to American culture. Joseph Papp first and foremost among them in a way. That was completely a life of the theater and not really about anything else. And he was a force for good—not only in the arts—but in the American cultural and political life as well. You always want a life to emulate—and that's a good life to emulate.

KM: Where do you think the most alive theaters are at the moment—you've mentioned a couple of places that you've enjoyed working with. What do you think are some of the most vivid spots in the theater scene right now?

TK: Well, in New York City, the theaters that excite me the most are New York Theater Workshop, which I think is an off-off-Broadway theater in the classic mold—a wide spectrum of performance and theater and very political and alternately sort of edging toward the mainstream and going very avant-garde. It's a real place where different kinds of people can work. I'm very impressed by Jim Nicola, who's the producer there. The other theater that I think is significant and probably—in my opinion—the most significant theater in the country right now is the Shakespeare Festival, under George Wolfe. I think what George is doing is thrilling. For one thing, it's multiculturalism in vigorous practice as opposed to halfhearted, apologized, tokenistic, wishy-washy "multiculturalism" which doesn't work, and then everyone says, "Multiculturalism, you know, is a terrible thing." But this theater is producing an astonishing variety—a genuinely multicultured menu of theatrical experience. And the audiences are becoming more diverse as a result of that. Younger people are coming. People from all parts of New York City are coming in, because this is beginning to be known as a place that does theater that speaks immediately to contemporary experience and life. It's an immensely exciting place to be. It's a kind of a model for that word—that much maligned but I think incredibly invaluable word—"multiculturalism." You know it's the beginning—it's utterly overcoming age—to paraphrase a line from a Mark Doty poem. It's about what's about to arrive, and that makes it tremendously future-oriented and exciting.

KM: I think it's true. You see it in the lobby of the theater. It's very alive. And it is very young, which is encouraging.

What do you think was your motivation for going into the theater in the first place? Is there one thing that you can think of, a play that you saw, a writer? What motivated you to begin to write theater?

TK: There are a lot of different things. My mother, who's a professional musician, was an amateur actress, and I'm sure that that's the deep oedipal reason for doing it—that I wanted, you know, to do what my mother was doing. And I loved watching her onstage and I know that I fell in love with the theater because she was in love with it. The classic theater queen's answer. I wanted to be sort of a serious political person, so when I was an undergraduate I loved going to the theater, but I thought this isn't the profession that one could really follow with much dignity if one wanted to be part of the political debate. Reading Brecht was the thing that gave me a sense of how one could be both serious about politics and serious about theater at the same time. Brecht had an immense impact in that regard.

The last thing—and it's sort of a tragedy—while teaching playwriting classes at NYU this semester, it struck me over and over again that the off-off-Broadway movement and the off-Broadway movement—which to a certain extent were a function of real estate in Manhattan—were destroyed by the depredations of the Koch administration and real estate speculation in New York. There are still incredibly vital practitioners, but the scene that existed when I first came to New York in the 1970s and that continued into the mid-1980s doesn't exist anymore. It's become absorbed more into the mainstream. It's not as clearly an alternate version of what theater is—and there's much less of it, it seems to me. I'm sure it will come back; it's not gone. It's still around, but it needs fresh blood and more real estate. That had a huge impact on me. I saw JoAnne Akalaitis's Mabou Mines production of *Dead End Kids* and that brought together the political theater—Brecht and the imagistic theater of the American avant-garde and extraordinary acting and a political response to an immediate crisis—that was just spellbinding, shattering, and a great challenge. I thought, "Well, OK, this is what I want to do."

KM: Whereas people talk about the change from the 1960s to the 1990s, you see a change in this past decade, when you've been involved in the theater. As we move into the 1990s, it becomes even more different.

TK: It's a combination of Ed Koch and AIDS also. I keep saying to people you'll never get to see what Charles Ludlum was like onstage, but he was the funniest person that ever lived. But saying that, of course, isn't even funny and you can't show what a Charles Ludlum did and there are so many—Ethel Eichelberger—there are so many people that have been lost. Ron Vawter, you know, has recently . . . Harry Kondolean. There are so many people who have died of the epidemic. And it also just becomes too hard when I say to my students, "Don't sit around waiting to be produced. Get a company together. Get some money together and go and produce it." Then I realize, of course, where are they going to do this? You can't go and rent a shoebox. We could go and rent a space for two weeks for five hundred dollars. You can't do that anymore. And I'm sure that during the 1950s and 1960s there was an infinitely more vital scene going on than there was when I got here in the 1970s and 1980s. But it was still at least dying beautifully and spectacularly. It feels now in the 1990s—New York having been completely sold out to real estate interests—it feels very hard to find and very scattered. When you asked is there a community—there is a theater community, but that sense of an avant-garde community is somewhat injured, and not particularly clear and vital at the moment.

Why Get Out of Bed?

Anna Deavere Smith

City Arts & Lectures in San Francisco brought together Anna Deavere Smith and Tony Kushner in a benefit program for The Women's Foundation, whereby all proceeds from the admissions fees went to the nonprofit, grant-awarding institution. Hosting the evening was Jaime Lujan, a board member of BRAVA! for Women in the Arts, a multicultural, feminist theater in the Bay area, celebrating its tenth anniversary of dedication to new works by and for women of color.

Introducing Smith and Kushner as "two of America's extraordinary and innovative voices" in the theater, whose "roots are in San Francisco," Luhan captured the theme of the evening's event by emphasizing how each artist's "work exemplifies the relationship between art and politics." The program began with Smith and Kushner alternately reading from their own pieces, followed by an extended conversation between the two.

ANNA DEAVERE SMITH: One of the adventures, I think, that both of us have been on, Tony, is this adventure of challenging form and changing form. When I saw *Angels in America* for the first time, which was in Los Angeles, I thought, "My God! This is like . . ." I remember reading

From City Arts & Lectures, Inc., Herbst Theater, San Francisco, April 12, 1996. This previously unpublished interview took place before a crowd of nine hundred people, each of whom paid $16 a ticket. Reprinted by permission of Anna Deavere Smith and the Watkins/Loomis Agency.

about Giraudoux that he did as much as he could to test everybody in the theater: the stage managers, the designers, the actors, the directors. When he wrote *Ondine* he put a waterfall in just to see if they could figure out how to make a waterfall. And it was a kind of a big deal in those days. Of course, there's so much about *Angels in America* that tests everybody. And each time that I've seen it I think about that. I was wondering if you could start by talking just a little bit about what it is to test not just yourself, but so many people. And ultimately, you've tested the theater.

TONY KUSHNER: There's something that Heiner Müller (the East German playwright who died in December this year), who I think is one of the great writers of this century, said: only literature that offers resistance to the theater is of any interest. It's a very Marxist idea of theater practice that whatever you do has to be difficult for conventional practice to absorb. It's the sort of sand-in-the-oyster idea that only by challenging do you cause the form to grow. There's always a kind of deadening complacency with received wisdom in theatrical form. I think it's what's killed the American musical and is actually now beginning to break up a little bit with something like *Noise/Funk* [*Bring in 'da Noise, Bring in 'da Funk*], George [Wolfe]'s new show on Broadway. There's a very quick leap to the formulaic, and hanging onto the formulaic. Commercialism in the theater guides that. It's also what I feel very much about your work. That in a certain way it confronts conventional theater practice and demands a rethinking of forms, a rethinking of what theater is supposed to do. That's the only reason, really, to do it—to see if you can figure out what direction it should be growing in, and how to participate in that.

ADS: When I saw *Noise/Funk,* as a matter of fact, I was thinking that's one of the good things about the theater. In fact, it's harder for people to do that in films. Some say the theater is dying. But if we realize how much space we really do have in the theater to test and change form, I think there's a lot of life in that.

TK: Yeah. You mentioned Studs Turkel [during Smith's reading earlier in the program] and there are certain performance artists, playwrights, and performers who have done work that's clearly antecedent to your work. *Angels in America* in a certain sense is a conventional narrative play. So there are always antecedents. You're referring back to something, or in *Noise/Funk,* which is basically a tap-dance show . . .

ADS: Right.

TK: . . . but creates an entirely new form by, in a sense, drawing very strongly on the past and looking at what was interesting in the past, and then seeing how to develop it. One of the things that we were talking about talking about . . . this sort of mutual conversation thing, it's very strange!

ADS: Well, let's test the form. Let's test the form of supposed real-life conversations in front of eight hundred people. *[Laughter.]*

TK: How's the apartment? How's the . . . *[Laughter.]* We decided to go after four big issues in the beginning. And one is the changing forms idea . . .

ADS: Connected to . . .

TK: . . . this question that you asked when we were sitting here doing mike checks, which is how come the two of us wound up onstage together? What is it that we share in common? Because we wound up together on several . . .

ADS: Well, you worked with me on *Twilight [Twilight: Los Angeles, 1992]*.

TK: I worked with you on *Twilight*. I came and sort of gushed all over you when I first saw *Fires in the Mirror*, which was one of the most important experiences . . .

ADS: I came and gushed all over you at that preview at . . .

TK: "Fabulous. Fabulous. You're fabulous, dear." *[Laughter.]*

ADS: We both worked with George [Wolfe].

TK: We've both worked with George. We both love George. I really loved your George tonight [Smith's performance of Wolfe earlier in the program]. *[Laughter.]* That was dead on. George in a more manic mood. We were talking about what sort of things we have in common. What kind of things in the past have fed the work that we're doing in the present. So why don't we do that a little bit?

ADS: I was hoping that this issue of form could somehow be related to that. One thing we know we share in common is a fondness for and a looking to Bertolt Brecht. So when's the first time you met him?

TK: Well, he died a month after I was born, so I never *[laughter]* did. But I encountered him at Columbia when I was an undergraduate and a Marxist art history professor of mine gave me a book to read, *The Necessity of Art* by Ernst Fisher, that made me incredibly angry, because I thought that it was Stalinist and dangerous. That started me on a path of looking around at different people that had written about art and Marxism, and trying to understand why this person whose political work I admired a lot liked this stuff. And that led me directly to Brecht and to Brecht's theories. I think I was looking for a model of a political artist who was engaged and committed politically, and who had generated, who had found some way of fusing integrally both politics and aesthetics, and Brecht really did. It's a really brilliant marriage of Marxist theory as theater practice. The first time that I saw *Fires in the Mirror* and the first time I saw you perform, I thought I'd never seen anything that I would really actually call Brecht onstage before, until I saw your work. What *is* your connection to Brecht?

ADS: It's really interesting, I think, if I could analyze both of us at the same time. *[Laughter.]*

TK: Good luck!

ADS: You came to Brecht from the theoretical, with a theoretical desire. I came to Brecht because of performance. I was in London when I was in college with no idea about theater at all. I wasn't a theater major. But we could go to the theater really cheaply. It was something like three shillings, six . . . that's not very much money at all. And I saw *Arturo Ui*. I don't think I'd seen any Brecht before that. I didn't know about Brecht. I just knew I had never seen performances like that.

TK: Yeah.

ADS: There was something about them which, as I look back on it now, I would say was probably less genuine than, say, other plays I'd seen in London. *Boys in the Band* was on that year—even *Hair*. There was still this commitment in those plays to have behavior that looked real. I'd been used to that commitment in the theater before, even sort of going to the all-black playhouse in Baltimore called the Arena Stage and seeing black people walk around and do *Dial M for Murder* in these British accents. I mean, there was still this *[laughter]* . . . this way that we thought it was real, you know? And we'd say, "My God, it was so real!" even though, you know . . . And the same person doing a British accent in that would do a very extroverted reading of Paul Lawrence Dunbar. It all seemed so real. So I'd never seen anything, if I look back on it now, that was in a way not doing that. And because it wasn't doing that, it seemed more naked to me. I was really excited by the theatricality and the color of it.

TK: The theatricality you were doing in the last monologue . . . [when] you got to the part where you were crying. I've always watched you, trying to think, "Well, is this in part because of some specific technique of yours as a performer, or is it simply because you're acting material that you have gathered in an interview and shaped as a writer?" But [it's to] the extent that the writing is quotation, that it's announced as quotation, that one is put into a very, very complicated relationship to the emotions that the emotions that you're expressing provoke. It is that kind of development of critical consciousness that Brecht talks about. I was very, very moved by what you were doing. And I was also thinking, "But of course, Anna is doing this person who was speaking to Anna and crying while she was saying these words. So we know that Anna is, in a sense, mirroring this person." It becomes both an inside and outside kind of performance at the same time that it's intellectually as complicated as it is emotionally complicated. That's something that one rarely sees in theater performance. That's why I think of it as incredibly Brechtian.

. . .

ADS: I always admire people who can keep their sense of humor in the most dire circumstances. When I interviewed Studs Turkel, he told me that his radio station told him that he just better calm down. He pretended he didn't know what they were talking about. They said, "Look, Studs! This is time for people to stand up!" So he stood up. *[Laughter.]* He said, "When I get in those kind of circumstances, I just can't help myself." *[Laughter.]* "I know I'll get in worse trouble, but I just can't help myself." And one of the things I admire about you is your bravery. To write to the president [Clinton] in such a way.

TK: He sent me back a copy of his State of the Union Address *[laughter]* signed, his own . . . *[Laughter.]* I wrote him a letter saying, "I hated your State of the Union Address so much that I almost sent this back to you, but I figured it would have cash value in a couple of years, so . . ." *[Laughter.]*

ADS: Backstage, as we were trying to find our talking points in this true-seeming conversation, we . . . you suggested to me—I'm obviously black and Tony is obviously Jewish—we haven't really talked about black-Jewish relationships before. You suggested to me that blacks and Jews are not politically at odds, really, unless you're talking about revolution. I thought that was really fascinating. And I wondered if you would expand on that, because I told you, "No, don't say anymore. We have to . . ."

TK: Yeah. It's tricky, because it was a remark that came after about thirty minutes of talking about it, so it's hard to sort of unpack it. We were talking about your view that the notion that there was at one point a period of union between blacks and Jews that disintegrated is, to a great degree, fictional, which I agree with. My point was that there has always been one kind of union, which is in terms of voting patterns, that blacks and Jews during the period of time that both groups have been enfranchised have always voted very similarly. More similarly than any other two groups on the American progressive Left. Both groups are situated on the Left. I mean, they vote progressively.

As I get older and older and older, my politics become more uncomfortable to me in the sense that they become more evolutionary socialist, rather than revolutionary socialist. I become more skeptical the more history I read about the effectiveness of revolution as a mode of political change, and more interested in the idea that evolution is a better model, that violent breaks in the political flow lead more often to aberrations than they do to real progress. I'm not sure that I believe that. But I think I believe that sometimes. To be comfortable with evolution you have to be physically comfortable, because it's going to take a while. Poor people are less physically comfortable. They can less afford the evolutionary process because they're starving to death, or they don't have a place to live, or they're subject to various kinds of oppression and brutalization. An appalling percentage of the African American population in this country lives in poverty. Consequently the comfort with evolution is something that Jews maybe are feeling more than African Americans. The question then becomes for me one of racism, which I believe is the most intractable form of oppression in this country. Is it breakable by an evolutionary development of pluralist democracy, or will there need to be an uprising, such as the one that you analyze and represent in *Twilight?*

ADS: Well, it's also will there need to be an uprising, or, like you say, there was an uprising.

TK: Yeah.

ADS: Do you know what I mean? And so what, right? There was [Louis Farrakhan's] Million Man March, which caused a lot of anxiety in many corners beforehand, and so what, right? I mean, part of this to me has to do with what is real and what is even symbolic. For example, the idea that Jews and blacks have lost something that they had. I'm struggling with that now, because I don't know if the union we had was real, or if it was symbolic. And the media very quickly takes what's real and makes it symbolic by trying to figure it out.

TK: Yeah.

ADS: You know. But not really figuring it out. Putting sentences, full sentences, on top of it, like "the uprising," right? So then we can put it in the can, right? And that's the end of that. It would take a lot, I think, before there were another such uprising.

TK: What are your feelings about the "uprising" since you first started working on *Twilight?* I've seen four different incarnations of the play. It was an enormous amount of material and the way that you've shaped it has changed each time I've seen it. I wanted to ask you about that, your changing feelings about the uprising. I mean, do you believe, finally, that racism in this country is conquerable by democratic means? You had said when I first asked you this question that you were feeling a certain despair. I don't want to put words in your mouth about the sort of death of multiculturalism as a part of the national discussion . . .

ADS: Well, I don't want to say it's dead yet. That's not really up to me, and it's not fair, because maybe people in this audience still believe in that possibility.

TK: Well, so, talk about it. In discussing affirmative action earlier, you also had mentioned it, and I think that's really important.

ADS: When Tony and I worked together on *Twilight* we spent a lot of time with George in New York trying to create a section of the play, which was kind of a multicultural dream. We looked very hard through all the material to find a really positive, good-thinking Asian American, Latino, white, black. And we constructed that. In this version that I've just completed, that is kind of not the case, you know. In its place I have something called a roundtable, which is just fragments of monologues. No conversation. Some of the events this year for me, the Million Man March being one of them, the O.J. [Simpson] verdict being another, really have tested this possibility of a conversation across the bounds of culture. And as I look at what's ahead of us, I think in affirmative action I see a lot of splintering. In *Twilight,* I kind of gave . . . maybe I thought it wasn't realistic anymore to put out all well thought-out, positive platforms.

TK: Yeah. So when you say that it's been tested, it's in terms of a watershed moment like the Million Man March or certainly the O.J. verdict. Can you characterize it in terms of optimism or pessimism now? Can you characterize it in terms of what you see in these events as predictive to a future course, or to what we should do politically in terms of shaping the . . . and who are you going to vote for in nineteen ninety-. . . . *[Laughter.]*

ADS: Right. I can't say. Yeah. Well . . .

TK: You can't say in the sense of . . .

ADS: I never say.

TK: Oh! OK. I'm voting for . . .

ADS: Who are you going to vote for in nineteen ninety- . . .

TK: Oh, I'm voting for Bill, of course! *[Laughter.]*

ADS: Not only that, you have strong feelings about what happens if it's not Bill, right?

TK: I think that if Clinton loses this election, we might as well all give up. *[Laughter.]* A Republican House, a Republican Senate, and a Republican president are absolutely the end of the last seventy years of progressive work in this country. It's like somebody just grabbing a handle and flushing the whole country. *[Laughter.]* This is the scariest moment in American political history in the last fifty years. Maybe I'm being hyperbolic but . . .

ADS: OK, so if we . . . Let's say that happens. Let's imagine . . .

TK: But you didn't answer those questions that I was asking.

ADS: What? Well, what I said in answer—I tried to answer them by saying that I think that the dream, you know, the multicultural dream maybe has to be reconceived. And that after the "uprising," I probably thought the dream was still powerful enough to pull us through. But it probably now has to be reconceived. In that way I am, as Cornel West is and as I quote him in *Twilight,* a prisoner of hope. As he says, whereas in optimism you look at the situation and you think it looks pretty good, and you figure it's pretty good by all the things out there that tell you it's good. But in terms of hope you look and you go, "Doesn't look good at all. Doesn't look good at all!" *[Laughter.]* And you decide that in spite of it not looking good, you're going to go forward, right?

TK: Yeah.

ADS: And I would say that's what I would have to offer.

. . .

TK: You would call yourself a political artist, I would assume.

ADS: Yeah.

TK: I would call myself that. I think that's one of the reasons that we're here. As a political theater artist, do you feel that it's necessary—that it's your responsibility as an artist—to provide your audience with hope? To imprison them in the same hope that you're imprisoned in?

ADS: Is it a responsibility or is it more like Studs Turkel? I mean, that you just can't help yourself? *[Laughter.]*

TK: Well, I don't know. That's the question. *[Applause.]*

ADS: It's very hard for me to have ended the reading that I did on such a sad note as Paulette Jenkins. If it were a show, I would end, you know, with the incarcerated woman who told me that what gets her through all this is when she wakes up in the morning and she hears the birds, and it reminds her of her grandmother and her grandfather to look at the birds, and the dawn as she goes to work. I would try to end on this; I can't resist that.

TK: Yeah. The line in the Cornel piece—which wasn't in the Broadway version, but which is in the Marines Memorial, San Francisco version of *Twilight*—the idea of being a prisoner of hope is a very powerful thought for me, because I do feel that in a sense audiences and people in this country expect hope almost as a kind of palliative.

ADS: What do you think about that? Is that good?

TK: I don't know.

ADS: People kept asking me that in my work, and they probably ask you, too. "Where is the hope?" You know, "Where is the hope, where is the hope?" Even when I watch the movies, there's this great dream for the hopeful. So many movies have, no matter what the circumstances are . . .

TK: And you sort of wonder . . . I mean, my friend, Kimberly Flynn, who also worked on *Twilight,* read me this great Walter Benjamin quote a couple of days ago saying that the biggest trap for people to fall into is not despair, but to be saying to themselves, "Well, we've hit rock bottom. It can't possibly get any worse."

ADS: Ah!

TK: And that in point of fact . . .

ADS: It could.

TK: . . . that's a mistake, because . . .

ADS: Right.

TK: . . . of course, it can and it will get worse. *[Laughter.]*

ADS: But! But! But the human spirit has always, you know, put its foot onto the worst. And the fact that we can go further and further down is some kind of a proof that we, you know, I don't know if we can come up, but that we can move! *[Laughter.]* You know?

TK: There's that great speech in *Mother Courage* when the chaplain talks about this man who's been to the wars, this war that never ends. He talks about him and his incredible ability to endure. You blow off one leg and he hops around on the leg that he's got left. You blow off both legs and he crawls. Through the course of the speech, and it's one of the great speeches of all time, I think, the character is transformed from a person into something that's not quite a person anymore, just by the sheer tenacity. You feel like it would almost be more human to die here, and that there is something that Brecht is saying, that at a certain point our ability to endure anything . . .

ADS: Right.

TK: . . . is somewhat obscene, and . . .

ADS: Do you think that?

TK: Well, I do think that in a sense to count on it is obscene, because we do. We are reassured by the fact that people who live in terrible, inhuman conditions of poverty keep going. And that some of them hold themselves together . . .

ADS: But many of them don't keep going.

TK: And many of them don't. But we always have those few people that the president hauls out on the State of the Union Address and says, "And here's Joe so-and-so, and we've made this person live in hell, and look, they're still smiling!"

ADS: Or read something . . . how it affects . . .

TK: Yeah, exactly. And that's kind of like, eeahh! You know? *[Laughter.]*

ADS: Do you want to ask your last question?

TK: Are we going to sing? We're going to sing . . .

ADS: Should we sing?

TK: . . . "Midnight Train to Georgia" now.

ADS: Yeah, good.

TK: No, we're not really going to do that. I'll ask you my last question, which is why get out of bed in the morning? *[Laughter.]*

ADS: It's a very simple answer, because I love life! And I think it's precious! *[Applause.]* Why get out of the bed in the morning, Tony?

TK: Well, on many mornings recently I haven't been getting out. *[Laughter.]* I don't know. I think I would answer probably the same thing. I love life and I love being alive. And I also think increasingly I get out of bed in the morning because I'm getting angrier and angrier, and I'm getting too angry to stay . . .

ADS: Right. You can't stay there.

TK: . . . in bed.

ADS: That's great! So you get up growling!

TK: Get up really nasty and mean and ready to . . .

ADS: Go to the phone.

TK: . . . read the newspaper and take somebody's face off. Absolutely! *[Laughter.]* So . . . *[Applause.]*

ADS: Thank you so much for joining us!

TK: Yeah, thanks everyone! *[Applause.]*

Poetry, Plays, Politics, and Shifting Geographies

Naomi Wallace

On March 9, 1997, Naomi Wallace's *One Flea Spare* opened at the Public Theater. A Kentucky native, Wallace had seen most of the world premieres of her work in England, from the Royal Shakespeare Company and London's Bush Theatre, to the Royal National Theatre. Along the way to New York, *One Flea Spare* had already won for its author the 1996 Susan Blackburn Prize and the 1996 Kesselring Prize, and before the season ended, it would be honored in New York with the 1997 OBIE Award for Best Play.

Kushner met Wallace during October 1991, when he was a National Endowment for the Humanities guest resident in the Department of Theatre Arts' Playwrights Project at the University of Iowa. Kushner taught a workshop and reviewed M.F.A. candidates' playscripts, including Wallace's, during his brief residency. Several years later (1995), Kushner directed the American premiere of Wallace's award-winning *In the Heart of America* at the Long Wharf Theatre (New Haven, Connecticut).

Kushner accepted the Public Theater's invitation to have a conversation with Wallace to be published, in part, in its March 1997 *Stagebill,* the program audience members would receive when attending *One Flea Spare.* The two writers got

From "We Are Not Only Ourselves," *Public Access,* March 1997, 10, 12, 14, 50. Additional material is from Wallace and Kushner's unpublished transcript of their November 9, 1996, conversation, from which "We Are Not Ourselves" is an excerpt.

together at Kushner's Union Square office and covered a wide range of topics.

TONY KUSHNER: The only other person I ever interviewed in my life is Liza Minnelli. What do you think of Liza Minnelli?

NAOMI WALLACE: I thought she was pretty cool, actually.

TK: I wanted to ask you, while we're on the subject of Liza Minnelli, about gay men in your plays. I'm going to go all over the place. It's interesting because in most of your plays that I know, there is a very strong element of male homoeroticism. Can you talk about that?

NW: Can I talk about that? I've always been interested in sexuality in my plays, and for me, writing from a different place.

TK: What do you mean, a different place?

NW: You know, me being [a] straight, white woman—I'd say bisexual, but I've been practicing straight for quite a few years, now—writing other sexualities that are in clash with mainstream views of sexuality. The first time I did that was *In the Heart of America* and I wanted to write about soldiers and it was scary for me at the beginning. I've always been able to write men, straight men, but to write gay men . . .

TK: Even with your straight men, there's an element of sexual tension. It's all about sort of power and sexuality.

NW: I've always been fascinated by the body and dealing with sexuality and the body; I feel like that's central and the body is a political being. Also physically damaged bodies, damaged through social roles or labor. It has something to do with a different kind of sexuality than the mainstream accepts, breaking down notions of what's proper or right, or disrupting norms of sexuality. I go for something other than straight.

TK: I've noticed that in your poetry you sometimes write from a male point of view, but primarily from a woman's point of view, whereas a lot of the plays are centered, in a sense, around men, and I wonder if that has something to do with the form if you feel more welcome as a woman in the world of poetry and wanted a male persona—it's something other women playwrights I know have done, especially really good ones.

NW: Actually, if I were going to critique myself and other straight women who write gay male roles, which is why in *Slaughter City* I did the other—I thought, OK, I'm going to write a lesbian woman. In mainstream culture the male body is power and is eroticized in a way that is powerful and opening up. If you're doing gay themes, because the male body onstage is power, there is more space, less invisibility there than the woman's body and especially the lesbian body onstage. There is more space for that in our culture.

TK: More space for what?

NW: Writing the gay male body onstage, certainly more so than the lesbian body, which is still completely invisible onstage. Because you have to work much harder to empower the female body onstage than the male, which is already granted power in the mainstream. Once I started dealing with women, issues that are close to me, I wanted to break down the idea that quite a few writers still have that only a woman can write a great role for a woman. I love it when I read a male who writes great roles for women.

TK: I've become very interested in the way that people—and it's something that we don't think about a lot in theater—but that people, when they're writing, are always building on antecedents and tradition and developing a tradition, even if they're making a radical break from tradition. And as a woman poet you're already heir to a rather old and prodigiously impressive tradition, while as a woman play-wright you're kind of in the second or third pioneer generation. But it is only very recently that there have been occasional exceptional women in history, but mostly it has been an outrageously male-dominated field, when you compare it to the novel.

NW: One likes to think you've made these choices of resistance and then I look at myself and I think, "Some of your work is accessible because you have these great male roles." What's important is the idea that our culture does not also attempt to construct or destroy the sexuality of straight men and gay men. Sexism in our culture and the way the body is abused are destructive to all of us. That's why I think it's important for a movement like feminism to show how sexism destroys both men and women. Social roles destroy our sexuality, and, for men, their sexuality is affected or deformed by mainstream culture. Feminism is always treated as "please do us a favor" and "support us," but men really should be as invested in feminist agenda because it affects them.

TK: The master is always, to a certain extent, destroyed by being a master.

Earlier, you mentioned the body as a political body, and in your plays the body is sort of a political battlefield. Do you believe in the existence of love and sexual love as distinct from expressions of power? There is a very complicated interweaving of class struggle, political struggle, sexual attraction, and sexual repulsion in your plays. I'm wondering, is that of the historical moment and something we are now stuck in, or is that, in a Foucauldian sense, a given, something that is eternal?

NW: What fascinates me is how much the body and politics are connected. The body that labors is also the body that loves. And if you live in a society where what you do for a living destroys the body, then that affects how you love sexually. On the first level, simply on the physical level, if you get carpal tunnel syndrome, that affects how you touch someone; also on a power level, it comes right into love. Can a love be possible between people from two different classes? In *One Flea Spare,* you have a sailor from the lower class and a woman from the upper class—there's a power structure they have to live with every day, and it doesn't disappear in their intimate moments; it isn't erased through sexual contact. Social roles damage our body, labor damages our bodies. That affects how we love. From the day the body is born, our body is pulled and stretched in different directions through the political values of our society.

TK: On the issue of Utopian possibility, has our time lost or through bitter experiences abandoned . . .

NW: You're not asking if love and sexuality are transformative?

TK: I'm sort of interested in its revolutionary potential, but that is a separate question. Your work is very unsparing; the places of resistance are the places where hope might be located and you have to think about where to locate them. There's no sop being handed to the audience to make them feel it will all be OK. And the plays are sort of tragic in that sense. Bodies are damaged, hearts, lives damaged . . . I've noticed many more people are in a deep state of despair in the early 1990s, so I'm asking . . .

NW: About hope? Well, I see my work as irresponsibly hopeful in a lot of ways. There are moments of possibility and transformation in my play where structures of power suddenly become visible and we see them and we think, "Aha, here is a place, a moment where something can change." *One Flea Spare* is a dark little play, but at the end here is this little girl who has survived all this, who says, "Yes, I am damaged, but I love these people." I hope the audience would see in moments like this that there is the possibility of change.

TK: Do you think that art has the power to do that? As a person with an engaged viewpoint, does art matter?

NW: Yes it does. I've been transformed in small and large ways by certain poetry or novels or theater. To me it's that moment when you're watching something and you feel like we can be bigger than we are. The best work does make us yearn toward that, toward change—not only political change, but changing ourselves. . . . And we're not meant to be alone.

TK: And we *can't* be alone. We're not meant to be alone—that's a fiction that is created by ideology. I asked Suzan-Lori Parks if she was an atheist and she said, "That's a white-people thing." It's another kind of category like materialist versus idealist.

NW: To separate those isn't right. Maybe the materialist part is there so that we can get to the other. I like to think I'm a mix. If I were only a materialist, things would not have turned out the way they do in my plays. There are moments when things would've gone in the other direction.

TK: So, you're not a determinist. I'm teaching Edward Carr's book *What Is History,* and there's a really shocking section where he talks about morality of history. Where do you think justice comes from? Carr says that suffering is indigenous to history and the hard thing about studying history is that there will always be winners and losers. He's a Marxist who thinks it will come through much bloodshed. Are there always losers in history?

NW: I would frame it differently. Look at people in power and people who are powerless. It does go against Utopian ideals, but I think if you look in history, there are times when there are not winners or losers. How big is the community you're looking at? You can look at a unit of two people, a city, a different time in history. What is important is the struggle and there is always a struggle. . . . It's important that there were times when people lived with more equality, more respect for each other and for their community. It has been better. There have been times in history when it was a lot less evil.

TK: And a lot less unequal. Do you believe in evil?

NW: The book of the Devil is so wonderful—the Devil is a rebel. I love reading about him but I think that the idea of evil is always ahistorical and isolating; I think it's trouble to say that anything is inherently this or that. When something is evil, you can't transform it.

TK: What about Slobodan Milosevic and ethnic cleansing?

NW: I think there are actions we can consider evil. I think evil may be even too small a word for something like that, but I don't believe people are evil.

TK: So you don't think that Milosevic is an evil man.

NW: I don't think that question is important in that way. We leave out what we should be looking at, a larger problem that this is horrible and must be stopped. If we give him all the power of what has happened, whether he is evil or not, does that mean if he were good this wouldn't have happened? It denies all the historical forces at work. Are there people who are evil or are they people who are destroyed and broken? To the point that the actions they carry out are no longer human. This may be romantic, but I truly believe that those who carry out inhuman acts have their humanity destroyed—either it was before or it is through those acts.

TK: So you believe that they are not human?

NW: No, I believe that their humanity is taken away and I feel very strongly about that.

· · ·

TK: It's daring to imagine the Other in a fictional context. Not simply writing what you know, but actually feeling that it is your responsibility to empathetically imagine important situations that are class positions and gender positions different from yours. Do you worry about that?

NW: No. To do so is absurd, reactionary, and simplistic—that we should concern ourselves only with ourselves. Rather, we are not only ourselves, we are who we interact with, we are who we live with. Saying we should only write about what we know is saying an individual is only what they experience themselves. It's risky. In *Slaughter City*, I wrote two roles for African Americans. I think a lot of times, white writers, privileged classes as well, have been stereotyped and racist. I think if one is attempting that, I like to stay very open to criticism and not get defensive. But I also feel as a writer for the theater, what am I going to do, write white roles for women? I want more roles for women, but I want to write good roles, and not just for whites.

TK: It's also nice being a playwright in that regard, because your work will inevitably pass through the minds and mouths and bodies of the actors who are playing them. So, if you write an African American part, it will pass through the mouth of an African American actor who is playing it. Do you find it harder to write across class barriers or are they all equally difficult?

NW: I'd say racial lines are the hardest. The community where I grew up, Kentucky, was mostly working class. My family was more privileged, but those are the young people I hung out with and I think that's something that I listened to all the time. I have never been afraid of class in that way. But we also don't do enough of self-critique, stepping back and saying, "What stereotypes might I be playing to?" That's exciting to me, especially if I find one in myself. I try to root it out.

TK: The tricky thing that I find is that when one is a member of an oppressed group and when one is working with one's own identity and transforming one's identity into a political issue, performing stereotypes is part of that politic; there is no such thing as an oppressed group that doesn't feel like, to some extent, part of their mission is to work with stereotypes. So when you see straight writers writing gay men, they seem like very nice people but they don't seem particularly gay, and as a gay man it is easy for me to know how to play that role. When I'm working with African American characters it's hard, and, of course, when people see my plays they know that a white gay man is writing them and when they see my African American characters on stage they know that a white gay man has written them. If it was a black writing them, you would assume different things at the beginning, so the dangerous game that is so much fun and so exciting is playing with stereotypes. It becomes very tricky when you're doing it for another group that you don't belong in.

NW: The idea of being two white people writing African American roles, we have to question if that's what we're feeling, if we're being generous or if it's some kind of charity writing roles for people of color. I feel like it's the education and a gift to myself to be able to write them. It's not a guilt trip as a white playwright. If anything, it's a selfish thing, because I need to learn more. It's who I can transform myself to be. To me, if you bring in spirituality and look for something common to all of us, you get rid of all the things that have oppressed and destroyed us, leading to a connection. That is where I feel the spirituality.

TK: Which Marx would have called essentialist at another time in history.

NW: There may be a sprinkle of that here.

TK: It's hard to stay away from that. . . .

You are a very American writer. [One Flea Spare] feels British. It's very convincing in its historical period. To what extent do you feel committed to historical accuracy or historical fidelity?

NW: The facts of history are much more imaginative than my own imagination, so that's where I go to be imaginative. I love historical accuracy, because it's so fantastical. It's magical in a strange way.

TK: It's frequently disappointing when you come up with a moment, then you read about it, and it is so much more interesting in the way that it actually happened. I showed my students the part in Brecht's journal where he talks about the exhibitionist urge being the urge in theater that replaces the urge to be ethnographically faithful. That the urge to create the effect or presentation is more important in theater. In *One Flea Spare* you manage to balance both of those things.

NW: It's not that I won't completely make up things. In terms of research—when it can work in my play, I prefer to do that. Small things, I'm always historically accurate.

But mainstream history has always covered up, always been about the wealthy. Power is the way it is because that's normal and natural and the way it always has been, and I think there's been an effort to bury and cover up and make certain events seem small. People have always struggled to change things and big events will only be given one line.

TK: Also groups that one thinks of as being completely right-wing, like the Mormons invite historical revision. In the beginning in Utah, they abolished private property and really had a communitarian society for a while.

NW: That seems like a crucial idea if you're ever going to look at Mormons, but it sounds like what is left out. The uncovering of those things is what gives one hope, and it can transform.

TK: Do you ever wonder that we should all be able to love how we want to love? I walk down Times Square and see these big Calvin Klein ads and kids being sexually overstimulated from always staring at the ads, and I think, maybe the sexual revolution was a mistake.

NW: I would call that socializing children in a wrong way—telling them to sell themselves to consumer culture.

. . .

TK: What does it feel like to write a poem? It's unimaginable to me; you are the only American playwright I know who is a really serious poet right now.

NW: I've always been interested in language. If you're talking about transforming power, transform the language. You have to change the language to make it be heard again. I know that, for myself, when I write poetry it's more scary. The space is so small in poetry. In plays, I feel bigger and less lonely. I feel smaller when I'm writing poetry. When I write plays I often write a few poems about the thing first, and I'll incorporate part of the poem into the play. But I've found I have to cut the poem out.

TK: Why do you think that is?

NW: I needed the poem to jump-start the play. I needed the emotion that was in the poem to stretch it out through the play, but then I needed a different language. You say you're not a poet? Look at your attention to language. Parts of *A Bright Room Called Day* are sheer poetry.

TK: In watching your evolution as a playwright, you keep cutting things out, because you've learned, play by play, the difference between literature and playwriting. A poem can be spoken aloud, but its primary life is on the page. There's a way in which there's an absolutely impatient demand that spoken language will not allow you to do certain things, even if it's beautiful. The audience gets annoyed with it: "Say what you are going to say!" When novelists write plays, they are horrified at how rude the audience is. Novelists take their time and chat and audiences say, "What is it?"

NW: It's interesting why we allow in our minds, when we read a poem, a certain language in poetry, but when it's on the stage we will not tolerate it.

TK: I think it has to do with passage of time. You have the luxury when you are reading a poem to take however many hours. You don't have that time when someone's onstage.

NW: That would be impatience. Although poetry could have been sung or spoken, it is not a physically visual medium. We have to create the visuals in our mind. The words create the entire world. In theater there are the words, the stage, the actors—the elements.

TK: In our society we have almost as much hatred for poetry as we do for children. It's kind of a dirty word. Poetical means you're a sissy. Richard Howard just did a speech that I thought was appalling, talking about how much he hated the poetry-in-motion series on the subway, which I love, and how he says poetry is not for the masses, it's not public art.

NW: He wants to privatize it, own certain words. The idea is that if the working, common people become involved in the arts, the quality will immediately sink. Elitism has been attached to poetry in our culture since it can't be consumed in a consumer society. You can't sell poetry like that. . . . Poetry carries just as much ideology as any art but it's often invisible. Poetry is above politics. But, if politics is how we live our lives, then poetry is above how we live our lives.

TK: And education does have a lot to do with it. People are so afraid of poetry. No one is trained to read it, so difficult poetry becomes completely out of the question.

You were talking about when you write a poem, it's like you're being diminished, something is being taken from you. You have a line in a poem, I paraphrase it horribly: "There's a child missing from your face, it's the child I'm holding in my arms."

NW: This is going to sound horrible and essentialistic—and it's that awful giving-birth metaphor, which I hate—but I remember feeling, after the birth of my second child, that same kind of emptiness as when I write a poem. You had something new out there, taken from you, but now there were two things, yourself and it, as opposed to only one before, an element of loneliness.

. . .

TK: I was thinking about the end of *One Flea Spare*. I was stunned by that kid [Morse], because it's the first treatment I've seen on stage of the children of war. All the children in *Mother Courage* are grown-ups. The kids we're so used to seeing on CNN are the children in Sarajevo and Baghdad—forty-five thousand kids die a month in Iraq of starvation. Children are the most disturbing casualty of all sorts of war, of the war that's called everyday life, or a plague. It's the mutilation of a future. What's brave about *One Flea Spare* is that you're tackling it head-on. In the astonishing monologue at the end, [Morse] loves these people but they have marked her. A terrible price has been paid by this love. It's a very careful balance—she's been loved or she's been marked? It's a very fragile kind of hope because of the horror.

NW: But hope is always terribly fragile. The last thread is maybe where the insanity starts. But we talk about possibility, those moments of transformation, which are so fragile and so quick. If one does not seize the moment, the power structure continues on. The girl is almost the most human in all these crises perhaps because she has lived through them. I'm always amazed by what is left over—not only in children, but that there can still be laughter. That is what makes me feel spiritual. It seems impossible that this child could ever laugh again, or this nation could ever find happiness, and then there is.

TK: Do you think there will be any life left on the planet in one hundred years?

NW: Yes, I do.

TK: Do you think it will be any fun?

NW: . . . I have a choice over my vision. I want to believe that what we're working toward is that we will save ourselves. There may be terrible periods of darkness, but why work this hour if we don't believe in some possibility that we can get together and make this change. How do you feel about that?

Calisto (J. Grant Albrecht), the prince, in *The Illusion*, freely adapted by Tony Kushner from Pierre Corneille's play. Produced by the Hartford Stage Company (December 1989–February 1990) under the direction of Mark Lamos. (*Photo by T. Charles Erickson.*)

Afterword

Tony Kushner

Introduction

Why, oh why, did I agree to this book? I have always worried that my confessional style is "of the repulsive sort that comes from an uneasy consciousness seeking to forestall the judgement of others." (That's George Eliot.) Now I feel utterly exposed, so much blah blah blah, will no one shut this clown up?!?! *Well, to confess, I agreed to the book for two reasons: Vanity, obviously, and because I have done so many interviews—one is forced to do them, really, because they provide free publicity for productions of one's plays, and since no nonprofit theater has an advertising budget, if you want ticket sales, you talk to the press— and the prospect of a book seemed like some way of reclaiming all that unremunerated clackering. I prefer my clackering to be remunerated, naturally. Come to think of it, I haven't been remunerated for this book, but at least it's an addition to the bookshelf, so I guess it comes back to Vanity. This must be what they call a low self-esteem day. Thank God for that, on high self-esteem days I buy too many expensive things. I often wish I was a Stoic, some sort of Roman who knew the virtue and value of suffering silently. But I'm not and I don't. I'm a modern man and I like to share—feelings, at any rate. Here, have some more, I have puh-lenty!*

I am grateful to Bob Vorlicky for being so patient with me (since after I agreed to the book I spent a year and a half fleeing from the prospect of it) and for seeing some value in what he's assembled here. I am grateful to the interviewers too, some of whom were wonderful at their task. A tip to interviewers from a subject: Never *ask a question and then glance around the room, or at your nails, or at your list of questions, while your interviewee struggles to answer while simultaneously struggling to believe he is not talking to himself; and use a tape recorder, so that when the interview comes out, the subject will recognize himself.*

I am, as always, grateful to Kimberly T. Flynn, from whom all the good ideas came, or at least many of them, and none of the bad ones, which were mine and those of the dumb devil who lives inside me.

A tip to the subjects of interviews: Never read them. *You will hate yourself; you sounded like an idiot, unless you are Jacques Derrida or Tony Benn; your speaking syntax is reminiscent of George Bush in his "halcyon salad days," like on his Japan trip when he did a* Bushusuru[1] *on the prime minister; you were misquoted; you were indiscreet; better you should look at your pores and your stretch marks and the hair in your nose in a magnifying mirror than you should ever read an interview of yourself. Only your reviews are to be more assiduously avoided.* Especially *don't read interviews when relatives call to say how smart you sounded.*

The following is a chapter from a book I'm working on, which may or may not be a novel, the title of which is The Intelligent Homosexual's Guide to Socialism and Capitalism, With a Key to the Scriptures. *Any resemblance between the protagonist of this excerpt and the clackerer in the interviews you've read is purely lamentable.*

"Waking Up"

The Intelligent Homosexual is midway through his fortieth year. I have been observing him all my life. He is busy with his life's work, a massive book running to many volumes entitled *The Intelligent Homosexual's Guide to Socialism and Capitalism, With a Key to the Scriptures.* He has been writing this book, day after day, for forty years; since parturition he's been writing it. He knows it to be incompleteable, he knows he will die writing it, he knows he is working himself to death—though he does not want to die.

Every book he reads is fed into this book, which is insatiable, if it makes sense to call a book insatiable. (And if you have ever read a really long, hard book or tried to write one of your own, you know it makes sense, insatiable.) If it reaches his ears it goes into his book: every droplet of conversation he overhears—and he is an inveterate snoop, a habitual eavesdropper, a nasty habit he deliberately acquired years ago to enhance his professional capabilities (he is, embarrassingly, a dramatist)—every casual exchange between strangers on a subway, every idea filched from friends, his lovers' chance observations about anything (in bed or out of it), an elegant British friend's shocking defi-

---

1. A word coined by the Japanese on the occasion of George Bush's remarkable visit to Tokyo, a variant of which is *Bushusita,* both meaning "to vomit."

ciencies in personal hygiene, the tricks he uses to catch the attentions of very young children, his nightmares, the death throes of his dearly beloved, newspaper accounts of calumny and torture, his weight, his bowels, his bibliomania, betrayals, loyalties, losses, generational shifts, night sweats, lapses in judgment and ethics and taste and kindness, films and television, wasted irretrievable hours, missed and misspent opportunities, laziness, cowardice, the lyrics to a thousand Tin Pan Alley tunes (one of his less secret addictions) committed indelibly to memory (*"So come and enlighten my days / And never depart / You only can brighten the blaze / That burns in my heart"*), the panic over a face remembered and a name forgotten . . . Well, you get the idea. Did I mention grinding green envy of others' successes, deep sorrow over the vanquishing of the valiant, overwhelming financial affrights, and expensive, exhausting psychoanalysis—his list-making compulsion . . . ? This book is his attempt to write the meaning of his life, to narrate life into coherence, history, theory even—doomed to certain failure at best. And at worst the whole thing will be revealed at the final terminal moment before his soul—if he has one (he's not sure)—leaves his body, the whole thing a mistake, a misunderstanding, socialism-slash-capitalism having been the wrong polarities, the wrong dichotomous premise, from which, dialectically, to proceed, and perhaps even dialectics itself being wrong, wrong, outdated and wrong.

I should pause here to explain why I call the Intelligent Homosexual the Intelligent Homosexual. I trust everyone present will know why I call him homosexual, which preferences, predilections, propensities, politics, peccadilloes, and sexual practices position him categorically as such. Though I myself am a homosexual and have been watching homosexuals all my life, even sleeping with more than a few of them, I don't feel adequate to define the word "homosexual," which is both readily understood and incredibly complicated and controversial. If you don't know what "homosexual" means, there are tens of thousands of volumes available on the subject, ranging from the grittily behavioral to the abstrusely abstracted. These last are written by extremely intelligent homosexuals called Queer Theorists. My homosexual is intelligent but not *extremely* intelligent, not a Queer Theorist; he is merely a queer in search of theory. Pity him.

To call our homosexual the Intelligent Homosexual is simply to note in passing that he is defined primarily by his desires and the tricky identity into which these desires have inserted him and that, adjectivally, his desire-based identity is modified, so to speak, by a mind that clamors, futilely, for attention and stands steadfast, wind-whipped and forlorn, against the gale force of his endlessly raging libido, his hunger. This mind seeks to efface everything; to rub and abrade everything it encounters into silky, silent, unarticulated smoothness; to caress with urgency, ardency, muscularity; to caress contrariety, dubiety, and ambiguity into finely sifted dust and ash, dust and ash spumed into the gentle rarified air of Eternity, Being eased, pulverized, atomized past any gathering-back and misted joyfully, lyrically into Oblivion. Every homosexual, heterosexual, and bisexual and every other shape, stripe, and variety of -sexual seeks this and this alone: not nihilism necessarily (though some *do* seek that and you'd best not date them), but dissolving, dissolution. Oneness if you will, the Big Embracer Embraced—Love, in other words, Love.

To which desire the historically constructed intellect, late in the twentieth century, bereft of its soul-certainty, nervously attaches itself, hoping all the while that even amorous Oblivion might prove containable ultimately in a book that will stand on a shelf in a library in Valhalla, a book to enter the eyes and the ears and the books of those who will come after and hence guarantee to the Intelligent Homosexual both universal unending existence *and* that specificity that we are terribly, understandably reluctant to surrender—since we have spent our whole lives shaping it. *The Intelligent Homosexual's Guide to Socialism and Capitalism, With a Key to the Scriptures*—for many, for most people, such a notional volume, if it ever flowers open in their minds, dismisses itself almost immediately with apologies for its improbability. For a few, however, the book rests atop the spinal column, like a tumor, the medulla oblongata its lectern, its foliage ever thickening, fed by blood, its bindings expanding, its table of contents groaning more and more loudly with rich edibles or lustrous riches, its indices more and more intricately cross-referenced, its footnotes sprouting footnotes like a vast network of tubers and its margins clotted thickly with tiny scribbled marginalia like stars in the summer sky, till wearily we come to imagine our deaths not as chilly, airy volatilization but rather as a pleasant crawling in between the sheets of this mighty volume, a drifting off into a safe, toasty, fetal slumber, in the depths of the book of our life, which has become, finally, our home.

Hence "Intelligent Homosexual" should be understood more as a diagnostic category than as any sort of boast. "Intelligent" here doesn't imply comparison or superiority, doesn't create an obverse class of the "Unintelligent." Well, of course it *does* create such a class, but we should try to understand intelligence in this context as a species of disease, chronic, congenital maybe, not fatal, incurable—like psoriasis or vitiligo, intriguing, on occasion unsightly, annoying. According to this definition of intelligence the Unintelligent ought to be ranked among the Blessed. And we will for the time being say nothing more about them.

Here's a sad little story from the early life of the Intelligent Homosexual. When he was a boy, his mother was stricken with breast cancer, and as a result of several botched operations and brutally excessive radiation therapy, she was badly burned and wounded and almost died. Already an experienced fetishist, the Intelligent Homosexual became obsessed during the frightening dark time of his mother's dangerous illness with obtaining for himself an old-fashioned pocket watch—the kind with a face cover that pops open when you depress the winding stem. When he finally succeeded in finding one and conning his father into buying it for him, he had the words *Cogito Ergo Sum* engraved on the back. He was a strange child, he hadn't read Descartes, he'd gotten the motto from a Marvel comic book. "I Think Therefore I Am." Of Cartesian idealism he knew nothing; thinking instead became, in the face of the threat of nonexistence posed by his mother's mortality, a retreat from which a fragile, frantic assertion of survival might be pronounced: a thinker or nothing, because the body, clearly, betrays.

The pocket watch must surely have been a vaginal symbol. When he was a very little boy he'd made a make-believe version of this timepiece out of one of his mother's discarded rouge compacts. And the desire to snap time shut in a tight gold case? Well, the Intelligent Homosexual was only twelve years old at the time of his mother's troubles, and he hadn't yet encountered Seneca's admonition that the wise man, who is never in any circumstance *reluctant,* escapes the necessity of death because he *wills* what necessity is going to force on him: if he must lose, then he chooses to lose; if he must die, then he chooses death. Now, at forty, he has read Seneca, but still, even at forty, the Intelligent Homosexual is *profoundly* reluctant and weak of will, and he wants badly to snap running time shut, immobile, between two covers, and hold it, cold, in his warm hand.

Even at forty! At forty Moses saw the Burning Bush, at forty Freud published *The Psychopathology of Everyday Life,* at forty Conrad wrote his first English sentences. The Intelligent Homosexual is waiting for his apotheosis, beginning now to worry that he will live out his days on earth apotheosisless, but he's noticed in the meantime one agreeable side effect of the aging process: he feels a newfound sympathy for the ungainly inept child he once was. Is this sympathy incipient wisdom or merely a softening of the brain?

Midway through his fortieth year the Intelligent Homosexual finds himself in a dark woods. And who doesn't, midway through his or her fortieth year? "Come," writes Wallace Stevens, "celebrate the faith of forty, Oh ward of Cupido!" And what faith might that be? wonders this particular ward. "The honey of heaven may or may not come," answers Stevens, "But that of earth both comes and goes at once!" What kind of faith, the Intelligent Homosexual asks himself, is that? The faith of a triceratops struggling in a quicksand bog. No wonder John Berryman mockingly called Stevens "the funny money man." The faith that faith goes unrewarded. The faith that, in this action-and-opposite reaction Red Queen universe, this *per*verse loony-tuniverse, faithlessness is the smarter option. As Ogden Nash put it, using a metaphor distinctly appropriate to the newly minted middle-aged: "I must admit I'm in despair / When I consider Human Hair; / Unbid it cometh, so it goeth, / And frequently it's doing boeth."

Human Hair, now. Hair has become a recent problem for the Intelligent Homosexual; I've noticed him looking more and more unpresentable. He hasn't had a haircut since his fortieth birthday. Before this he wore it stylishly short, but now he can't bring himself to enter a hair salon. The short cut, he has decided, is too Chelsea Boy, too blatantly sexually advertising, like tight jeans, unseemly in a man of his years. The long hair, he knows, makes him more frowsy, less sexy according to the fierce fanatic standards of tightness and hard-ness of his community, the rebellion against which and the freedom from which he enjoys, and which also causes him anguish—he *wants* to remain an Intelligent (adjective) Homosexual (noun), a modifying mind in a sexual body; he fears that, barely quadragenarian, he is being ushered prematurely by the relentless clock and calendar to a new unwelcome identity: the Homosexual Intellectual or, worse, the Homosexual Intelligence, carnal become immaterial, all thought and no body: "I think therefore I am *alone*."

Maybe his brain *is* softening, maybe his hair growing wild signals a regression, back to the sixties, back to the seventies, back to his youth. It's so complicated: short hair means young nowadays, but he's noted that when his hair is very short, his face by contrast looks older, more gaunt, more lined, while longer hair distracts unwanted scrutiny from his withering time-scoured physiognomy and indicates almost convinc-ingly a youthfulness, if not youth, a youthfulness generationally appro-priate; we know he looked something like this way back when he was young, like one of those middle-aged film actors playing their character's younger self in a wig that neither succeeds nor completely fails to make the aging star seem younger. The long hair marks the attempt to turn back the clock, the pathetic best anyone can do.

Or maybe his hair's gotten thick and wooly—"Does it work for me?" he asks querulously when we meet, and I don't know what he wants me to answer—because, a Jew in his Moses year, he's decided to obey the stern injunction of the Creator of the Fruit of the Vine not to cut his hair and is offering up this rug, this mop, this burning bush of hair in place of the *payes*, the sidelocks he is too much an assimilated, almost assimilationist, Diasporan humanist socialist Jew to wear convincingly or comfortably. Maybe it's all for G–D. But this is getting shaggy. Enough with the hair already. Back to those dark woods, that other, denser, more tangled thicket.

A few years ago he was in a small bookshop in a town in West Yorkshire, in England. The Intelligent Homosexual is a bookstore rat. He is happiest when browsing and buying books. His home is walled in books. He hasn't read a tenth of them, like the Nobel laureate Czeslaw Milosz, he responds, when asked if he has read them all, "No, and so what?" And the legions of books unread, awaiting, torment him marvelously, mock the innumerable importunate distractions and emergencies that prevent him from reading as much as he ought; and the cleft between mind and body of which I have been speaking that has made the Intelligent Homosexual rather a slow reader, too excitable, too ready for distraction, too easily flamed into flights of digressive fantasy by an exciting thought or strange new word or some lingual association that conjures up a face or a body his memory has stored. His choice now which book to read next is determined largely by trying to guess which one, unread, should he die tomorrow, would most reproach him. These books, into which after all thousands upon thousands of hours of lives of labor, intellectual and physical, have been condensed, these books that have trapped time between their covers and, by outlasting their authors' and their authors' antecedents' demises, have thwarted death—and I think I should interject here that all his bemoaning his growing old doesn't become the Intelligent Homosexual, who, a gay American male at the end of the twentieth century, should be weak-kneed with gratitude that the Grim Reaper somehow overlooked and passed over his house as it gleaned its superabundant recent harvest—these books that mock death constitute at the same time a mountain unscalable by any measure of human strength or endurance—certainly by *his* weak measure—and so his large library has made him mortal. Or he imagines his library ransacked, or burnt, or abandoned by him should he, like many of the writers he most admires, have to become a refugee—unlikely, but did any of those writers really think it likely?—and he knows himself to be mortal through his investment in these things and so knows himself to be a fetishist, a perishable fetishist. All the lessons of history, politics, poetry, and passion he has learned from reading notwithstanding, mortality is perhaps the clearest and most dismal dismaying thing his books have taught him.

Back to the West Yorkshire bookshop, in which the Intelligent Homosexual, shopping for books as usual rather than staying home reading them, or writing his *Guide*, retreats to the back room to escape the smoke of the bookshop keeper's cigar, which smells to the Intelligent Homosexual of saltpeter, forest mulch, and animal dung rolled tightly in sheets of asbestos insulation. The asphyxiating industrial-strength fumes remind him of the new cigar-smoking fad back home; he finds it typically sinister-retrograde-American that, while the Helms-Burton Act is throttling Cuba, our populace has developed a taste for bootleg Cuban cigars or their more noisomely malodorous Miami cousins, in imitation of Bruce Willis and Demi Moore and Mel Gibson and Arnold Schwarzenegger, and other derriere-garde crypto-barbaric phallo-porcine putschists, all epigones of the Reagan/Gingrich/Limbaugh/Kristol and Himmelfarb-crazy Christian counterrevolution, an aggressively ego-anarchist/individualist identity assertion in the face of the progress of the antismoking crusade, the only instance of genuine political wisdom and progress nineties America has been able (so far) to maintain in the face of corporate and the aforementioned neo-con Forrest Gumpist opposition.

In the bookshop's back room he finds a shelf labeled "JEWRY" and, pausing a moment to reflect on the history of British anti-Semitism, which digression you, gentle reader, will be spared, he finds and purchases a book for a mere thirty pounds (the unfavorable pound-to-dollar ratio calculations necessary to justify such a purchase inspiring another momentary digression concerning the meaning of fluctuating international monetary rates, both as personal portent and as ideological puzzle, which nanosecond's reflection again is marked here but not expanded upon, for your sake, gentle reader, whose patience and skills at quilting disjunctive narrative have already been so strenuously tested and so sorely tried). For a mere thirty pounds, or about $54.78, as he calculates it (he who has never been even remotely competent with numbers), the Intelligent Homosexual purchases four English and Hebrew volumes of Jewish Law, which was first laid down by God in the Pentateuch, then collected and expounded upon in the years before and after the commencement of the Diaspora in the vast Talmud, and then in the twelfth century reclassified and codified by Maimonides as Mishnah Torah, or Yad-Hazakah, and then re-reclassified and rearranged by Joseph Caro of the sixteenth century into the Shulkhan Arukh, and then in 1870 rendered into a layperson's multivolume, two-thousand-page version called the Kitzur Shulkhan Arukh, of which now for $54.78, approximately, the Intelligent Homosexual finds himself in possession. And immediately upon possession he feels himself to be more deeply a Jew, though he has yet to read a single statute: ownership, he recalls Walter Benjamin having written, is the most intimate relationship a person can have to objects. He knows that it would probably have been more Marxist/Leninist appropriate to write that use, rather than possession, constitutes the most intimate relationship between a person and an object—appropriate, politically correct. And the Intelligent Homosexual strives mightily to *be* politically correct and despises the unthinking mockery made of what seems to him only to be a shorthand way of saying that he wishes to be *moral* and *just*. And he knows from his sexual habits and experiences that intimacy and political correctness are uneasy—frequently unhappy—bedfellows. And he knows that Benjamin, like his adoring fan the Intelligent Homosexual, was a self-confessed book fetishist—his fetishism, Benjamin noted, standing out in sharpest, most distinct relief contrasted against the sky of its sunset, at the twilight of its last possible moment of historical justification.

The Intelligent Homosexual begins, several weeks later, to browse through the Kitzur Shulkhan Arukh. Four laws into it, this is what he finds:

Immediately upon awakening from sleep a man must rise quickly and be ready to serve his Creator, blessed be He, before the evil inclination is given the opportunity to prevail over him with claims and designs not to rise. In the winter for instance the evil inclination attempts to persuade him with the subtle argument: "How can you arise so early in the morning, now when the cold is so intense?" In the summer he uses this argument: "How can you arise now when you have not had sufficient sleep?" For the evil inclination knows well how to catch a man in his nets. You must arise in the morning as if your property were burning in a fire and you make haste to rescue it; as if the King had summoned you for a task and you make haste so as not to be accused of negligence: so you must arise every morning.

In a way the Intelligent Homosexual has always known this was what God expected; and so he begins every morning suffused with guilt and regret. He is, as I have said, reluctant by nature (or by design) (since, Seneca, when someone's not free, aren't they reluctant about everything?) And he hates waking up; the Kitzur Shulkhan Arukh has his number. When it's cold, when it's hot, when he's in bed with a man and can curl up against him, breathe in the milk smell his skin's effusing in the bedroom's curtained dark, hold him while they both drift an hour or so longer in the shallows of sleep off the shore of consciousness . . . But beware the Shoals of Conscience, against which your pleasantly bobbing raft will wreck, pitching you into cold saline tumult and turbulence, undertows of regret and dismay at finding the land unchanged and awful as when you left it; buffeted against the grit and gravel of the beachy bottom, tossed ashore festooned with seaweed, eyes burning, body clammy, lungs full of sea foam and salt, a Caliban gawping with horror at the newly dawning day.

Index